Advance Praise for Demystifying Demons

"An excellent and courageous work. …Virtually everything described in this book is consistent with what I have learned in four decades of listening to persons relating their internal struggles in the course of psychotherapy. …It especially has the potential to be a significant resource for those initiating psychotherapy. Also, it can be helpful for young psychotherapists who are looking for ways to organize thinking without becoming narrow or dogmatic."

--Gary Mac Smith, M.D.

Clayton Morgareidge enlists insights from poets, artists, psychoanalysts, and from his own field of philosophy to map a path through the darker terrain of the human soul. He explains how many of the torments of mind––the demons that overtake people––have their origins in what is most fundamental to the human condition. In this journey through the difficulties of being human, the author offers solace without sentimentality. He is most fascinated by the paradoxes of mind and how desire and dread for human connection are particularly intertwined. It's a lovely book written by a sage and savvy philosopher.

-- Janice Haaken, Ph.D., Professor Emeritus of Psychology, Portland State University

Demystifying Demons

Demystifying Demons

Rethinking Who And What We Are

Clayton Morgareidge

ISBN-13: 9781544027807
ISBN-10: 154402780X

Table of Contents

Preface

THIS IS THE book I wish I had read a long, long time ago: a book for people troubled by inner demons, and disturbed by the darkness of the inner space where demons hide. I grew up wanting to do what the adult world asked in exchange for recognition and praise. At the same time, I was besieged from within by a resentment of that adult world, and I tried to escape from it into fantasies of some idyllic paradise where I ruled supreme. Sometimes unruly thoughts came to me of vandalizing or sabotaging something the adult world thought was important. It felt as if a foreign agent that did not wish me well had invaded my mind. No one around me spoke of such mysteries, so I was left to ponder them in isolation.

Underlying this mystery was a larger question: What is this inner space in which demons live and flourish, and how can it be so obscure? What does it mean to have a conscious mind, or a soul, and how can that mind not know itself? Who are we, what are we made of, and how are we put together? What happens in the world to make us who and what we are? Questions like these drew me into a long academic career studying, writing, and teaching philosophy. But it wasn't until I retired from teaching some fourteen years ago that I was able to work on the mysteries of the soul in a way that would produce this book, the book I wanted to read.

In spite of my academic background, *Demystifying Demons: Rethinking Who and What We Are* is not addressed to philosophers or psychologists, but to the troubled souls the book is about and to those who care for them. This is one troubled soul talking to another. The book's goal is to lay out a sketch of the human soul (using "soul" in a completely secular sense that will be explained in the first chapter) and how it is formed in the interaction between the infants and children we once were and the family and social settings in which we have lived and still live. My hope is that when we understand what makes our inner demons so demonic, they will be less frightening, rather as a child's bedroom at night is no longer so scary when a nightlight is installed. Moreover, in the story told here, we are all deeply entangled in each other's lives and embedded in the social order of our times. So we have less reason than we usually suppose to blame people, including ourselves, for our sins and errors, and more reason to treat each other with mercy and compassion.

The years I spent teaching and doing philosophy taught me two things about the capacity of language to both obfuscate and clarify our thinking. First, the language of philosophers (and other theory-makers) can often be a barrier for those without special education. So in the course of teaching, I learned how to restate philosophical ideas in language nearer to the experience of my students. This is what I have tried to do in this book for the often obscure language of my sources. But sometimes ordinary language is the problem. Everyday terms can lead us astray when we are thinking about such notions as time and space, money and value, consciousness and the unconscious, thought and emotion, and body and soul. So in writing about how our souls work and how they are formed, I have tried not to assume a common understanding of words like 'soul', 'consciousness', 'the unconscious', 'emotion', and 'feeling', and to offer fresh ways of understanding what they refer to.

Just as our lives cannot be separated from our world, so the completion of this book is the product of its author's relations with others. My thinking has been shaped by a diverse cast of characters in the philosophical tradition. Friedrich Nietzsche, George Herbert Mead, Ludwig Wittgenstein, J.L. Austin, John Dewey, Michel

Foucault, and Slavoj Žižek have deepened my understanding of how the lives of individuals are shaped by language and evolving social arrangements. I have worked to go beyond the abstractions of philosophers by drawing on work in psychology and the social sciences, especially psychoanalysis for its investigation of the unconscious and disavowed elements of our lives. R.D. Laing, Daniel Stern, and Jacques Lacan (filtered through Žižek) are among the psychoanalytic writers who have contributed to my understanding of how the soul is constructed. Marxist studies of ideology have helped me to think about how we are shaped by the economic and political organization of our society.

This book has been over a decade in the making, and a number of people have helped and encouraged me by reading and commenting on earlier drafts. Gary Mac Smith is first and foremost among these; he read many drafts, engaged in hours of conversation, suggested sources, and helped me to see how valuable the work could be for the many troubled souls there are in our world. I have also learned a great deal about life and emotions from conversations and shared experiences with my life partner Jackie Lemieux. I could not have arrived at this point without her support. Others who commented on early drafts include my brother Kenneth Morgareidge, Phil Lewin, and Sevin Koont. Rick Holmes, Monica Villhauer, John Erdman, Peyton Stafford, and Robert Vance read and commented on later versions.

Some of my earliest attempts to write about consciousness and the unconscious were presented in philosophy colloquia at Lewis & Clark College and Willamette University, and I learned a great deal from those discussions. Criticism from philosophers at Lewis & Clark in particular impelled me to rethink and reformulate my ideas on these topics. My many years of association with colleagues at Lewis & Clark, Sevin Koont and Bill Rottschaefer, and more recently, John Fritzman, have also had a major impact on my philosophical outlook. I also owe a great deal to A.Z. Zehava and Luisa

Zini, core members of a philosophy discussion group that has been meeting for over ten years. Together we discussed many of the books I have drawn upon here as well as earlier drafts of this one.

None of these folks should be assumed to agree with everything, or even anything, in the book, and any errors of fact or logic that remain after all this help are my sole responsibility.

I also want to acknowledge the role of my students in the philosophy courses I taught over the years at Lewis & Clark College where I learned whatever I know about how to present ideas clearly. Finally, I am grateful to the Ugly Mug Coffehouse where I did much of the reading and thinking about the topics of this book.

Portland, Oregon
April 2017

Part 1: The Soul in Society

1

Introduction: Troubled Souls

Troubles

THIS IS A book for troubled souls. We all have troubles—like unpaid bills, illnesses, or problem children. But troubled souls are those who are troubled by the *senselessness* of their troubles. Beset with nameless fears, unreasoned anger, unexplained guilt and self-loathing—troubles that disturb our sense of who we are. The troubled soul is *deeply* troubled, shaken at its foundations. Many of us are such souls, and this book is for us and for those who care about us.

The feelings, attitudes, emotions, and thoughts that torment the troubled soul are *opaque*. We may know that we feel anxious, guilty, angry, or sad; or we may only be vaguely aware of being "stressed" or "down." And if we know that what we are feeling is, for example, anxiety, then we often cannot say *why* we are anxious or what we are anxious *about*.

Where do these inner demons come from? They seem to arise on their own, independently of our will. We would like to disavow them, but who else is there to blame for them? We might say, "I am divided within myself, split between who I mean to be and some other unintended, unsavory, and obscure part of me." Or we might think, "I have been invaded or colonized by a foreign agent, a saboteur who does not wish me well."

We call these dark and alien forces within us "inner demons" because they are scary and mysterious. They hide in the dark, they frighten us, and we cannot understand where they came from or what we might do to bring them into the light or exorcise them. Their obscurity makes them a constant source of anxiety.

We're all, to some degree, like the guy in Butch Hancock's song:

My mind's got a mind of its own;
Takes me out a walkin' when I'd rather stay at home,
Takes me out to parties when I'd rather be alone,
Oh my mind's got a mind of its own.[1]

People in emotional turmoil may describe their minds like this:

My thoughts had still to be kept on a leash, and there were long dark passages down which they were straining to run.[2]

Or like this:

My brain is a hothouse, but when I get nervous ideas run through me in a vertiginous ballet; in spite of which, or perhaps just because of it, I have learned to govern and order them rigorously; otherwise I believe I would soon go crazy.[3]

So who am I? Am I the thinker of these confused and fractious thoughts? Or am I the one who is frightened by them? If it isn't I who thinks them, then who does?

---

1 Composed by Butch Hancock, but Jimmy Dale Gilmore is best known for performing it. It appears on his album "After Awhile".

2 Murdoch, Iris, *The Sea, The Sea.*

3 Sabato, *El Tunel / The Tunnel.* My translation.

The fact that our souls are dark and inhabited by demons can discourage us from reflecting on ourselves, afraid of what we might find. But what if knowing more about how our souls are constructed would make them less scary, rather as turning on the lights in the bedroom chases away the monsters that were peering out of the closet? This book is premised on the proposition that a big part of what troubles our souls is our confusion about how the soul is put together and how its disturbances were formed. We do not have an adequate conception of our souls, and this is why many everyday experiences can seem baffling.

- Parents find themselves swept up in anger and shouting at their kids things their own parents said, things they swore never to say to their children. Somehow our parents live on in us, continuing to run our lives and those of our children. As one patient in therapy said, "I like to think that I can be tolerant to a problem child and to the problem child in myself, but I can't. I am intolerant and aggressive to myself and though I disagree with the way my parents brought me up, I operate *en bloc* all their standards against myself."[4]
- Our emotions seem to have a will of their own, separate from our own. Hours, days, or even years, after the situation that provoked us to anger or shame has ceased to be important and we are trying to get on with daily life, the emotion continues to haunt us, nagging in the background, distracting us from the tasks at hand. Listen to Willie Nelson's song "Local Memory" for a description of this experience.
- Some people feel that they are fakes, that their personalities are just acts they put on for others, that behind the mask, they are nothing. If they are successful, they worry that they will be exposed as imposters. Though they know they are

---

4 Guntrip, *Schizoid Phenomena, Object-Relations and the Self.*

adults, they still think of themselves as children who have only managed to impersonate, so far, competent grownups. It's not that they are torn between two views of themselves: their core belief is that they are just pretending to be adults, and only luck or the kindness of others keeps them from being exposed and punished. They feel unreal, as if they didn't really exist.

- Then there is the "internal saboteur," or the inner critic. In the 1971 movie *Who is Harry Kellerman and Why is He Saying Those Terrible Things About Me?* Dustin Hoffman plays Georgie Soloway, a successful songwriter who is consumed by self-loathing. Whenever he begins a promising relationship with a woman, someone named Harry Kellerman calls her and warns her (falsely, we assume) that Soloway is violent and abusive. In the end, we learn that Soloway himself is making those calls. He is his own worst enemy under another name. The internal saboteur need not, of course, masquerade as someone else. More often, we speak in our own names when we say terrible things about ourselves.

The weirdness of these experiences suggests that our default notion of who we are, of how our souls are constituted, is misleadingly simple. What is this default picture of the soul?

First, we imagine, or try to imagine, that our souls are open to our own inspection, that we have the ability to "see" (and therefore control) what is going on in them. This is the illusion of *transparency*. How can I have a motive (for example, to sabotage myself) I am unaware of? It seems crazy that I could believe something (that I must be punished, for instance) without knowing that I believe it.

Second, we suppose that there is just one actor, or agent, in charge in this mind. It makes no sense that there might be an internal saboteur within me that makes me fail at things *I* really want to do. To take another example, it should be up to me to decide how to treat children, or the child in myself. It doesn't make sense that the attitudes of my parents, which I have disavowed, should be controlling what I think and say to my kids or to myself. There is just one thing that I name when I say 'I', and that is the agent who thinks my thoughts and makes my choices. I am *I*—the *one* responsible for my actions. Call this the illusion of *unity*.[5] This illusion also carries with it the idea that I am—or at least I should be—*independent* of other people. I am who I am regardless of my relations with others.

Most people today know, when they are thinking scientifically about psychology or the science of the brain, that the human being is a complicated system about which there is still much to be discovered. We know that a great deal of what makes us who and what we are is unconscious. How we see and react to the world is largely determined below the level of consciousness by parts of the brain we share with lower animals. National Public Radio often reports on studies showing that people's real reasons for voting as they do or buying what they buy are quite different from what they themselves think.

Nevertheless, when it comes to our everyday understanding of ourselves and each other, we usually fall back on the simple picture. There is a disconnect between what we know, in theory, about ourselves, and the way we experience and present ourselves. There is a reason for this. We think of ourselves as transparent, unified, and independent because the social world in which we live turns on holding individuals solely responsible for their thoughts and actions. You cannot hope be taken seriously and recognized as a real player in the social world without accepting the myths your society lives by.

---

5 Unity and transparency are central features of Descartes's conception of the mind. He resolved "to believe that nothing except our thoughts is wholly under our control..."Descartes, Rene, *Descartes*.

He also claims that knowledge of himself as a thinker "does not depend on things of whose existence I am as yet unaware." There can be no unconscious thoughts or motives for Descartes. Descartes, *Descartes*.

We hold ourselves to the standards of the simple model of the soul when we blame ourselves for our sins and errors and give little or no regard to how external events have affected us; we impose this model on others when we do the same to them. We insist that we—ourselves and others—are rational agents who know what we are doing, and if we act badly, it is by our own, individual, conscious choice. Our whole way of organizing society seems to depend on this assumption.

Nevertheless, when we can step away from the pressure of social obligations, talking with friends or writing in a private journal, we can often reject the simple model of the soul and accept that the soul is not a clean and well-lighted place, and that we are often divided. We are neither transparent nor unified. We are often disturbed by thoughts we wish we didn't have and feelings we cannot identify. We find ourselves doing and saying things we intended not to do or say. This richer understanding of our souls is often demonstrated in literature and film and in songs. This book does what it can to make this understanding deeper and more systematic.

The Soul

Since this book is an exploration of the *soul*, I owe you an explanation of how I will be using the word. To begin with, I must ask you to set aside, at least for now, any religious or metaphysical associations you might have with the word 'soul.' The soul is not an immaterial thing that exists, or could exist, independently of the life of the body (We will see later[6] why it's natural to think the soul lives on after death.) Indeed, the soul is not a thing, an object, or an entity at all—material or immaterial. What, then, you may be asking, could it be? Here is an analogy.

---

6 Chapter 15, Appendix.

Like the weather, the soul is not an object or a kind of object, but rather a general *topic*. What do we talk about when we talk about the weather? The weather is really a range of topics having to do with what's going on outside: amounts and kinds of precipitation (rain, snow, sleet, hail), wind, pressure, temperature, humidity, storms, clouds, sunshine and even pollution. So the weather is not an object or entity, but rather a topic. And it is not just *one* narrowly defined topic, but a whole grab bag of them. So what are we talking about when we talk about the soul?

Rather as 'the weather' directs our attention to what's happening outside, 'the soul' points to what's going on in a human being.[7] (We might even speak of an "interior" weather, the weather of the soul.) We use the word 'soul' to refer to the essence or the *core* of something, like the soul of music, or the soul of a novel. The word points towards something important and valuable that goes beyond what we can fully articulate. Similarly, when we speak of your soul or mine, we are trying to get at more than what is obvious on the surface.[8]

Understanding a soul is also rather like understanding a novel, for a person has a story, or many stories, to tell. We ask of a novel what the words and deeds of the characters *mean*—how they fit into the rest of the story, and this is also what we want to know about what we and other people say and do. What's missing from our stories that leaves us in the dark about why we have the inner demons we do?[9]

---

7 I don't wish to deny that animals have souls, but our focus here is on the souls of human beings.

8 Soul is a concept with an open horizon. Philosopher Wilfrid Sellars defines the *nature* of a thing as that which, if we but understood it, would explain why a thing does what it does. A person's soul is, in that sense, the nature of the person. This book is a guide to exploring the farther horizons of our souls with no expectation of a final and complete accounting of a soul.

9 I once had a conversation with an academic social psychologist who, when I told her I was interested in psychoanalysis, said "That's more like literature than science." Thinking about it later, I realized I should have responded, "Well, thinking about a person is more like thinking about a novel than like thinking about the objects of natural science."

There are some further reflections on the soul in the Appendix to this chapter.

Beyond the Brain

Since we are working towards a secular way of understanding our souls, one that is compatible with the modern scientific view that human life belongs to the natural world as it evolved biologically, it might seem that neurophysiology—the science of the brain—should offer us the most fundamental and complete explanation of the ways we think and feel. There is much to be learned about our souls from neuroscience, and I will occasionally make use of it. But our souls as we know them are missing in purely physical explanations of human life. We can be persuaded as we read books about neuroscience that our painful and joyful experiences are all explained in terms of the functioning of neural networks in our brains and throughout our bodies. In the same way, we can learn from chemistry and physics that the water we drink and bathe in is made up of atoms of hydrogen and oxygen combined as H_2O. But we do not experience water as a chemical compound, and we do not experience our thoughts and emotions as the work of the neurons and chemicals in our heads. This is not to deny the validity of these theoretical explanations; it is only to say that the approach of this book is different—more clearly connected to our experience (more "user-friendly") as I will now try to explain.

Our aim is to understand our inner demons, the painful and mysterious things that go on in our souls. Neuroscience begins by changing the subject: it tells us about an incredibly complex organ in our skulls and then tells us that the functioning of this organ is what is ultimately responsible for the demons—and the angels—in our soul, just as the way water behaves is ultimately explained by water really being H_2O. The neuroscientist says, "Obviously the way we ordinarily talk about our experience is inadequate, for it leaves us in ignorance about why we are beset by demons. So let's approach our experience in terms of its ultimate material foundation, namely the brain." My approach is different. Yes, it's true that the ways we ordinarily think and talk about our experience leaves us in the dark about ourselves. But instead of changing the subject, let's *begin* with our existing ways of talking about ourselves—about our thoughts, feelings, and attitudes. We will explore how we painfully bump up against the limits of these ways of understanding ourselves, and then we will expand and enrich them. We will ask what it is that our ordinary concepts of our mental and emotional lives fails to include, and what are the reasons for that blindness. Then we will build, step by step, on our existing understanding to develop a richer and deeper understanding of our souls.

To put it another way, the language we mostly use to record and communicate what we think and how we feel, a language inherited from our ancestors, leaves us unable to think clearly about the troubles in our souls, and this compounds our troubles. We don't make sense to ourselves. But rather than abandon this language in favor of scientific discourse about the brain, it might be possible to sharpen and expand the language we already know. That is what this book tries to do. As we proceed, we will be better able to make sense of experience that now seems senseless.

We will be making some use of an established psychological theory, one that in fact developed along the lines just suggested—psychoanalysis. Psychoanalysis is the analysis of the soul (the Greek word 'psyche' means *soul*)—how it is put together, why it is in conflict with itself, and how it got that way.[10] It's true that psychoanalytic writing is often dense and full of jargon. It seems to put forth a model of the "psychic apparatus" in which it seems hard to find a place for our souls as we know them. However, Freud intended many

---

10 Freud regularly uses the German word for soul (Seele), which his translators unfortunately either omitted or translated as 'mind'. See Bettelheim, *Freud and Man's Soul.*.

of his writings to be accessible to the general public and helpful to anyone who wanted to think about the soul. Psychoanalysis does not need to be couched in technical language, and I will use very little of it, attempting always to use and to build upon the language in which we ordinarily express ourselves.[11]

About this Book

The book is divided into two parts. In Part One, we will remind ourselves of how deeply we are embedded in our social life with each other. We will explore the paradox that we could not be who we are without being able to see ourselves through the eyes of those around us, and yet at the same time, the social world is often a heavy and painful burden. We are essentially social beings at odds with our social selves, leading us to wonder if there is a "real" self underneath the social façade.

Part Two expands and deepens our ways of thinking about our souls—again without retreating into a "foreign" theoretical language. This expanded conception of ourselves should help us to understand how our inner demons come to dwell in the darker corners of our souls.

Although this is not a self-help book, my experience is that the ideas developed here—in more than a decade of work—can render

---

11 It is difficult for us as English readers to find ourselves in psychoanalytic writings because Freud's translators, in an effort to make psychoanalysis seem more "scientific," used technical-sounding Latin words to translate Freud's more ordinary German words. Where we read that the structure of the mind consists of the 'ego,' the 'id,' and the 'superego,' in Freud's German, we would have 'das Ich' (the I), 'das Es' (the it), and 'das über Ich' (the Over-I). So instead of these theoretical objects—ego, id, and superego—we have, first, the ordinary word 'I' by which we normally affirm and identify ourselves. Then there is the *it*, which is familiar to us in contexts like "it came over me that I was very uncomfortable." And the Over-I is just the voice we take on when we speak to ourselves in the voice of authority—as an overseer. For example, "Why did you___, you idiot!." For a clear and readable account of all this, see Ibid..

our inner demons less demonic as light is cast upon them simply because what seems understandable is less frightening than what remains mysterious and dark. Reading this book will not reveal your particular collection of demons and their claims on you, but it might put you in a position to begin figuring them out yourself, perhaps with the help of a good friend or a therapist.

So this book is not a course in do-it-yourself therapy, but an exploration of the way our souls work. Two other things separate this work from self-help. First, it is written from the perspective of a particular kind of troubled soul and does not claim to address every way that souls can be unhappy or in pain. I think it illuminates the human condition in general, but it does so from the point of view of people who can identify with the troubles described in the first pages of this Introduction. If you find that it has no bearing on you, or that it is speaking to someone you feel no connection to, then put it aside. I have no wish to force anyone to wear shoes that don't fit.

A second difference from most self-help books is that the mood here is not relentlessly upbeat and optimistic; I do not sugar coat human life. The human condition is fundamentally tragic, and whether any of us can have a good life and a good soul is to a very large extent a matter of luck. I nevertheless do believe that having a clear-eyed, honest view of the world and where we are in it can make life better. This book's contribution to that goal is to sketch a map of the soul, illuminating the territory where we might find and come to accept parts of our souls that have been lost to us.

Self-help and Other Short Cuts

Self-help books, of which there are thousands, often with the word 'soul' in their titles, promise a quick and easy path to enlightenment and an end to the troubles of our souls. This book, as already mentioned, is not a self-help book. It may help, but it offers no guarantees and makes no promises. The path we will follow here is a more difficult one with more questions and fewer answers than self-help books. To explain why this more winding and ambiguous path is worth taking, I would like to show why the promises made by self-help books are deceptive and likely to give only short term and unreliable relief.

One of the more intelligent and well-written self-help books is *The Untethered Soul: The Journey Beyond Yourself*, by Michael A. Singer.[12] Both his book and mine begin with the same problem expressed in different words: While I call attention to our inner demons, like guilt, self-loathing, and anxiety, Singer points out the voices we hear in our heads giving us unwanted advice and criticism. Both books also pursue the question, Who am I? But here the differences emerge. Pursuing this question takes up most of the rest of my book, and the answers are tentative and incomplete. Singer, on the other hand, leads the reader quickly to a definitive answer that, he claims, provides the key to enlightenment and the silencing of the inner voices. Here is how he proceeds.

Pressing the reader to answer the question, 'Who are you?', Singer refuses any response that refers to your relations with others, anything about your body, and anything that you have done or that you are experiencing. All of that can, and does, change, while you remain the same you. Everything that goes on in your mind—your feelings, emotions, and your thoughts—are just objects you are observing. They are not parts of the essential you. So what is left to be you? Simply the pure consciousness that is doing the observing. This pure, unencumbered, "untethered" self is free to choose to have, or not to have, fears or desires towards whatever passes before it. Since nothing in your mind is really you, there is no need to go on defending all that extraneous material you used to identify with. "The reward for not protecting your psyche is liberation. You are free to walk through this world without a problem on your mind."

---

12 Michael A. Singer, *The Untethered Soul*.

Moreover, there is no danger that you might be troubled by demons you cannot see or control, for nothing within us is hidden from the enlightened and fearless consciousness. "Because there is no part of you that you're not willing to see, the mind is no longer divided into the conscious and subconscious."[13]

This reduction of the soul to a pure act of consciousness is an attempt, reminiscent of Descartes, to remove us from the real human condition of flesh and blood bodies desiring the help, companionship, and love of others and who depend on the soil and weather of the earth for comfort and survival. Singer, like many others writing in this vein, seduces us into picturing ourselves *abstractly*, secure in an imaginary existence apart from anything in the world that can cause pain and suffering, including our own desires. The pure self we are asked to believe that we are is *nothing*: an immaterial, solipsistic non-entity with no qualities and no motives for acting one way or another.

The idea that this pure, disengaged consciousness is *us* (our souls) has no relationship to what we know of our lives in a material—biological, chemical, and social— world. It gets its confirmation only in the fleeting experience of readers who succumb to a fantasy of total freedom from anything beyond their control and are thus momentarily empowered by a baseless self-confidence. The possibility that we are conscious of only a very small part of our souls and that our inner demons many be grounded in parts of ourselves beyond our grasp can never be taken seriously once pure consciousness is defined as the totality of what we are.

Let us take ourselves as we really are. The difficulties and obscurities that arise when we try to answer the question Who am I? point to something deeper than consciousness, and it will take a careful inquiry to get even a rough idea of who and what we really are.

---

13 Ibid., p. 61.

I do not claim that it is impossible to fundamentally change our mental and emotional habits by means of proactive, intentional action, whether by some "spiritual" practice like meditation, resolving to replace negative thoughts with positive ones, or following a twelve-step recovery program. But many people begin such practices only to give them up after a few days, weeks, or months. Why is this? As we will see in Part Two, every word we utter, and every gesture and posture of the body, interacts with the fabric of feeling and expectation, fear and desire, that was woven into us before we had any ability to perceive or control ourselves.[14]

Trying to give conscious direction to our souls is rather like trying to use wrenches and screwdrivers to manage the flow of water in an ancient swamp. Some people do come to feel more in charge of themselves, less controlled by alien forces, when they deliberately decide to think and act differently under the guidance of someone who tells them what to do. But I think the odds of success and the ability to sustain such changes will be improved by the sounder grasp of how our souls are put together that is offered in these pages.

---

14 Here is some useful realism from psychiatrist Arthur Kleinman:

> Psychotherapists and other healers can reject clichéd soap-opera solutions to personal crises, which reinforce the politically expedient and commercially profitable illusion that we live in a domesticated "natural" world of expectable order in which disorder is atypical and need not be endured. In the place of this illusion, psychotherapists and other healers can offer the hard-won critical—and therefore moral as well as political—awareness that our experiences are difficult, uncertain struggles with menace and loss in local life worlds over which we exert imperfect control, sometimes hardly any, and in which the transformations of impending chaos into transient order is, for the most part, a precarious victory to be won (or lost) every day with usually inadequate resources and within an intimate circle of interdependence on them.

Arthur Kleinman, *Rethinking Psychiatry: From Cultural Category to Personal Experience,* p. 129.

We are going to try to make sense of ourselves and our lives. If nothing else, I hope you will come away from this book with "a deep appreciation of the awesome complexity of the human soul."[15]

The least we can do for each other in a world where life is short and difficult is to try to understand and love each other.

One final comment about how to use this book. While no background in philosophy or psychology is necessary to follow my main argument, some of the chapters have appendices that expand philosophical ideas related to the discussion. These can be safely skipped. Some of the footnotes also make connections to philosophers and philosophical questions; these, too, are optional reading.

Appendix: Only a Soul Can See a Soul

We sometimes use the word 'soul' to indicate what we find most valuable in a thing. When Freud used the word ('Seele' in German), he meant, according to Bruno Bettleheim, "that which is most valuable in man while he is alive."[16] So, to call up another analogy, let's think about how something becomes valuable—money, for example.

What makes a piece of metal or paper become money? All by itself, as a chemist might describe it, or to someone from a society that did not use money, such an object has no value; it is not money. But it is not just our minds or imagination that turns it into money. It gets its value from the ways in which it is woven into our daily lives and into the complex system of social practices that constitute our economy. Two factors embed it in our lives: desire and force. Because money is the key to all our desires for material things, it becomes itself the primary object of material desire. Our practical, day-to-day lives revolve, to a very great degree, directly or indirectly, around the desire to obtain or hold on to money. And the value of money is protected by force; like the border between the U.S. and Mexico, the value of money is made real by laws and the enforcement of those laws by guns and the walls of banks and prisons.

---

15 Paraphrased from Mitchell, *Hope And Dread In Pychoanalysis.*
16 Bettelheim, *Freud and Man's Soul.*

Granted, there is something unseemly about comparing the soul of a human being with the value of money; there is something soul-less about a life devoted to money. No analogy is perfect, and that is the limit of this one. What it suggests, though, is that the human soul is what a human being has because of the way we are woven into each others' lives. We are bound up with each other in institutions like the family and the workplace, and by a complicated mix of habits, interests, desires, and love. When we recognize another human being as a person, as having a soul, we are counting him or her as part of the human community. This is why we often say of our enemies in war that they are inhuman: we do not want to recognize them as having souls.

This helps us see why the soul is not just the activity of the body as it is described by chemistry and biology, or just a function of the brain. That would be like supposing that a dollar is just a piece of paper or metal or some electronic traces in a computer server. Only people who live in and depend on an economic system involving money can see money. Only people who can read and get caught up in stories can recognize a long string of words as a novel. And only a human being among other human beings can see a soul. Only the soul has eyes to see a soul.

Reducing the human being to nothing but the human body and brain as described by natural science forgets that human beings *are us*. We can empathize and identify with a soul, but not with a mere *thing* like the structure of the brain. Reduction of the human to the body bleeds out the investment we have in each other, in our common life. This is what we mean when we say that the soul is missing from a purely physical or natural or objective account of a human life. A human being is someone who signifies—makes meaning—and who is significant, who plays a central role in our lives.

The soul, then, is not a metaphysical entity separate from our bodies and our lives together. And yet our souls are not just our bodies as physical, chemical and biological systems. Similarly, the meaning of a word is not some entity separate from the sound or look of the word, and yet is more than just the noise or sequence of letters we use to make the word. A melody is not just a sequence of tones, but it is not some extra material feature of that sequence. To say a word has meaning is to make it part of our way of communicating with each other. We call something a melody when we take it up in our musical life. To say that someone is a person—has a soul—is to take that creature up in our social and emotional lives. We will see how we are woven together by language and social practice in the next chapter.

2

Soul in the World

Alas for me! The more I seek my solitude, the less of it I find. Whenever I look for it, my shadow looks with me.

FERRAN[1]

Self-consciousness exists in and for itself when, and by the fact that, it so exists for another; that is, it exists only in being acknowledged.

HEGEL[2]

Introduction

WE NOW BEGIN a step-by-step inquiry into how our souls are put together. Each step by itself will seem insufficient, and that insufficiency will lead to the next step. We start with the most visible thing about what makes each of us a person—that we can be identified

---

1 A Spanish writer quoted by Nat Hentoff in liner notes for "Sketches of Spain" with Miles Davis and Gil Evans.
2 Hegel, *Phenomenology of Spirit,* §178, p. 111.

and recognized in social space. In the next chapter, seeing that we are more than just what our documents say about us, we consider the fact that we often act spontaneously and unpredictably. This is followed by the question of how we interact with social forces to become the social beings we are. And so on. At each step, we have an incomplete picture of our souls, but each step is intended to add to the picture, filling in the gaps.

Personal Identity and Social Location

When we search our souls, asking ourselves "Who am I?" where are we looking? Where do we turn our mental gaze—inward or outward?

It is natural to suppose that our thoughts and feelings are inside us, that our souls, or minds, are interior spaces into which we look when we try to know who we really are.

If who I am is something contained entirely within me, then my soul is mine alone; I am ultimately responsible for what I think, feel, and do. The rest of the world may limit me, it may offer me opportunities and temptations, but at my core, I am in charge of myself. As a famous poem puts it,

> It matters not how strait the gate,
> How charged with punishments the scroll,
> I am the master of my fate:
> I am the captain of my soul.[3]

Yet if someone asks me who I am, I naturally begin with my place in the world. My name already locates me in a web of family relations. My nationality, my occupation, my interests and ambitions involve me in networks of social life, and they all are part of who I am.

---

3 "Invictus by William Ernest Henley."

You might say that's true from a sociological perspective, but not from a personal one. Of course, I have a *social location* (name, address, social security number, credit rating, etc.), but who I am in society is not my soul. Wouldn't I still be *me* even if I occupied an entirely different social location?

I don't think so. My social location consists not only of the terms by which society, official and unofficial, identifies me, it is also central to how I identify myself. We can no more understand ourselves in isolation from our social existence—looking only within—than we can understand an organ of our bodies—the heart or the brain—without knowing anything about the rest of the body and its physical environment. What we find within us is a snarl of mental knots and emotional tangles. It would be hopeless to try to untangle them without knowing that they consist of cords whose other ends are tangled up in the lives of others. Although as we will see in the next chapter, our souls *resist* the world in various ways, we are nevertheless in and of the world.

When we look within, what we find there keeps drawing our attention to sources and connections far beyond us. Consider two constant activities of our souls: desire and thought.

Desire

We are never free from desire, and what it is that we most desire? In her book *The Hidden Life of Dogs*,[4] Elizabeth M. Thomas says that what dogs want more than anything else is each other. Isn't this true of that other social animal, the human being? What we spend most of our energy plotting and striving to do is to get into the right relations with other people. Even bare physical survival is accomplished for the most part through arrangements with others, but we want much more from others than just the food, shelter, and sexual sat-

---

4 Thomas, *The Hidden Life of Dogs*.

isfaction they can provide. Let us say, for starters, that what we want from each other is *recognition*. According to Jacques Lacan, "man's desire finds its meaning in the desire of the other, not so much because the other holds the key to the object desired, as because the first object of desire is to be *recognized* by the other."[5] Or, as Slavoj Žižek writes, "The problem with human desire is that, as Lacan put it, it is always 'desire for the Other' in all the senses of that term: desire for the Other, desire to be desired by the Other, and, especially, desire for what the other desires".[6]

Our deepest fear is loneliness; death is terrifying when we imagine it to be eternal solitude. It is no accident that the most serious punishments (short of the ultimate loneliness of death) have always involved solitary confinement and exile. And the worst thing we can do to another person in social life is to ignore her, to withhold recognition, to act as if she doesn't exist.

Thinking

Since our relations with others are of ultimate concern to us, they are what we think about most of the time. Most thinking is problem-solving, and most of our problems concern our relations with others.

True, not *all* thinking is problem solving, and not all problems are about others. I may contemplate something beautiful or wonderful without trying to decide what to do or say about it. Curiosity is the desire to know something for the pleasure of knowing it. Nevertheless, more often than we realize, our curiosity has the ulterior motive of preparing ourselves to deal with people in some way, for example, to be able to describe it in a way that would satisfy or interest them. Similarly, problems that seem to have nothing to

---

5 Lacan, Écrits, cited in Murphy, Glowinski, and Marks, *A Compendium of Lacanian Terms*.
6 Žižek, *Violence*, p. 74. We will find in Part Two that our desires for each other go beyond recognition..

do with others—questions of mathematics, physics or biology, for example—are also guided by concerns about what others want to know and about one's own ability to explain.

To answer the question "Who am I?" I have to *start* with facts like these: I am a 76-year old American male with a PhD in philosophy who spent 37 years teaching at a liberal arts college in Portland and who is now writing a book about the soul. It is also central to who I am that I *want* to be known and perceived in certain ways by others—with the dignity appropriate to my station in life. People regularly risk, or even give up, their lives to maintain their reputations. And I cannot avoid the fact I am afraid that I may *not* be perceived in those ways—that people might see me as an awkward, solitary old man or as having lived a mediocre and undistinguished life. All these aspirations and fears are in me, and they are ways in which my soul is woven into the social fabric made of other souls.[7]

Entangled in Language

So far I have been trying to show that we cannot know ourselves without knowing how we are mixed up in each others' lives. But it turns out that we would not be able to reflect on ourselves at all except for our engagement with others through language.

---

7 There are two other important ways in which our thoughts and action are woven into the social network. First, we move and act in a world that is largely the product of human activity. Thus our actions and what they mean to us are shaped by the architecture of our world, just as our speech is shaped by the language we speak. For example, we work and consume within the framework of the money system, and we travel from one place to another in the transportation system consisting of streets, highways, traffic laws, airline schedules and airport procedures, and all of this (working, commerce and travel) are regulated by calendar and clock time. Secondly, every thought we have about the world and about ourselves gets its meaning from —and thus is the thought that it is because of—the common categories of our language. When I perceive something as, say, a bus or a tree, I am claiming that it is what others would recognize as a bus or a tree. That is, my perception is appealing to the language we share. Thus thinking is an implicit act of communication, a social act.

When I ask myself who I am, I am using concepts that already locate me in social space—the concepts of *who* and *I*. 'Who' means *someone*, a person with a name and a social location. 'I' means one who *says* 'I'. We use the first person pronoun to identify the one (among others) who is speaking, and speaking is a communicative act. It *addresses* others (*I* speak to *you*). To say 'I' is to enter into a transaction, a "language-game,"[8] in which those to whom I speak can address me as 'you', and can refer to me as 'he' or 'she' when addressing others. Moreover, as one who says 'I', I can become part of a *we* in contrast with more distant others, and part of a *they* from the perspective of those distant others.

To be a person, then, is to be a participant in the game of personal pronouns by which we identify ourselves and are identified by others. To speak and be spoken to is a crucial sign of the recognition that is the first object of our desire.[9] If someone refers to you as 'it', that would be a chilling signal that your voice will not be heard and you will not be spoken to.

To be a person, rather than an *it*, one must be either *he* or *she*. The grammar of our language requires that every person be either male or female, since no one can refer to you in the third person without deciding whether to use 'he' or 'she'. This makes gender and all its cultural baggage the axis of who we are. Everything about me is *inflected* by my gender, as I and others perceive it. In many languages, the gender to which I am assigned inflects all the nouns and adjectives that describe me. In a similar way, whether I am male or female inflects how I and others interpret my actions, and this interpretation influences the actions themselves. This strict male/female dichotomy is being challenged by the LGBTQ (lesbian, gay, bisexual, transsexual, queer) community, but it is still a powerful part of our cultural grammar.

---

8 Wittgenstein made this phrase famous in philosophical circles in the early pages of his *Philosophical Investigations*.

9 This mutual recognition can also be accomplished nonverbally—with looks and gestures.

Gender is just one of many ways our language, institutions, and practices organize what and who we can be. Our society has a whole system of identities built into its language and institutions. Race is a powerful example. If you are identified as "black," for example, then many doors are, if not closed, then either hidden or just much harder to open than they are for those seen as "white". And many dangers await, not least of which is being perceived as dangerous or expendable, and therefore justifying preemptive violence by police or others.

Being Self-conscious

The human soul has the ability to reflect upon itself; we can criticize, condemn, praise, and guide ourselves. We can even ask, "Who am I?" We are *self-conscious*. But how can the soul, catch itself in the act of thinking about itself? The eye cannot see itself; how can the *I* think about itself? And yet we do it. We are conscious of ourselves whenever we remember what we have done, think about what to do now, or wonder why we feel the way we do. How is this possible? How do I become both the subject and the object of my thought, the thinker and the thought-about?

The *I* cannot know itself directly, just as the eye cannot look at itself. But the eye can see itself in a mirror or a photograph—a "selfie" or a self-portrait.[10] Similarly, we make stories about ourselves.[11] These stories are recorded in our common language. We see, remember,

---

10 As Ariel Hirschfeld notes,

> The portrait, the appearance of man's face, cannot be seen by him. He sees everything except for his face. Man must go out and become an other. The self portrait is departing one's eye sockets and disguising oneself as the other. The other that is within him, leaps forward to his consciousness, and through his otherness he is able to see himself. (quoted at http://www.mots.org.il/Eng/Exhibitions/WorkItem.asp?ContentID=58)

11 It follows that we do not catch ourselves in the act; we do not see ourselves in action, but only after the fact, in retrospect—in the story we then tell. The eye can see itself in the mirror as it is in the moment (setting aside the nanoseconds it takes

and evaluate ourselves with the concepts bequeathed to us. We are not alone within our souls. We learn to monitor and care for ourselves by first being cared for and monitored by others. Just as the eye must be reflected in something outside itself, so the *I*, to be self-conscious, must be reflected in and through another *I*.

What happens when I realize that I am angry and start to reflect on it? Let's say that being angry and being reflective about being angry are two different performances, two different roles that one can play. So when I reflect on my anger, I step out of one role and into another. I step out of the stance of being angry and take up the attitude of observing one who is angry. In this way, I get some distance from the one who is angry.[12]

Standing aside from my anger by thinking about it does not necessarily mean I cease being angry. The urge to present myself as angry can very well persist along side the desire to understand it. (My mind has a mind of its own.) More exactly, I am often of two (or more) minds, and which of them gets to be *my* mind is often in doubt.[13] Moreover, the mind that observes me being angry may itself become angry that I am angry!

---

for light to travel and the brain to process visual signals), but the *I* can only know itself as it was. Self-knowledge begins with memory.

12 In philosophical terms, the performance of anger becomes the object of reflection for the one who is reflecting, who is now the subject. The angry subject has now become the angry object because a new subject position has entered the scene, the reflecting subject.

13 Nietzsche makes a powerful case that there is no single ego or executive agent which unproblematically makes decisions. Rather, within each of us there is a complex of *many* tendencies, wishes, impulses, concerns, worries, and goals which are in tension and opposition with each other. We identify with, and call "I", that one force which, at the moment, has achieved hegemony and which the others have, again for the moment, obeyed.

> In this way the person exercising volition adds the feelings of delight of his successful executive instruments, the useful "under-wills" or under-souls—indeed our body is but a social structure composed of many souls—to his feelings of delight as commander. *L'effet c'est moi.* What happens here is what happens in every well-constructed and happy

To become conscious of something is to make it available for discussion, to put it on the table, to bring it into the conversation, even if the conversation is only between you at one moment and you a moment later. So we become self-conscious by making something about ourselves, something we are thinking, feeling, or doing, a topic of discussion, even if it's a discussion we have only behind closed doors or closed lips. Why do we do this? What's the purpose of self-consciousness? The example of anger suggests that it's a matter of self-control, a way of tracking and guiding what we are doing. Instead of just acting on impulse and instinct, we act under advisement.

Critical Self-consciousness

But the advice that comes to us when we pass our lives under review is not always friendly, as these lines from T.S. Eliot suggest:

> What is this self inside us, this silent observer,
> Severe and speechless critic, who can terrorize us
> And urge us on to futile activity,
> And in the end, judge us still more severely
> For the errors into which his own reproaches drove us?[14]

Where does the advice we give ourselves come from? How do we learn the role of self-critic and self-adviser that we enact in response to things we have done or might do? We often speak of "internalizing the attitudes of others," but how does this happen?

---

commonwealth; namely the governing class identifies itself with the successes of the commonwealth. Nietzsche, *Beyond Good and Evil §19*.

That bearer of ultimate responsibility, the agent, is thus the fragile result of a temporary balance of power. This point will be further developed in Chapter 6.
14 "The Elder Statesman" (a play). Quoted in Briggs, *Ruined Time*. Page number unknown.

George Herbert Mead argues that the foundation for that inner dialogue that goes on in self-consciousness begins with the child's game of pretending to be other people, in particular, parents or other grown-ups.[15] Children play at being their parents and order themselves about as their mothers or fathers would. As we grow up, we learn to do this as a matter of habit—to comment upon and to guide our own actions from the point of view of others. Sometimes we are influenced by people who are significant to us in one way or another, whose approval we desire—family, friends, or colleagues, for example. Their attitudes can affect the way we think and act even when we are not with them and even without our realizing it. Sometimes we are moved by a general, and again unnoticed, concern for the image we present to the world at large, and this guides the way we carry ourselves when we're out in public.[16]

We take up the attitudes of others usually without being aware that they are borrowed, with the result that we either treat them as our own when talking to ourselves, or, like Eliot, we experience them, as alien forces that have somehow invaded our souls. Self-consciousness is not conscious of its sources: we are self-conscious because we take the attitudes of others towards us, but we are not aware that we do so. Much more than we admit, we are deeply social beings, for we are constantly acting in light of the attitudes of others, in the gaze of the other. We have strong ties and deep conflicts with each other, and if we try to live as if we didn't, we lose sight of much of what makes us what we really are. And this gives rise to demons.

---

15 Mead, *Mind, Self & Society,* p. 152.

16 Sometimes, even as children, we are aware, and even appreciative, of lessons we have learned from others—our parents, for example. *The Great Gatsby* begins "In my younger and more vulnerable years my father gave me some advice that I've been turning over in my mind ever since." Fitzgerald, *The Great Gatsby.* The central concern of *this* book, however, is what we have learned without knowing we have learned it.

Appendix: How we say who we are (the vocabulary of the soul)

Besides the word 'soul', discussed in Chapter 1, there are several other words in this and later chapters that focus attention on one or another facet of our existence. I try to use them in ways that I think will make sense to readers and without reference to special psychological or philosophical theories. For readers who find the following terms confusing, I offer these notes on how I understand them. They are not precise terms, and they overlap and blend into each other.

Social location: First, how you are identified in social systems and institutional records (name, date of birth, Social Security Number, credit rating, criminal record, education, employment, marital and family status, age, military record, etc.). Secondly, your social status, how you are perceived and received and valued by others.

Personal identity: Your story about yourself—what you can tell and what you keep to yourself, what you are clear and/or confused about. What you think of yourself. Your "sense" of who you are.

Persona: The way you represent yourself to others. It can be compared to a mask that portrays you as you wish others to see you, or to the performance of an actor in a play. It covers over some or most of what you think and feel; you may even be taken in by it yourself. Some people are comfortable in their personas, at ease with the fit, or lack of fit, between who they are and who they are supposed to be, believing, perhaps, that they wear no mask. This book doubts that; in any event, it addresses those whose masks weigh heavily and painfully on their skins.

The self: To begin with, the word 'self' is just a grammatical particle for referring back to something already mentioned, as in 'The building collapsed in on itself'. In psychology and philosophy, it functions as another word for whatever 'I' refers to, so its meaning depends on the theory being put forward. However, 'self' is often strongly contrasted with 'others' or with 'society', thereby implying, misleadingly, that the self is to be understood apart from relationships with others. I make no special use of 'self' in this book.

Ego. In psychology, the (often considerable) theoretical weight of the word 'ego' varies from one theory to another. It does not play any role in this book and appears only in a few quotations from others.

The body. The soul is not distinct or separable from the living human body, so 'body' is not to be understood in contrast with 'soul'. When I refer to 'the body', it is to draw attention to processes and events in their organic dimension, occurring independently of our conscious will. For example, emotional reactions to events, of which we may or may not be aware, occur in the body before, and whether or not, we take note of them. You can see that someone is shocked or puzzled when she herself is unaware that she is. As Wittgenstein says, "The human body is the best picture of the human soul."[17] We can say that our souls are written in, or on, our bodies.

I also use the phrase 'animal soul' to refer to what we think and feel unconsciously. 'Body' and 'animal soul' remind us that a great deal goes on in our bodies that we do not notice and could never articulate, which nevertheless has a lot to do with how we feel and what we think and do.

---

17 Wittgenstein, *Philosophical Investigations* II, iv.

3

The Task of Being You

I'm not really Mr. X; I just play him in real life.

FROM THE JOURNAL OF MR. X

Introduction

THE LAST CHAPTER focused on how wide and strong are our connections with each other and with the social fabric that weaves our lives together. "The self is not something that exists first and then enters into relationship with others; ... it is, so to speak, an eddy in the social current and so still part of the current," writes George Herbert Mead. But he goes on, "It [the self] is a process in which the individual is continually adjusting himself in advance to the situation to which he belongs, and reacting back on it."[1] We are certainly in the social current, but we also respond to it and contribute to its movement. We are more like fish in the river than driftwood at the mercy of the currents of our culture and social order.

---

1 Mead, *Mind, Self & Society*, p. 182.

All The World's a Stage

I have an identity—that is, I can be identified and identify myself—because I have a location in social space where I can be addressed and located. I am *I* only because there is a *you* to address me as "you" and to whom I can identify myself as "I". Like the words we use, you and I are social beings. The marks on this page would not mean what they do if were not for the language we speak. They are the words they are because of their relations to the other words of our language and the roles they play in human social life. I would not be who I am apart from the network of relations I have with others.

> All the world's a stage,
> And all the men and women merely players:
> They have their exits and their entrances;
> And one man in his time plays many parts.[2]

We are indeed players, not just some of the time but all of the time. We never act or think or feel without the eyes of others upon us. Yet that does not mean we are *merely* players.

To see what more we are, let's think through this idea that we live our lives on stage and play many parts. Is *everything* we do scripted by the roles we play in our lives? Certainly not in the way that an on-stage character's words and actions are scripted by a text that has been memorized and rehearsed. And yet there are similarities: Our parents drill us in the civilities of life. They tell us, "Say 'thank you' to the nice man!" and then a gift or a kindness becomes the cue to repeat our lines.

But most of the scripts governing us in social situations are much looser and give us more room to be inventive. In a meeting or on a date or standing in line at the coffee shop, there are norms, rules, expectations, practices, and implicit understandings that roughly

---

2 William Shakespeare, "As You Like It," Act II, 7.

define the boundaries of what's acceptable. In many situations the participants are trying to achieve something, either together, as in a meeting, or in competition, as in a game. Therefore they need to be inventive, to come up with something not previously scripted by the situation. Most real-life scenarios call on the actors to be original—as in impromptu theater.

"All the world's a stage" means that we are always responding to the demands and expectations of fellow actors in some situation in terms of which we must act. Every situation is a scenario, like a moment in a game that invites or demands some response from us. I am the batter and the pitch is on its way. You have asked me a question or complimented me or stepped on my foot. What do I do next, and what do I expect you to do? Moreover, I am aware of, and responsive to, not only the other actors on the stage, but to the audience—the bystanders. In the theater, of course, the audience usually remains outside the action, but on the street or in the kitchen, those who are in the audience at one moment may become part of the action in the next.[3] Most scenarios not only permit, but call for, some degree of spontaneity—actions that are not, and could not be, predicted.

Some of the many parts we play in our lives we play only in certain limited situations, like being a member of a concert audience. But other roles are more defining of who we are, and once we take them on, they become part of our identity. Being a father or mother, for example, affects the way I conduct myself for the rest of my life, as does being the child of my parents and being an American. These roles, too, leave plenty of room to invent oneself.

---

3 For an extended discussion of human social life in these terms, see Goffman, *The Presentation of Self in Everyday Life.*

Stage Fright, Stage Presence

You are not just the roles you play. Not only do you invent your own way of playing your part, but you also react to the parts you play or might play. You are comfortable doing what some situations require of you, and uncomfortable with others.[4] People mostly gravitate towards roles they like to play, and avoid those that embarrass or frighten them—though you may have reasons for voluntarily taking on difficult parts. It may pay well, or you might want to overcome your embarrassment at appearing before an audience.

We play many parts, some just for the moment or for a day, and some for life. But there is also a sum of our parts—the part of being _____ (insert your name here). We can call this image that you (inconsistently, of course) try to project and to live up to, your *persona*, a word that also has the meaning of *mask*. Personas are "those larger than life masks that conceal all the wild inconsistencies within."[5] And just as with your smaller parts, you have to work at maintaining that mask, at being _____. Moreover, you do it in front of an audience, under the gaze and judgment, real and imagined, of others. It isn't always easy being you.

> ...and finding a way to smuggle your name
> from one day to the next
> is a real puzzle.[6]

---

4 In his book *Faking It*, Ian Miller remarks that there must be a "real me, a very embarrassable real me, who drew the line at...how loud I would not cheer at a pep rally, or how nothing in the world could get me to say 'groovy.' My true inner self sets limits and draws the line at certain kinds and amounts of faking...." (Miller, *Faking It,* p. 229). However, as we will see, there is nothing especially "real" or "true" about this "embarrassable" me. It is simply the other side of the self that does the faking. They both result from the same activity.

5 Robinson, *Red Mars* p. 200.

6 Rutsala, *The Mystery of Lost Shoes*, p. 12.

Just as our smaller roles, like our shoes, can fit us well or badly and give us pleasure or pain, so there are, or at least there seem to be, people whose personas fit them comfortably, who are always at home in their skins. They seem to really and spontaneously be what they pretend to be; they *seem,* even to themselves, not to be pretending. But there are many others whose personas fit them badly, as did Richard Nixon's, at least as observed by Norman Mailer:

> ...Nixon has character-armor,[7] hordes of it! Several schemes of armor are stacked all on top of one another, but none complete. It is as if he is wearing two breastplates and yet you can still get peeks of his midriff. He walks like a puppet more curious than most human beings, for all the strings are pulled by a hand within his own head, an inquiring hand which never pulls the same string in quite the same way as the previous time––it is always trying something out––and so the movements of his arms and legs while superficially conventional, even highly restrained, are all impregnated with attempts, still timid—after all these years!—to express attitudes and emotions with his body. But he handles his body like an adolescent suffering excruciations of self-consciousness with every move.... It is as if his ...brain...is off on a journey of inquiry into the stubborn refusal of the body to obey it. He must be obsessed with the powers he could employ if his body could also function intimately as an instrument of his will... but his body refuses. Like a recalcitrant hound, it refuses.... Stubborn as an animal, the body does not give up and keeps making its disjunctive moves while the will almost as quickly snaps them back.[8]

7 As Mailer acknowledges, "character armor" is Wilhelm Reich's metaphor for the way we manage our bodies to present our public images and hide our disreputable desires and impulses.

8 Mailer, *Some Honorable Men* pp. 472-723.

It was, apparently, hard work being Richard Nixon. Many people know from their own experience what a burden it is to be who they say they are, how much anxiety, even panic, is attached to the feeling that they *must*, at any cost, act the part they have been assigned without betraying the terror that threatens to melt them down to jelly. They must not display this terror, or even admit it to themselves, and that commandment only heightens the fear. In moments of reflection, people like this may say to themselves, "It isn't easy being Me! I am a heavy burden to myself!" And they may well feel estranged from themselves—as if there really isn't anyone named _____, in spite of the charade they are putting on. ("No doubt others are snickering behind my back at my ridiculous attempts to pass off this fictional character as a real person.") We[9] are the hollow men, as T.S. Eliot wrote. This book is an attempt to understand why this is so, and to see if there are ways to ease that burden.

Who Am I, Really?

If being you or Richard Nixon is just a façade, an act, then who is the creature putting on the act? Is there someone, or some thing, that you *really* are?

In Mailer's description of Nixon, the bearer of the burden of being Nixon is "an animal," "a recalcitrant hound," "the body." But Nixon and his body are not two things; neither could exist without the other. They are two sides of one thing, as with any human performance: the dancer and the dance, the singer and the song, the speaker and her discourse. They are distinguishable, and yet they are inseparable, like a word and its meaning.[10]

---

9 Recall that this "we" is meant to include only those who can identify with the state of mind being described here.

10 Usually, when we are in the midst of life, we focus on the personas of people; we see them as the characters they are enacting. But sometimes from a distance, we can see them otherwise, as does Kate Brown in Doris Lessing's novel *The Summer Before the Dark* as she looks down on a theatrical production: "But what

A good actor may subtly suggest the animal within even when it's hidden by a smoother performance than Nixon's. Film critic Stephanie Zacharek comments about Michael Caine's portrayal of Alfie in the 1966 movie of that name:

> ...as Caine plays him, [Alfie's] coldness wafts off him like vapor off dry ice. He has a sensitive side, but it's fully veiled by that polar smoke—we may get glimpses of the anguished, *animal shape of his soul*, but by design, we can't get close enough to smooth down and calm its fur. Still, we know it's there—that kind of subliminal conviction is just part of what an extraordinary actor like Caine is capable of.[11]

If we could find ways to get close enough to each other to "smooth down and calm" our agitated fur—to trust others to be that close to us—would that ease the burden of "being me"?

Our souls have two sides: First, there is the posture we adopt for public presentation, the stance we take for others. Then there is the *animal* shape, the *contortion*, that results from the effort of maintaining that posture or stance, the strain, for example, of holding the smile required of a cocktail waitress. This contortion of the body has several layers: the muscular effort of putting on the public show; the fear of failing at it; the pain of embarrassment or anger at having to perform; the further effort of hiding or disguising that pain; the resentment, directed against one's audience, that one is

---

a remarkable thing it was, this room full of people, animals rather, all looking in one direction, at other dressed-up animals lifted up to perform on a stage, animals covered with cloth and bits of fur, ornamented with stones, their faces and claws painted with colour." Cited in John Leonard, "The Adventures of Doris Lessing," *New York Review of Books*, Nov. 30, 2006, p. 46.

11 Zacharek, "Alfie.'"

required to exert that effort; the effort of hiding *that* resentment; and so on and on.[12]

Our relations with others are usually beset with some degree of performance anxiety. Perhaps we feel only slightly nervous that we might say or do something slightly foolish or careless, like spilling coffee or talking with a mouthful of food. Or we may be intensely afraid of being exposed as an incompetent or a complete fake. Like all emotions, these feelings do not lie passively inside us waiting for permission to show themselves. They are like dogs locked in the basement: they want out. But these dogs are not separate creatures that can be confined by shutting a door. They are *us*; like breathing, they are what our bodies *do*. So the labor of hiding our feelings is the labor of disciplining our bodies, ourselves, to engage in a life-long battle against doing what bodies want to do. And this work, in turn, gives us more to fear and more to resent.[13]

What is especially scary is that while we *feel* all this distress, we don't let ourselves understand it, and that prevents us from doing anything about it. We feel beset by invisible forces within us we call our "demons." Most of what goes on in our hearts and minds does not require us to be conscious of it; consciousness is an optional feature of our emotional life and of much of our cognitive activity.[14] Thus the feelings of anxiety and resentment that surround our social performance have a life of their own whether we are paying attention to them or not. It is not out of carelessness that we don't notice them. It is because we are afraid to look; we are frightened

---

12 This makes clear that it is not the "natural" body that resists what the public requires, but the body that has been bruised and scarred by its experience as a public body—a body on display.

13 The animal shape of our souls need not always be so afflicted. Some of us, perhaps, are, at least some of the time, with people we love and trust, people with whom our performances can be playful rather constrained by fear, and then the animal breathes freely and rejoices.

14 It might seem impossible that we should have thoughts we are not aware of. We will take up this seeming paradox in a later chapter.

of not really being what we pretend to be, afraid of not living up to expectations, afraid of being exposed as "hollow," afraid of not existing. As a result, we have trained ourselves to carefully control what our bodies say and display; we must monitor what we say and what is implied by what we say (and don't say) and how we say it. We must also govern the sound of our voices, the play of expression on our faces, our gestures and our posture. All this work would be impossible if we had to do it consciously. Even when it's set on automatic, it's still a struggle, and it produces battle fatigue, or stress. And that, too, must be hidden and denied.[15]

Who are we afraid of?

We have been describing lives lived in fear, fear of not living up to expectations, fear of being exposed as fools or failures. But whose expectations are these? Exposed to whom? If we were just afraid of being seen in a bad light by people we meet, by real people, then it seems our anxieties should disappear when we escape into our own rooms and close the doors behind us. Alone, I should no longer face the struggle to be me, to "smuggle my name from one day to the next."

---

15 In *Swann's Way*, Marcel Proust describes Swann's way of dealing with an embarrassing mistake involving Odette:

> He did not talk to her about this misadventure, he himself did not think about it further. But now and then his thoughts as they moved about would come upon the memory of it which they had not noticed, bump up against it, drive it further in, and Swann would feel a sudden, deep pain. As if were a physical pain, Swann's mind could not lessen it; but at least with physical pain, because it is independent of thought, thought can dwell on it, note that it has diminished, that it has momentarily ceased. But with this pain the mind, merely by recalling it, re-created it. To wish not to think about it was still to think about it, still to suffer from it. Proust, *Swann's Way*.

There is nothing more alone than being in a car at night in the rain... Between one point on the map and another point on the map, there was the being alone in the car in the rain. They say you are not you except in terms of relation to other people. If there weren't any other people there wouldn't be any you because what you do, which is what you are, only has meaning in relation to other people. That is a very comforting thought when you are in the car in the rain at night alone, for then you aren't you, and not being you or anything, you can really lie back and get some rest. It is a vacation from being you. There is only the flow of the motor under your foot spinning that frail thread of sound out of its metal gut like a spider, that filament, that nexus, which isn't really there, between the you which you have just left in one place and the you you will be when you get to the other place.[16]

Or so thinks Jack Burden, the narrator of *All the Kings Men*, as he drives from one social location to another, from his mother's genteel home where he grew up among old Southern aristocracy back to his job working for populist governor Willie Stark.

But is it really that easy to retreat from oneself? Many people find that it's when they are alone in a car or in bed at night that lots of regrets and *what ifs* come pouring back, and so you don't really get any vacation from being you. You are never really alone; you're always thinking and feeling as if someone else is present—as an Iris Murdoch novel asserts:

There are mysterious agencies of the human mind which, like roving gases, travel the world, causing pain and mutilation, without their owners' having any full awareness, or even

---

16 Warren, *All the King's Men* p. 128-29.

any awareness at all, of the strength and the whereabouts of these exhalations. Possibly a saint might be known by the utter absence of such gaseous tentacles, but the ordinary person is naturally endowed with them, just as he is endowed with the ghostly power of appearing in other people's dreams. So it is that we can be terrors to each other, and *people in lonely rooms* suffer humiliation and even damage because of others in whose consciousness they scarcely figure at all. Eidola [phantoms] projected from the mind to take on a life of their own, wandering to find their victims, and maddening them with miseries and fears which the original source of these wanderers could not be justly charged with inflicting and might indeed by puzzled to hear of.[17]

Psychologist Harry Stack Sullivan puts it more dryly:

It is a notorious fact about personality problems that people act as if someone else were present when he is not—as the result of interpersonal configurations which are irrelevant to the other person's concern—and to do this in a recurrent fashion without any great difference in pattern.[18]

In anxiety, for example, we generally don't know what we are afraid of. The anxiety may be set off by someone's failure to show us the respect we feel we deserve. This perceived insult doesn't have to come from someone who is present, or alive, or even real, but can come from "eidetic people," those "which each of us carries with us and lives with."[19]

We have seen that everyone (not just those with "personality problems") acts always under the gaze of others. That we do so is

---

17 Murdoch, *The Nice and the Good*, pp. 152-54.
18 Sullivan, "The Illusion of Personal Individuality, p. 222."
19 *Ibid.*, p. 248.

what makes us self-conscious. To be able to see ourselves at all, we must be able to see ourselves as others, real or imagined, see us. But others have *attitudes*, and so our sense of who we are is always saturated with the attitudes that we imagine others take towards us.

We are not only beset by the attitudes, real and imagined, of our friends, neighbors, and coworkers, but we are haunted as well by the attitudes of some who are no longer with us. Eidetic people are immortal; they live on after they are parted from us by geography or by death. Their personalities survive within us, represented by their gaze which we still feel upon us and by the weight of their judgments. The force of these attitudes returns us to the situations of childhood in which we first met them. As we will see in more detail in Part Two, much of the anxiety, the nameless dread we feel as would-be adults results from finding ourselves back in that "garden of infantile catastrophe —terror, dread and trauma"[20] where we were helpless against the hostility, indifference, and betrayals of those who ruled our lives. These events and these situations are, along with their casts of characters, also eternal, for we find ourselves unknowingly always among them. Our normal condition, of course, is that we feel the terror and the dread, but cannot consciously remember the garden where the traumas occurred.

The scenes of our childhood affect us rather like a movie with a strong, compelling atmosphere, for example the *Godfather* films. For an hour or so after you leave the theater, the world has changed: violence lurks behind every door. But you are an adult; you know where this feeling comes from, and you have not forgotten the movie. As a child, however, you absorb the atmosphere of your family and society before you have the resources to keep track of and take exception to it. And unlike you as you emerge from a three hour gangster

---

20 Psychoanalyst James Grotstein used this phrase at A Conference on Evil in New York City in 2005, remarking "Evil flourishes in the garden of infantile catastrophe: terror, dread, and trauma." It describes one side of childhood. Childhood can be other things as well, leading, sometimes, to happy adulthoods, but the catastrophes have to be acknowledged.

movie, the small child has no alternative world to return to. As a result, our feelings about what happens in our daily lives continue to be reactions to situations and people we cannot see.

To Sum Up

What I've tried to do in this chapter is to introduce the idea that being who you are is a *task*, and I have tried to describe what that task is and what it costs us. The task is to *be someone,* just as an actor must convincingly portray a character on film or on stage. Our parts, however, are not written down in detail, so we are expected to be creative and spontaneous, though more so in some situations than in others. Most situations are like games of skill in which there are definite rules defining the object of the game and what can and cannot be done to achieve it, but leaving lots of room for the development of our own skills and strategies. The *spontaneity* we display within the structure of social life reveals the presence of an actor behind the mask who has gut reactions to the parts assigned to it, including the fear of failure, the fear of being scorned, unrecognized, ejected from the game. These fears follow us into our private moments and continue regardless of our relations, or lack of them, with real people, reminding us again that we are deeply social creatures who are never alone. We are always in the company of others, under their gaze and judgment. And in fact, the important judgments upon us come from people who may be dead and far away, and they were delivered to us in situations which we no longer remember. It is to those people in those long-ago and forgotten situations that we address ourselves in our every action. So I perform my part, my role as me, not only for the people I currently live with, but for a timeless audience that makes the most powerful demands upon me.

Whatever possesses us to take up these roles? That's the question we must turn to next.

But first, a word. Because we are trying to understand our inner demons, we naturally focus most of our attention on unpleasant experiences. But not all our social performances are painful or uncomfortable. Much of our social activity, many of the postures and gestures we use in our social games with each other, are deeply· pleasurable. A mother's embrace, a lover's kiss, the well-run footrace, making music in a group, learning a poem—all these can be joyful social performances. They also shape our animal souls and our emotional reactions. Let's not forget this even as we continue to focus on the traumas that become our demons when we hide them.

Appendix

We can distinguish two perspectives from which to see how we are always embedded in society and are never alone:

Sociologically: I am always in social space. My every act, word, and thought (including my name and the word "I") gets its meaning from the language game going on in me and around me in the discourse and social activity of my world.

Psychologically. First, my thoughts and feelings are always shaped by the presence of others—not only those I am addressing or for whom I am performing, but also those who are, or may be, observing me from a distance or at a later time. Second, there is the *eidetic* other—the world at large whose opinion and expectations often sneak into my own. I will have much more to say about this "other" in Part Two.

4

Becoming Ourselves

Photo by Alan Wieder

[...at the age of fourteen, he] "at once began to develop the carapace, the façade, which, if our sanity is to survive, we must present to the outside and usually hostile world as a protection to the naked, tender, shivering soul."

LEONARD WOOLF[1]

A Case of Mistaken Identity?

SO ALL OUR identities are *assumed* identities. This raises the question, How do we come to assume them? In what settings, and by what methods, do we learn to be what we are supposed to be? This is not the kind of learning that happens through any kind of formal education—by being told what to believe and on what principles or values we should act. Nor are we, like actors in a play, given a script to follow. We might, instead, say that we are "hailed" into our social position.[2]

In reality, this induction into our social position happens gradually and before we have the capacity to reflect on it. But we can get a better view of it by imagining it compressed into a moment in an adult's life. Consider this bit of guerilla theater:

You are sitting in a bar waiting for a friend. A couple of strangers carrying gifts and party hats come in, and address (or *hail*) you as "Ted," even though your name is Charley, and wish you a Happy Birthday. They persist in acting as if they know you, and are soon joined by thirty or so others, all having the same and over-lapping stories about your life as part of their social circle. They laugh off your protests, and eventually you find it easier to go along and accept the role they have assigned you as the birthday boy for the evening. This actually happened––a prank staged by Improv Everywhere and

---

1 *Sowing* (1960); cited in Furbank, P.N., "The Love of a Pessimist: Review of Leonard Woolf: A Biography by Victoria Glendinning."

2 As explained in the Appendix to this chapter, this concept comes from Althusser.

reported on the NPR program *This American Life*.[3] Charley found the experience disturbing, afraid he might be losing his grip on reality: could it be that he is "Ted" after all?

Who we think we are depends on continuing support from the world around us. Our identities and our beliefs are not things we do individually but in ensemble with others. Becoming who we are is a matter of getting tangled up in relationships.

By hailing us, other people pull us into parts in the scenarios they are enacting. At the moment of birth, the infant is given a name by which it can be drawn into a position that has already been prepared for it: a family with a history and a certain economic and social status; a nationality; an ethnicity and a gender.[4] Unlike Charley, AKA "Ted," the small child has no previously formed identity to conflict with the one the world assigns to it. Throughout our lives, every scene in which we appear, every situation in which we might be addressed or expected to participate, calls out corresponding behavior in us, hails us into the position demanded by its storyline––pitcher, center-fielder, father, daughter, teacher, student, clerk, customer, soldier, prisoner, guard.[5] We take up these position in our own fashion, often diffidently or resentfully. Nevertheless, they are our tickets to ride in the only game in town.

Identification and its Discontents

How does each of become the person we are, the person we mean by 'I', the person who carries our name? Take my case, for example. My name is Clayton Morgareidge, or C.M. for short. I have been brought

---

3 "Mind Games." See also http://improveverywhere.com/

4 I refer to the child whose gender is still being formed as 'it' because to use 'he' or 'she' (or even 'he or she') would be to suppose that gender is natural from birth. (Gender is a social identity, as contrasted with sex, which is regarded a biological feature of the body.)

5 For some philosophical discussion of this process, see the Appendix for this chapter.

up to *be* C.M.. I am not just *called* "C.M.": I just *am* C.M.. That is my identity. There are, it seems, no more layers to peel off.

But is that true?

If I am C.M., it is because I *identify* as C.M.. With every word and gesture, with every silent thought, I present myself as C.M., not as an actor or imposter playing C.M.. But what does it really mean to "identify" as someone?

Do I become C.M. (or do you become you) in the same way that an actor becomes a character on the stage? Not exactly. Even the "method" actor, the one who tries to get into a character by reliving situations from her own life similar to those her character finds herself in, is aware that she is an actor playing a part. If she loses herself momentarily in the part, she reverts to her own identity when the curtain falls or the director says "cut."[6] Yes, like actors, you and I have to *learn* how to be who we say we are, and, like them, we have to work at it. But unlike the actor, we have no underlying identity to fall back on if we come to doubt that we are the characters we enact in everyday life.

Should we say that I believe I am Clayton Morgareidge in the same way that while we are watching a play, we take the actors to *be* the characters in the story? In the theater or watching a movie, we are said to "suspend disbelief": we allow ourselves to be taken in by what we see before us, accepting it as real, even though we also know that it isn't. A method actor might do the same—she suspends her own identity in favor of the character she is portraying.

---

6 In the film *A Double Life* (1947), Ronald Coleman plays a stage actor playing the part of Othello. The actor, increasingly immersed in the role, eventually strangles the actress who is playing Desdemona during the death scene. It is the actor's wife (Shelley Winters) who plays Desdemona. The border between who are and who we pretend to be can be a hazy one. "We must be careful who we pretend to be, for we become who we pretend to be," says Howard W. Campbell, an American in Kurt Vonnegut's novel *Mother Night* who at the (top secret) behest of US intelligence, becomes a Nazi propagandist in Germany during WW II and after the war finds he is recognized only as a Nazi. Vonnegut, *Mother Night*. See also the film, *Mother Night*, with Nick Nolte.

Is this what I do as I enact the role of C.M.? But what identity do I have to *suspend*? If I lack an identity that is more real than C.M., the only alternative to keeping up the act is to cease to exist. This is why doubts about who I am are so terrifying: they lead to the unthinkable.

This makes it a matter of desperate necessity that I stay in character no matter how badly the character armor slips and slides around. I *must* abandon any doubt that I am more or less than C.M..

And yet I cannot abandon those doubts, because I am aware that I have to use all my intelligence and training to stay in character. I can't help but have doubts, for I *am* both more and less than Clayton Morgareidge! Moreover, I must also use all that skill and energy to silence those doubts. But silent or not, they do not disappear. They hide in the dark where they become my *inner* doubts, my demons.

These doubts about who we are can be frightening, but their value is that they call upon us to stand back from the identities (or personas) we normally put on even when we're alone. So this book offers us a new position from which we can take stock of the work we have to do to be who we say we are. Perhaps we can say it hails us into a new, and less confining, position, a position from which we can accept that our identities do not belong to us as individuals: we acquire and live our parts in our relations with others. We sustain each other's existence.

Of course, this means that we can also destroy each other. "There seems to be no agent more effective than another person in bringing a world for oneself alive, or by a glance, a gesture, or a remark, shriveling up the reality in which one is lodged."[7]

What keeps us secure in our selves is being recognized by others, and it is the lack of recognition that threatens to destroy us. So we turn now to what it means to recognize and be recognized.[8]

---

7 Goffman, *Encounters* p. 41; cited in Laing, *The Politics of Experience*, p. 33.

8 In Part Two, we will see that there may be another cause for confidence in our own existence besides living up to a prescribed social identity.

Appendix: More on Being Hailed

The process of being hailed into a social position is called *interpellation* by the philosopher Louis Althusser in his classic article, "Ideology and Ideological State Apparatuses (Notes towards an Investigation)".[9] Althusser's notion is that we are created as citizens, for example, by being addressed—"hailed" as such, by authorities of the state—a policeman, for example. When I turn to answer the policeman's call to me on the street ("Hey, you there!"), I am assuming the role of the citizen who is subject to police authority. More generally, it is by being swept up into the network of social activity, attached by my name to a position and a status, that I come to know and to be who I am.

Early in Walter Mosely's novel *Little Scarlett*, detective Easy Rawlins is interpellated by the law:

> "Ezekiel Rawlins?"
>
> It was a question asked in a voice filled with authority. It was a white man's voice. Putting those bits of information together, I knew that I was being addressed by the police.[10]

Of course the voice of the policeman does not create Easy Rawlins out of nothing; the voice hails a subject who has been interpellated many times before in the white society that assigns him his status as a black man subordinate to the white cop. Rawlins contests that status vigorously throughout the novel.

Savoj Žižek draws on the Hitchcock film *North By Northwest* to develop this idea with different theoretical language. In the film, Roger O. Thornhill is mistaken by Russian spies for an American spy named Kaplan. The Russians kidnap him and take him to a hide out where they grill him for information about his espionage. Žižek writes,

> Thornhill's situation corresponds to a fundamental situation of a human being as a being-of-language.... The subject [the person] is always fastened, pinned, to a signifier which represents him for the other, and

---

9 Althusser, Louis, *Lenin and Philosophy*.
10 Mosley, *Little Scarlet*.

through this pinning he is loaded with a symbolic mandate, he is given a place in the intersubjective network of symbolic relations. The point is that this mandate is ultimately always arbitrary.... The subject does not know why he is occupying this place in the symbolic network. [He asks] the hysterical question: 'Why am I what I'm supposed to be, why have I this mandate? Why am I (a teacher, a master, a king ... or George Kaplan)? Briefly: 'Why am I what you (the big Other) are saying that I am?'[11]

We, you and I, are the subjects now asking that "hysterical question."

---

11 Žižek, *The Sublime Object of Ideology*, pp. 125-26

5

Recognition and Confession

To be is to be perceived. And so to know thyself is only possible through the eyes of the other.

SONMI-451 IN *CLOUD ATLAS*[1]

The Need for Recognition

THE QUESTION 'WHO am I?' arises most urgently for people who have doubts about who they are; they suspect—or feel certain—that they go through life under false pretenses, secretly terrified of the thought that they do not exist, that there is no one there behind the outward show. They may wake each morning faced with the frightening and never-ending task of defending themselves against prosecution, against objections to their very existence. Each day they must create themselves out of nothing, keeping the thought that they are unreal at bay by means of work, play, conquest, entertainment, shopping, or drugs. This book is written for such people and for those who care about them.

---

1 A film by Tykwer, Wachowski, and Wachowski.

Who we are is a matter of where we belong in the scenarios that make up our lives, scenarios that are performed by a large cast of characters. So the doubts we have about our existence are doubts about where—or whether—we belong. What if we are liable to sudden expulsion from every scenario that sustains us? What if no one really knows who we are, what if we pass through life unrecognized? This is the unthinkable thought that draws us to a song like "Eleanor Rigby". We might feel sure that our funeral, unlike Eleanor's, will be well attended, yet we may still feel like one of the lonely people no matter how hard we try to divert our attention with the noisy march through our busy lives.

Formal Recognition

At one level, recognition is a social formality. I am recognized when people call me by my name, or even just wait on me when it's my turn in line at the check-out counter. I am a citizen of my nation because the name conferred on me at birth is recorded in various documents that are recognized by authorities. I am recognized when people speak to me, respond to what I say, and make a place for me in their activities at work, at home, and in organizations I belong to. In each of these venues, I am some-*one*: I am addressed as 'you', included in their 'we' and I am heard when I say 'I' and 'you'.[2] I know who I am when I say 'I' because it evokes a 'you' of recognition in those to whom I speak. The lonely people are afraid to say 'I' because they expect the response 'And just who do you think you are?' Each of us is daily created and re-created in this continuous exchange of names and personal pronouns—or we are lost in its absence.[3]

---

2 See Chapter 2, "Entangled in Language"

3 Modern societies turn people loose from older ties of family and community, leaving many more empty spaces in which people can be lost and unrecognized than did traditional societies. Every need, activity, and relationship increasingly revolves around money and recognition, and the sense of belonging is tied to material wealth rather than to deeper and more secure bonds among us. A character

These formalities are important, even comforting, when they run smoothly. We need to be recognized and welcomed. It is worse than frightening to be unrecognized and unwelcome, to find oneself in a social setting where no one will look at you or speak to you. You can then feel annihilated, deprived of your existence. This exclusion can be subtle: You may be unrecognized, under-recognized, or mis-recognized because of how others perceive, and feel about, your poverty, your race, gender, dress, or accent. How others see you infects the way you see yourself; attitudes are contagious. Your recognition by banks or government officials can go off the rails through identity theft or misplaced documents in a bureaucracy, and you can feel that you've lost control of who you are. The truth is, though, that you never control who you are. Being who you are requires the cooperation—the recognition—of others, and that can fail.

But even when it doesn't fail, this formal recognition is not enough. We all hope for a deeper kind of recognition. We want to be known for who we *really* are –– "deep down inside," as we sometimes say. Moreover, we may want to know ourselves this way as well. All the outward forms of social recognition may be working smoothly, and yet you may still feel *hollow*, privately convinced that no one really knows you, that you don't know yourself—that there might be nothing there to be known. Richard Corey, in the well-known poem, was thought to be "everything to make us wish that we were in his place," and yet "Richard Cory, one calm summer night, went home and put a bullet through his head."[4] Behind the suave social performance everyone envied, this man was like most men, who, as Thoreau put it, "lead lives of quiet desperation and go to the grave with their song still in them."

---

in Jane Gadam's novel *Old Filth* remarks, "You know…, the withering of the family tree is one of the saddest things ever. Who else can you turn to when you're old and sick without having to feel grateful?" (p. 175). We will have more to say about this in the final chapter.

4 Edward Arlington Robinson, "Richard Cory".

To Be Understood

What is this deeper level of recognition we crave? What more do we want from other people besides that they call us by name, remember our place in the world, and include us in their work and games? What is missing from the lives of those who live, and sometimes end, their lives in quiet (and sometimes not so quiet) desperation? Clearly, there is more to being recognized than we have seen so far. We can know that we are well recognized and still have the feeling that no one *understands* us. We often hope to find the right person who can take us in as we really are—a "soul-mate," perhaps. Writers and artists try to convey something deeply personal to a wider audience through self-expression. The narrator of Rebecca Goldstein's novel *The Mind-Body Problem* confesses that "the end of all this scribbling [is] to give you myself as I am to myself, the *en soi*, the *être intime* of me." She wants us, her readers, to "begin to know what it's like to be me." [5] Her hope is to be known, and to know herself, by finding the right words to communicate her very soul.

Confession

Guilt is often a reason for wanting to bare our souls; we confess in hopes of being forgiven for our failures and mistakes. A 1965 song by The Animals goes like this:

> I'm just a soul whose intentions are good
> Oh Lord, please don't let me be misunderstood[6]

Or take the case of Jim in Joseph Conrad's novel *Lord Jim*.[7] Jim talks for hours to the novel's narrator Marlow trying to explain how, as the young first mate on a broken-down steamer loaded with Muslim

---

5 Goldstein, *The Mind-Body Problem,* p. 84.
6 "Don't Let Me Be Misunderstood"
7 Conrad, *Lord Jim.* Numbers in parentheses refer to this book.

pilgrims, he deserted the ship along with the rest of the officers when they all thought the ship was about to sink. "I don't want to excuse myself," Jim says to Marlow, "but I would like to explain—I would like somebody to understand—somebody—one person at least. You! Why not you?" (76) And when Marlow has listened patiently for many pages, Jim says gratefully, "You don't know what it is for a fellow in my position to be believed—make a clean breast of it to an elder man. It is so difficult—so awfully unfair—so hard to understand" (122).

Jim wants to reclaim his right to a place in the community that has cast him out. He knows he is finished as a sea man (his mate's certificate has been cancelled), and he knows his father would never understand. But if he can explain himself to Marlow, a representative of the seafaring community, he might receive a kind of virtual redemption. So Marlow is aware that Jim is not just talking to him. "He was not speaking to me, he was only speaking before me, in a dispute with an invisible personality, an antagonistic and inseparable partner of his existence—another possessor of his soul (87)."

We have met this possessor, this partner in our soul, in earlier chapters: It is Harry Kellerman from Chapter 1, who says "all those terrible things about me;" it is T.S. Eliot's "severe and speechless critic, who can terrorize us" with his reproaches (Chapter 2). It is the critical audience to whom we appeal for recognition as we perform our parts in the social scenarios that make up our lives. Our every word and deed seeks the attention of this critical mass—the collection of our significant others, our moral reference group (or the "big Other," as we will call it in Part Two of this book). This is the audience for our every word and gesture. The performance of our lives is addressed to that audience and demands its uptake, its recognition. If we believe that that audience never listens, or hears us with contempt—if what we say and do has no effect, then our lives are meaningless and we are nothing—just one of the lonely people who belong nowhere.[8]

---

8 This Audience is like a chorus of Eidola, or eidetic others (see Chapter 3), an echo of the attitudes of those we care about.

Disclosure and Evasion

This Audience, before whom we always appear, and to whom we always appeal, even when we are by ourselves, puts us in a double bind. I want it to know me and accept me as I am without my defenses and pretenses. But to win its applause, I groom myself to be what I think it wants. To evade its contempt, I lie about myself. I am torn between two powerful desires. I want to confess, to be real, to lay down the burden of maintaining a false front and multiple cover stories like a spy in a novel by John LeCarré or Graham Greene. But I also want to live up to what the Audience expects of me. Do I trust the Audience enough to confess my sins, throw myself on its mercy, and hope to be forgiven? Or do I keep my guard up and massage my image to match what I take to be the Audience's expectations, even as I carefully confess? As he listens to Jim, Marlow is aware of this tension: "Didn't I tell you he confessed himself before me as though I had the power to bind and to loose? He burrowed deep, deep, in the hope of my absolution" (91). Yet Marlow sees Jim's unconscious self-deception: "I didn't know how much of it he believed himself.... for it is my belief no man ever understands quite his own artful dodges to escape from the grim shadow of self-knowledge" (75).[9]

Is there a third possibility: that the Audience itself might become either less powerful in our hearts, or more benign and forgiving and thus more worthy of trust?

Confession, then, is rarely simple and straight-forward. As we admit to our transgressions, we look for ways to excuse or justify them as "human all too human" (as in the Animals song), or as the fault of others. At one point, Jim blames his leap from the ship on the men who were calling from the life boat, *Jump!* "It was their

---

9 Confessing my sins and hiding them are not the only options; I may decide to *magnify* them! Why? To receive the highly charged attention that comes with being chastised or punished. This is a masochistic strategy for achieving recognition.

doing," he tells Marlow, "as plainly as if they had reached up with a boat-hook and pulled me over" (118).[10]

We began this chapter with the doubts about our existence that nag at us behind our public faces, worries about whether we really belong in the scenarios in which we play our parts. We are always in need of reassurance that we are welcome in spite of our failures—past, present, and future. And so we are moved to reveal our flaws and failures to a sympathetic ear (a therapist, for example), hoping to be accepted by someone for who we are. At the same time, if we are uncertain of the other's tolerance or love, then we will rein in, or stifle, our impulse to confess. Full disclosure requires trust.

However, as Marlow observes about Jim, when we confess before another human being, we are playing to a larger audience as well, the eidetic Audience that is one of the partners in the operation of our souls. It is this always-present Audience that is the ultimate arbiter of sin and salvation. This imaginary Other, my constant over-seer, is the one whose forgiveness and love I eternally seek. So while I might be respected and even loved by most of the people I live with, I may still feel like zero, or worse, in the eyes of the Audience that ultimately matters.[11] I can no more set myself apart from this judge than I can from my own eyes and tongue, nor can I separate his opinions from my own. By confessing, coming to know myself, I am trying to set right my relationship with the Audience by clearing away the accumulation of lies and cover-ups I have been using to maintain the image I thought the Audience wanted. Again, since this Audience is my other half, coming clean to it is necessary for the healing of my soul. The full recognition I seek in order to feel secure in my existence must come from this Other within me.

---

10 Ironically, the men in the boat were not even calling to Jim, but to another man who lay dead of a heart attack.

11 It will be obvious that this Audience, a product of the human condition as it evolved on earth, is a major motivation for the belief in God.

But full disclosure requires trust, and what if we don't trust the Other? This Audience enters our lives, takes its seats in the theater, before we are old enough to exercise discretion over who is to be admitted. How do we learn to trust? More importantly, when is an other, or the Other, trustworthy?

More about these questions lies ahead. But first we need to think more about the flip side of recognition: how do we perceive a soul?

6

How to Understand a Soul

Beyond the Last Word

As WE HAVE just seen, we want more than just recognition: we want to be understood. We often seek to fulfill this desire by baring our souls to another person, sometimes in confession. Let's look at what this desire demands from the one who listens. How much of another person is it really possible for us to understand? Can we meet this central need of others to be known for who they really are?

Jim begs Marlow to understand him. But Jim's soul remains shrouded in mist for Marlow. After some two hundred pages of Jim's confession, Marlow says,

> ...the last word is not said,––probably shall never be said. Are not our lives too short for that full utterance which through all our stammerings is, of course our only and abiding intention? I have given up expecting those last words, whose ring, if they could only be pronounced, would shake both heaven and earth. There is never time to say our last words—the last word of our love, of our desire, faith, remorse, submissions, revolt.[1]

---

1 Conrad, *Lord Jim*, pp. 216-17.

Does this mean that no one ever really understands another, and we are all ultimately condemned to loneliness? This is apparently Marlow's belief:

> It is when we try to grapple with another man's intimate need that we perceive how incomprehensible, wavering, and misty are the beings that share with us the sight of the stars and the warmth of the sun. It is as if loneliness were a hard and absolute condition of existence; the envelope of flesh and blood on which our eyes are fixed melts before the outstretched hand, and there remains only the capricious, inconsolable, and elusive spirit that no eye can follow, no hand can grasp.[2]

The words that pass between Jim and Marlow do not communicate Jim's soul. Why is that? Why would it be that we can never really tell anyone who we are?

Some descriptions of ourselves are obviously too small for us. I will certainly not feel adequately recognized if I am known only by such bureaucratic or formal markers as my social security number, address, gender, occupation, and the like. And you will not feel that I know you if I see you through some stereotype—as a pretty girl, a teenage punk, a homeless panhandler, or a lonely old man.

A character in Iris Murdoch's novel *Bruno's Dream* remarks, "A human being hardly ever thinks about other people. He contemplates fantasms which resemble them and which he has decked out for his own purposes."[3] And of course, we don't just "contemplate"

---

2 Ibid, pp. 172-73.

3 Murdoch, *Bruno's Dream*, p. 208. Here is the context of this quote: Diana's husband Miles has fallen in love with Diana's sister, who has gone away rather than break up Diana's marriage. Diana can't face living with Miles. "He'll despise me," she tells her friend Nigel, "I cannot bear his thoughts, his thoughts about her, his thoughts about me." Nigel replies, "A human being hardly ever thinks about other people. He contemplates fantasms which resemble them and which he has decked out for his own purposes. Miles's thoughts cannot touch you. His thoughts are about Miles." This advice is intended to comfort Diana: when Miles thinks about

the people in our lives. We argue and fight and work with them, love them and hate them, and make life-changing decisions that affect them directly and indirectly. But in doing so, it seems we are guided less by who they are than by our images of the heroes or villains we hope or fear them to be.

So do we live our lives in the company of fictional characters—people we create for reasons of our own? It would be better to call them *semi*-fictional, since they are based on at least some facts and experience we have of the people who go by the names we use to refer to them. Still, if we all see each other through a fog of phantasies, then we cannot trust that anyone else sees *us* as we are. Since we see ourselves through the eyes of others, this makes our own sense of who we are shaky. And yet our desire to be recognized is so powerful that we often try to convince those who misrecognize us that we really are just what the other seems to imagine. We may shape our actions and reactions to conform to the expectations of others, with the result that we *misrecognize ourselves.*

But is there such a thing as what we *really* are apart from, or prior to, the images we project of ourselves, underneath the masks we put on? What is it that gets *mis*-recognized, and what would it take to recognize it? What does Goldstein's narrator, mentioned in Chapter 5, mean by "myself as I am to myself, the *en soi*, the *être intime* of me" that she hopes her reader will come to know by reading her work? Part Two of this book will be an extended answer to this question. But for now, let me come back to the point made in Chapter 1: that the soul, who and what we really are, is not a fixed object that can be

---

Diana, he is not thinking about the real Diana—Diana as she is to herself, but about Miles's own fantasy of Diana. Diana, for Miles, is a fictional character in the story he makes up about himself, and he tells it for reasons of his own, to make sense of—to justify—his own life, and there is no reason why Diana should identify herself with that character. But while this distinction between Diana as she is to herself and Diana as Miles imagines her protects Diana from being drafted into Miles's self-serving scenario, it deprives her of the recognition she once thought she was getting from her husband.

sharply distinguished from its surroundings, including the souls of others. Proust remarks,

> ...None of us constitutes a material whole, identical for every-
> one, which a person has only to go look up as though we were
> a book of specifications or a last testament; our social per-
> sonality is a creation of the minds of others.[4]

Here are three things about knowing a soul.

First, I do not exist at any moment of time in which I could be known. Like the proverbial river that you can never step into twice (for new waters are ever flowing in upon you)[5] you and I are always in flux, outpacing whatever has been said or thought about us. Whatever lives is not a thing but a performance.[6] It is not just the tissues of our bodies that change, but the shape of our lives in the world. The truth about me is always unfolding and never complete, which means that any truth about me must be partial, incomplete, and tentative.[7] This is not a grand, metaphysical notion. It's simply that I am alive and active, full of desire, and living in a moving world peopled by other living beings. I am always initiating changes that affect my world, and I, in turn, am affected by changes begun by others. My hopes and plans carry me forward, but never along exactly the path I intend. What I do is affected by what others do, as well

---

4 Proust, *Swann's Way*, p. 19.

5 According to the early Greek thinker Heracleitus.

6 In a book about trees, Colin Tudge asks "––what is a tree? His answer, which pertains to all life including ourselves, is profound. Living tissue, he says, is constantly replacing itself, even when it seems to stay the same. It is *not a thing but a performance.*" Flannery, "What Is a Tree?"

7 Joan Didion gave a talk to her daughter's junior high school English class about how she became a writer, and reflecting on it later she writes "I suppose that what I really wanted to say...is that we never reach a point at which our lives lie before us as a clearly marked open road, never have and never should expect a map to the years ahead, never do close those circles that seem, at thirteen and fourteen and nineteen, so urgently in need of closing." Kerr, "The Unclosed Circle" p. 19

as by unforeseeable events—which include my own unpredictable fears, desires, impulses and compulsions. There is no fixed or final object of knowledge, for me or for anyone else, as my "true self" or "the real me." I am always under construction with no end in sight. That is the truth about me: I never exist complete in any moment.[8]

Secondly, I am not an object apart from the rest of the world. Who I am is inseparable from the vast, interconnected community of human and non-human life in which I live. I cannot be myself outside the scenarios, with their props and supporting casts, in which I do what I do. As Neil Young sings,

There's a world you're living in
No one else has your part[9]

No one else has your part, yet your part is a part of the world.[10] Willie Mays was like no other baseball player, but he played ball. Whatever we know of his unique achievements and personality is bound up with what we know about the history, culture, and institutions of

---

8 Sartre says "Man exists as project." This is true, but we also exist as *accident*, as what befalls us that we did not project. "Life is what happens to us while we are busy making other plans" (Old Sufi saying often attributed to John Lennon.)

9 Neil Young, "There's a World," from *Harvest*.

10 "To draw a carp, Chinese masters warn, it is not enough to know the animal's morphology, study its anatomy or understand the physiological functions vital to its existence. They tell us that it is also necessary to consider the reed against which the carp brushes each morning while seeking its nourishment, the oblong stone behind which it conceals itself, or the rippling of water when it springs toward the surface. These elements should in no way be treated as the fish's environment, the milieu in which it evolves or the natural background against which it can be drawn. They belong to the carp itself, insofar as it is not defined as a distinct form capable of a set of movements or as a particular organism performing a series of functions. Instead, the carp must be apprehended as a certain power to affect and be affected by the world. In other words, rather than a formed and organized individual, the brush should sketch a life, since a life is constituted by traces left behind and imprints silently borne." Feher, Kwinter, and Crary, Zone 1/2 p. 10. emphasis added.

baseball. You and I can only be the individuals we are because we are in our social world as it is at this moment in history.

Finally, let's look again at that last quote from Conrad's novel. After hours of heart-to-heart conversation with Jim, Marlow suggests that when we look beyond "the envelope of flesh and blood on which our eyes are fixed," the "spirit" that remains is so "capricious, inconsolable, and elusive that no eye can follow [and] no hand can grasp [it]." The more we find out about someone, the less we seem to know. This is not only because people change in unforeseeable ways and because they are but eddies in the social current. It is also because what is meant by the *words* we use to describe ourselves and each other is not fixed, is not "determinate" (as philosophers would say). Whatever words you might use to describe yourself, to say who you "really" are, are subject to the way they are received by others—even to the way you yourself receive them.[11] Anyone who keeps a journal may have the experience of being unsure just what she meant by words she wrote last year or even yesterday. There is no fixed or authoritative meaning that words have independently of the occasions when they come to life in conversation or in practice; and how they are then used depends on the shifting experience and imagination of the users. I write these words now, hoping they will help you to think about the soul; what you actually do with them is beyond my control and is not rigidly legislated

---

11 That the "last word is...probably never said" is, paradoxically, illustrated in Orson Wells's film *Citizen Kane* (1941). The story revolves around a reporter's fruitless investigation of what Kane meant by his dying word "rosebud". At the end, another reporter says, "If you could've found out what Rosebud meant, I bet that would've explained everything." The investigator replies, "No, I don't think so; no. Mr. Kane was a man who got everything he wanted and then lost it. Maybe Rosebud was something he couldn't get, or something he lost. Anyway, it wouldn't have explained anything... I don't think any word can explain a man's life. No, I guess Rosebud is just a... piece in a jigsaw puzzle... a missing piece." We the viewers may think we have the explanation since we know that the word "rosebud" was on the sled from his childhood. But even though we have the missing piece, we don't really know where it goes in the puzzle of Kane's soul. http://www.imdb.com/title/tt0033467/quotes

by any ultimate authority. Words take on the meanings they do in the interconnected lives of those who pick them up.

Consider, for example, what you know of the two boys who did the shooting at Columbine High School in 1999. News reports described them as "bullied," "loners," and "goth". What these words convey to you about Eric Harris and Dylan Klebold and the reasons they did what they did will depend on your particular experiences of high school, resentment and authority, and on your moral and political beliefs about law and order, responsibility, education, and child-rearing. As you read or hear more about them, and talk with people whose views are different, your conception of, say, "goth" and "bully" may grow, becoming more complex, and perhaps both less clear *and* more informative.

What these reflections[12] show is that who I am—my soul—is not something that can be communicated, not an object that could be understood or grasped like the objects defined in geometry. Neither can it be located and investigated like a material object. The words 'my soul' no more refer to an object than does 'today's weather'.

What are we doing, then, when we talk about ourselves to a sympathetic listener? We are seeking recognition. What does Jim hope for when he talks to Marlow? We have seen that he wants "redemption," *forgiveness* from someone representing the community from which his own act has divided him. While Marlow does not forgive Jim in so many words, his willingness to listen without condemning him offers at least an implied forgiveness. Redemption does not come as a judgment or a verdict upon his confession; it comes in being able to confess at all, in being *listened to*. When Jim says he's glad for Marlow's belief in him, what is he is grateful for is Marlow's full attention to him. What we want from each other is to belong at the table, to be acknowledged, heard, recognized. It matters less *what* people say to us than that they listen and look into our faces. Of course sometimes we do want our

---

12 Which we could sum up in theoretical jargon by saying that the soul is disseminated in time, in social space, and in semiotic space.

friends or our therapists to see us more clearly than we can ourselves, or even to tell us just what to do. But often, we finish our story and, before the other says anything, we say "Just talking to you has helped me see what I need to do."

This is not to say that all we have to do to understand another person is to shut up and listen, although that often helps. But it does tell us that we don't understand people by finding accurate descriptions of them. Knowing a person is like knowing a city; you know a city by knowing your way around in it, knowing how to get from one place to another. It's a skill. Your knowledge of your closest friend is not a body of truths, it is your ability to get along with her, to do things together, including talking about her life. You deepen your knowledge of her, and help her to understand herself, by finding together new ways of talking and feeling about her situation. You and she try out different attitudes, fresh stances, to take towards what she is facing. And that's the kind of recognition we want from each other—companionship in the struggles of life. This is the only way to understand creatures like ourselves who are always changing, about whom any definitive description would be false and constraining—one more reason we don't want to be "understood" in terms of stereotypes or the fantasies of others. It is more important that others be *understanding* than that we be *understood*.[13]

Misrecognition

But why is this so hard, and so rare? Why is it that so many people, as we saw in the last chapter, are left in a lonely limbo where they feel unrecognized and unreal even in the midst of a busy social life? Why does recognition fail to guard us from the abyss? All we have to do is look around: most of our relations with each other are not about

---

13 "As soon as I am sure that I know you, that I know what you will do next, I have stopped having a relationship with you and instead have a relationship with myself, with my own projection onto you. When I think that I know you, our relationship is over." Oliver, *Witnessing* p. 210.

supporting and getting *along* with others, but at getting *ahead* of them by exploiting and manipulating them. This may sound harsh because most of us aspire to do better, and may imagine that we do. But it's not an exaggeration.

Consider, first, the interactions among supervisors, bosses, employees and co-workers; citizens, cops and other officials; military officers and enlisted personnel; military personnel and the people in occupied areas; and clients, customers, and sales-people. These settings are venues for some kinds of recognition. Even paying bills provides me with some sense of having a place in the world. But these exchanges take place in institutions in which definite rules and conditions dictate what behavior will be accepted, sharply constricting how we can present ourselves. We have to tailor our personas to be functional in those settings, which are, after all, the places where most of us spend most of our lives; even when we are not in them, our performance in them has a major impact on the rest of our lives.

Even when we are less constrained by our institutional roles, we are likely to think about people we don't know well by means of ste-reotypes. For example, many people assume that increases in immi-gration lead to higher crime rates when in fact just the opposite is probably true.[14] Stereotypes about black people led the news media to portray them as looters when they took food and clothing from stores in New Orleans in the aftermath of Hurricane Katrina, while white people doing the same thing were just gathering supplies for their survival.

14 "*Salon* spoke with professor Robert J. Sampson, chairman of the sociology de-partment at Harvard University and most prominent member of a new school of academics who say that, contrary to widespread public belief, immigrants may ac-tually be the secret to decreasing crime in the U.S. Sampson et al. believe their research shows immigrants are less likely to commit crime than native-born Americans, and that immigration itself may actually play a role in lowering the overall crime rate." Koppelman, "Memo to Bill O'Reilly."

And then what about the people with whom we spend our leisure time—friends and family? Don't they often see us through their own very definite ideas of what a good wife or husband or child ought to be, rarely listening to what we have to say about the matter? Since we want to get along with them, we often suppress our doubts and objections and try to live up to what others expect. Those of us who have one or two others in their lives who listen closely and cooperatively to us are fortunate indeed.

You want someone who believes in you. What is hard is finding someone who believes in *you*, rather than in "you" as they imagine you, someone who believes in *you*, rather than in some fantasy of you (even your own) driven by expectations, hopes or fears. Someone who believes in you does not have to believe what you believe about yourself. We all have our own fantastical self-images born of our hopes and fears, and it does us good if someone who loves us can gently help us to see through our own bullshit.

Who, then, am I? (Really)

We have learned now that to this question there can be no spoken or written answer. There is no *I* that can be analyzed and defined. The soul I wish to understand is less an object to be known than it is a process to be engaged with. I understand someone by learning how to be with her, not by developing a correct description of her. In the next chapter, we will take up the challenge of listening to someone.

7

X, The Estranged One, Speaks[1]

*In every man's memories there are such things as he will
reveal not to everyone, but perhaps only to friends. There
are also such as he will reveal not even to friends, but only to
himself, and that in secret. Then, finally, there are such as
a man is afraid to reveal even to himself, and every decent
man will have accumulated quite a few things of this sort.
That is, one might even say: the more decent a man is, the
more of them he will have....Now, however, when I not only
recall them but am even resolved to write them down, now
I want precisely to make a test: is it possible to be perfectly
candid with oneself and not be afraid of the whole truth?*

DOSTOEVSKY, *NOTES FROM THE UNDERGROUND*[2]

---

1 While this is the most personal chapter of the book, Mr. X is not identical with
me: at most, he is a partial version of an earlier me, exaggerated to make the condition of estrangement stand out. Moreover, whatever portion of him I share, I am
also the author––the one who can write about and reflect upon him, and much
of the time refuse to be him. (This chapter, including the preceding part of this
note, was first written seven years ago, and coming back to it now, I realize that I
am much less like X than I was then. I hope that testifies to the therapeutic value
of the parts of this book that are still to come. Of course the value of reading may
be less than the value of writing it.)
2 Dostoevsky, *Notes from Underground, p. 39*

DOSTOEVSKY'S CHARACTER IS known as the Underground Man. We may call the one for whom this book is written, the one who urgently asks the question "Who am I?" *the Estranged One*. Such a character, Mr. X, has already appeared in this book: an excerpt from his journal appeared at the top of Chapter 3. This chapter belongs to him. Here he will speak at length, trying to understand *why* he must ask who he is and how he might answer.

Like Dostoevsky's Underground Man, he will try to "be perfectly candid" with himself, and with us. It may well be that if we could look at ourselves without concern for our public self—for our "decency"—we might all recognize a good deal of ourselves in X. Like Ralph Ellison's Invisible Man (modeled on Dostoevsky's Underground Man) X might say to us "Who knows but that, on the lower frequencies, I speak for you?"[3]

Me? Am I on? Well then, here is my life as I see it when I put aside my pride and put words to my darker moods. I will talk without censorship. As Dostoevsky says, we all have layers of protection that hide what we don't reveal even when we're alone because it's so horrifying and shameful. You know it's there, like a heavy ache in your heart that never lets up, but you can't let yourself name it. Maybe there are no names for it. But with a mixture of interests that are not just scientific and philosophical, but that might include the desire to heal, a noir-ish fascination with the morbid, and a bit of exhibitionism, I am going to let my soul talk without the usual worries about propriety or saving face. At least I'll try.

I ask myself, Who am I? But how strange that I should have to ask that question! It's not as if I have amnesia, or might have been switched with another baby at birth, or suspect my parents of having adopted me. There is not some other misplaced identity that is rightfully mine. My problem is that I have no identity. I am no one; I do not exist—or, if you prefer, I am unable to believe that I exist, which seems the same as believing that I do not exist.

But what kind of "believing" is this? How can I believe something that I do not act upon. I don't act as if I don't exist. I don't send my bills back

---

3 Ellison, *Invisible Man 2nd (second) Edition*, p. 581.

marked "No such person." A normal belief is one where what we say, how we act, and how we feel go together. I believe that today is Wednesday: I say this, act on it, and feel comfortable in doing so. But in the case of my own existence, saying, acting, and feeling are at odds with each other. I don't act or talk as if I don't exist. But I feel uncomfortable when I say I exist; I am emotionally certain that I do not exist. What is this feeling?

Whenever I say "I," or my name, fear springs up in me. When I was much younger this fear had no object. Fear just loomed up, senselessly when people looked at or spoke to me. Now I realize that what I fear is that I'll be exposed as an imposter with no right to my name—or any name. When other people address me, or refer to me, by name or by pronoun, they seem to be blindly assuming the reality of a fiction. Or perhaps they are just pretending to see something more than an empty shell. For my part, I am quite sure that that's what I am—a fake who is on the point of being discovered and punished as an incompetent who somehow managed to slip unnoticed into a respectable position. I have to go on acting the part of X even though I am privately quite sure that I'm a fake, that X is no more real than Goldilocks or James Bond. I fear death only because I'm afraid I will die without finally demonstrating that I had a right to live in the first place.

In fact, my reality seems much less convincing than James Bond's. I am sure that no one is taken in by my performance of X as they are by Sean Connery's portrayal of Bond. When fans of 007 see Thunderball, they see James Bond on the screen. When I appear in public, my audience sees a bad actor trying to be X, but botching the job. At least that's what I see them seeing, which becomes one of my ways of seeing myself.

I know all this, but I don't say it, even to myself. I just know it the way you know anything you can't bear to face. It's there, like the shame we feel for foolish childhood acts, like our regrets for roads not taken long ago. My lack of substance, my failure to be anything worth being, is a constant weight, a din of accusation in the background of my life. It leaves me, like Mailer's image of Nixon, always hesitating, a question in my voice and a hitch in my gestures, always calculating before acting, envying spontaneous people whose words *and actions seem to pour out of them without having to get past so many guards and censors.*

Our author argues that no one is ever alone, for we are in the presence of others even when no one else is near. Every act and every thought has a social significance that matters to us whether any one else actually sees or hears us. And yet I feel very alone, whether others are near or not. Isn't that what it means to be estranged—to be isolated from those you're with? Lonely when you're alone and lonely when you're in a crowd? It has been written that "… One can only stand being alone in outer reality if one is never alone in inner reality." [4] *Well, I'm not alone in "inner reality," so how come I feel so alone "in outer reality"—and, for that matter, in "inner reality" as well? I must be with the wrong people when I'm alone.*

But who are they—these people who are always with me even when I'm by myself in the woods or in a quiet room? They don't seem to love me: when they are not pointing out my sins and errors or my character flaws, they pointedly turn their backs to signify that I am nothing. Ostracized in my own soul!

I want to flee from public places where others snub me, but when I get to a solitary place, their attitudes and their silences follow me. Other judges start yammering at me, reminding and accusing me of a lifetime of failures and warning me of shame and disasters yet to come. Who are they anyway?

They are tricksters: they speak in the first person, claiming to be me; I identify with them. [5] *I can recognize the attitudes of my mother or a seventh-grade teacher in the words I find myself saying to myself. Pretending to be a wiser me, they address me as a child who needs to be taken down a peg, and so I feel like a child. Of course I have my little strategies for muffling these*

---

4 W.D. Winnicott, cited in Guntrip, *Schizoid Phenomena, Object-Relations and the Self* p. 286

5 Sometimes, however, the inner critic wears other masks, like Harry Kellerman who was the alter ego of Georgie Soloway in the Dustin Hoffman film discussed in Chapter 1. In George MacKay Brown's novel *Greenvoe*, a woman sits every after-noon in her parlor, which is transformed in imagination into a courtroom where a prosecutor builds a painstaking case against her for an infidelity of many years past. Brown, *Greenvoe.*

inner saboteurs: obsessive abstract thinking, work, play, sex, and the judicious application of alcohol.

I want to feel at home in the world. I read somewhere that at birth, we enter an "elated, euphoric phase of discovery in which the infant is delighted with the world and himself, discovering his own agency as well as the fascinating outside." [6] *Did I really start out life in love with the world? I'd like to find that love again, to always hear the world saying to me what Paul Simon sings,*

Never been lonely
Never been lied to
Never had to scuffle in fear
Nothing denied to
Born at the instant
The church bells chime
And the whole world whispering
Born at the right time.[7]

But if the world is telling me anything, it's that I was born at the wrong time, or was not born at all.

Here are my questions: Who are these hectoring voices in my head that badger me, how did they get there, and why do they have such a hold on me? And who am I really—that is, what would I be if I could see myself without all that inner criticism?

And with that, I'll stop so our author can get on with it.

The case of X may seem sad, yet he is ahead of many other people in his self-understanding. He does not simply *give in* to the feeling that he is incompetent and has no right to exist; he knows such feelings

---

6 Benjamin, Jessica, *The Bonds of Love*, p. 34.
7 Paul Simon, "Born at the Right Time," from his 1990 album "The Rhythm of the Saints."

are his *feelings* and not objective truths. He seeks an explanation that might help him in some way, whether by enabling him to change the way he feels, or at least to accept that they are not of his own making and he does not bear sole responsibility for them. Nor does he, like many, just deny those feelings, pretending with all his power to think and act as if he were exactly as he pretends to be when dealing with the outer world.

What might X, or someone like him, have learned so far? We have not really answered his questions or explained the inner demons that surfaced in Chapter 1. We have, however, located our souls in the larger context of social existence. So we should now understand that we are not, at least not entirely, to blame for the unhappy state of our souls, since our souls are what they are in relation to the many souls of others and to the culture in which we live. We do not create ourselves all by ourselves; we are largely drafted, before we are in a position to think about it, into the many social roles that are demanded by the scenarios going on around us and to which we have had to adapt.

But while it seems to X that at least some other people feel at home in their social lives, he does not. He feels disconnected, alienated from the social life going on around him, and since he is inseparable from his social life, this means he is disconnected from himself. He finds himself taking positions hostile to himself, or positions that he later regrets or feels ashamed of. When he begins a situation by playing the responsible adult, he often finds himself overtaken by the part of a vindictive, punitive critic, attacking himself or someone else. If he attacks himself, he may then identify with the victim of the attack, appearing on both sides of the bench, condemning himself and feeling condemned. Although he tries to take a third position which stands calmly above the fray, he doesn't manage to remain there long, finding himself sucked back into the anger or the shame. He seems to be too many people at once, all working against each other, and he himself—if there is such a thing!—seems to have no control over who has the floor. He looks for a description, a recipe for sanity or a model of wisdom and peace in philosophy, literature, and film, or even in "self-help" books, and sometimes feels he has found it, but it vanishes as his actual life reasserts itself and the book or movie fades. He realizes that there are voices within him that he often finds himself channeling—voices of his harshest critics. Apparently there is more than one "antagonistic and inseparable partner of his existence."

We might say that the first part of this book has approached these issues from a sociological perspective. It is time now to move to a more psychological perspective, one that looks at what happens in the lives of individuals like X that leads them to have these burning questions.

So to sum up X's questions: First, he wonders why he has so little control over the positions he takes, and thus over his own thoughts and attitudes. Why is so much of what he thinks and feels so opaque, so obscure, so irrational, so unconnected to understandable motives, so contrary to what he supposes are his real interests?

Second, *who are* all these "others" that take charge of his soul? How did they get inside of him and get so much authority?

And finally, who or what is the creature, or the force, behind all this thrashing about and its attendant suffering? Who, or what, is it that feels compelled to judge me worthless? Who or what is it that feels the shame and the fear? Is there a real "me" underneath all this drama?

Part Two of this book will try, as far as possible, to answer, or at least illuminate, these questions. We will see how others become part of us—how we become who we are by taking others on board. We will then think about why our souls are so unknown to us. One reason will be that we try to use adult language to understand experience that is in fact *infantile*. After all, we first came to terms with the world before we were able to shape it with adult categories. When we did start thinking as adults are supposed to think, we lost track of those experiences that wouldn't fit adult logic but which continue to happen –– and to matter.

Adult thinking goes on under the gaze of an inner judge, and in later chapters we will be looking at where this judge comes from, its role in setting up our inner demons, and the possibilities of getting the judge off our backs.

Part 2: The Making of the Troubled Soul

8

The Big Other

There must be something somewhere that makes me want to
hurt myself real bad.

JOHN PRINE[1]

He was not speaking to me, he was only speaking before
me, in a dispute with an invisible personality, an antago-
nistic and inseparable partner of his existence, another
possessor of his soul.

JOSEPH CONRAD

A person is always a feigned or artificial person, persona
ficta. A person is never himself but always a mask; a person
never owns his own person, but always represents another,
by whom he is possessed. And the other that one is, is always
ancestors; one's soul is not one's own, but daddy's.

NORMAN O. BROWN[2]

---

1 "There She Goes," from his album *Burnt Orange.*
2 Brown, Norman O., *Love's Body,* p. 98.

Noticing the Big Other

WHO OR WHAT is this partner of our existence before whom we seem compelled to justify ourselves, or to humble ourselves, with self-loathing and guilt?[3]

We all know the pressure we feel to look presentable and act properly in public places (though people vary greatly in how much of this pressure they feel and in their sense of what this actually requires). But it is not only the expectations of the other people around us that we feel we ought to live up to. Even our silent, inner monologues are judged by the invisible, and often antagonistic, "partners of our existence." Implicitly, we ask ourselves, Is what I'm thinking true, grammatical, logical, sensible, sincere, kind….? Do I look silly, or cool, doing this or wearing that? Our every gesture, even in privacy, takes place under the critical eye of an invisible monitor.

> Even the most intimate moments in our lives structure themselves around a public look, even when that look is absent. The subject in a private moment continues, albeit most often unconsciously, to act and present her/himself for an imagined look.[4]

---

3 To repeat something I've said before, not everyone suffers from anxiety, guilt, self-loathing and ontological insecurity in the same way and to the same extent. Some happy people, perhaps, hardly experience these emotions at all, at least not to speak of. And some people have such feelings but are not unduly disturbed by them because they are able to manage them, or distance themselves from them. When I say "we," as I did in the text, I mean to take in those of us who *suffer* from these existential feelings. By saying "we," I do not mean to conscript anyone who feels fine into a pathological condition. If the shoe fits, wear it—and may it be helpful. If it doesn't fit, then use what is written here as a guide to understanding those of us it does fit.

4 McGowan, *The Impossible David Lynch*, p. 4. McGowan continues,
This a point Jean-Paul Sartre stresses in his chapter on "The Look" in *Being and Nothingness*. For Sartre, the subject cannot avoid its fundamental situatedness, which means that it cannot avoid the Other's look, which follows the subject everywhere. As Sartre puts it, "The Other is present to me everywhere as the one through whom I become an object." (BN, p. 373) We perform our intimate activities in way that confirm a certain idea we have ourselves, and this self-image implies

This silent judge is not just some mixture of the identifiable and particular other people in our lives. It's true that we are influenced by real people in subtle and complex ways of which we can never be fully conscious. We react to other people out of murky motives of envy, jealousy, fear, and desires for recognition, admiration and love, giving rise to the "eidola" Iris Murdoch describes in a passage quoted in Chapter 6. But our anxiety about how to act, feel and think refers to something over and above what we are afraid that the real people in our lives will say or do; we are also anxious about how we will be judged by that "invisible partner of our existence."

Slavoj Žižek, following Jacques Lacan, calls this presence the big Other.[5]

While talking, I am never merely a 'small other' (individual) interacting with other 'small others': the big Other must always be there.

When I talk about other people's opinions, it is never only a matter of what I, you, or other individuals think, but also of what the impersonal 'one' thinks. When I violate a certain rule of decency, I never simply do something that the majority of others do not do—I do what 'one' doesn't do.[6]

---

an external look—what Freud calls an ego ideal—that apprehends it. The implicit on-looker gives meaning and structure to the private activity. Without the implicit onlooker or ego ideal, we would have no sense of how to act in private, no method for organizing our private lives.

5 We can clarify this concept: we often refer to what "others" will think without specifying exactly who these others are. We may mean just the actual people we are normally in contact with, or we may mean the general run of people. The phrase 'the Other' can have this second meaning. The *big Other* goes further, as we will see, to indicate a virtual ever-present monitor or overseer of our every word, thought, and action. It is the big Other that accounts for the inner judgments being made in the passages cited in the following note.

6 Žižek, *How to Read Lacan*, p. 9 and p. 11. Here are some more examples from fiction:

This demanding presence has an eerily ambiguous location. Is it an "inner voice," a part of ourselves? Or does it come from above, from a higher authority?

The Big Other

The big Other (which I will sometimes call simply "the Other") does not exist in the way that you and I do, and yet it is not just a figment of our imaginations. We might say that the big Other is a *virtual* reality, meaning that it exists because we talk and act *as if* it existed. In that sense, the big Other is like the dollar or the border between the US and Mexico. We do not, however, normally speak of the big Other, as we do of borders and the dollar. As it was once forbidden to look at the King, so the Other commands us not to name it—a command that this book will disobey.

What is the evidence that we feel the weight of the big Other, besides the feelings of being observed and judged by something— which some of us may refuse or be unable to notice? If we listen closely, we will find that we often refer (and defer), more or less covertly, to the big Other in guiding or criticizing what we and others do.

Laidlaw sat at his desk, feeling a bleakness that wasn't unfamiliar to him. Intermittently, he found himself doing repentance for being him. When the mood seeped into him, nothing mattered. He could think of no imaginable success, no way of life, no dream of wishes fulfilled that would satisfy. McIlvanney, Laidlaw, p.8.

To whom does Laidlaw want to repent? Who or what is it that must be satisfied by some yet-to-be-imagined way of life? Or consider George Falconer in Tom Ford's movie *A Single Man* getting dressed for work in the morning:

It takes time in the morning for me to become George, time to adjust to what is expected of George and how he is to behave. By the time I have dressed and put the final layer of polish on the now slightly stiff but quite perfect George I know fully what part I'm supposed to play.

For example, we make use of the passive voice in order to convey a demand to someone while obscuring the question of just who makes that demand. We say, "You are supposed to arrive on time," or "Men are required to wear jackets at dinner" and usually no one asks who it is that supposes or requires this.[7] Even to raise that question undermines the aura of the Other[8]—like what happens in *The Wizard of Oz* when the curtain is drawn back and an ordinary man is revealed producing the effects of wizardry.

When we use passive verb forms like 'you are required to' or 'it is expected that', it is not difficult to make the verb active and ask "Who?": Who requires, or expects, us to do such and such? But often we express these general norms or expectations in ways that offer no obvious opening to the question of who exactly is behind the norm. We say, for example, "one must," and "it is important that..." and "It is necessary to...". Not to mention, "One ought to..." Or "we have to...".

We implicitly invoke the big Other when we explain the meanings of words. Someone asks, What's a parka? Or what does 'parka' mean? And we say, "A parka is a long hooded jacket that protects the wearer against rain and wind," or "'Parka' means a long hooded coat." Or we point to a picture and say "That's a parka". Even though we probably know better, these explanations give the subliminal impression that there is some essential and even mysterious connection between the word 'parka' and the concept of parka—or the class of all parkas. In this way, the meanings of words become objects in their own right.

---

7 Edith Wharton's novel *The Age of Innocence* and the 1993 Martin Scorsese film adaptation brilliantly expose the rigid social rules of wealthy 19th Century New Yorkers that everyone knows but no one ever speaks. Wharton, *The Age of Innocence*.
8 What if someone did ask? The accurate answer might refer, in the first case, to a supervisor and then to company policies laid down by upper management. And in the second case, to the manager and/or owner of the restaurant. But the authority (the compelling effect) of the demand laid down in the original passive-voice statements is diluted by these down-to-earth explanations and that is why they are avoided.

Wittgenstein reminds us that we refer to the meaning of a word in order to explain how the word is used, bringing us back to the passive voice.[9] But if we go on to ask, "used by whom?" we really have no clear answer. If we say, "native speakers of the language," we can't mean every such speaker, since we know there are many people who misuse the word or have never learned it. We are driven to say, "This is how the word is used by educated speakers, or by those who speak correctly." Yet we have no independent way of identifying those speakers other than that they are those who speak correctly. We make our standards of correctness seem objective (and therefore mandatory) by appealing to the authority of a fictive community defined only by its allegiance to those standards.

Here are some other virtual authorities—we might think of them as "departments" of the big Other—which are often appealed to in support of our claims about what is really true and right: The American People, Destiny, The Economy, The Market, The National Interest, Science, The Law, The Constitution, The Dictionary, Grammar, and last, but far from least, "Society". Any of these things, and more, can be the big Other depending on what dimension of our lives we are talking about.

We can also say that they are all aspects of the *Symbolic*, for they oversee our signifying behavior, i.e. all our socially significant behavior, which is to say all our behavior.[10]

---

9 Wittgenstein, *Philosophical Investigations* §43. "For a *large* class of cases—though not for all—in which we employ the word 'meaning' it can be defined thus: the meaning of a word is its use in the language."

10 See Žižek, *How to Read Lacan*, pp. 9-10. Everything we do and everything that happens to us has social meaning, even if the causes are purely biological or mechanical. For example, the meaning of a fart depends on where it takes place and one's relationship to those who are nearby.

The Symbolic

The big Other is the authoritative presence, the virtual personality behind our sense of what is correct (or fitting or decent or right) in what we do and say. The Symbolic is *what* the big Other demands, the content of the big Other. It is "the invisible order that structures our experience of reality, the complex of rules and meanings which makes us see what we see the way we see it (and what we don't see the way we don't see it)."[11] So it includes all the "oughts" by which we feel bound, and which if we don't follow them, we feel compelled to punish ourselves with guilt.

Is the big Other really God? Or is God really the big Other? Perhaps the attraction of believing in God is that he puts something like an idealized human face—or something like a human personality—on the otherwise faceless Other. The "something somewhere" that watches and judges us becomes someone who might forgive us, even love us; and who even if He condemns us, at least he does it justly, as a good but strict father would. We can address our confessions and pleas for forgiveness to the One who has the ultimate power to make us whole, or to justly condemn us to everlasting torment.[12] In D.H. Lawrence's *Sons and Lovers*, Miriam, praying, "fell into that rapture of self-sacrifice, identifying herself with a God who was sacrificed, which gives so many human souls their deepest bliss."[13]

---

11 Žižek, *Event*, p. 106.

12 Of course many of us deny, or are skeptical of, religious beliefs, and many who say they believe have a stronger living faith in the value of material wealth and status than they do in the God to whom they pray on Sundays. But the virtual reality of the big Other remains in force even for non believers and those whose belief has become a mere formality. God may be dead, as Nietzsche claimed, but what God personified lives on beyond our grasp, leaving us only with the wounds we inflicted on ourselves in his no-longer-utterable name: guilt, anxiety, self-loathing, and ontological insecurity.

13 Lawrence, *Sons and Lovers*, p. 172.

The Inner Bully

Why do we punish ourselves so viciously when we fail to live up to the demands of the big Other? We can think of this as a form of *bullying*. People bully those who are weaker than themselves. What makes people weaker, in this sense, is that they have a lower social status and so fewer allies who will defend them. In other words, the big Other does not like them. Bullying, then, is the claim that *I am not weak*; I am on the side of the powerful big Other. So when we attack ourselves for having done something stupid or terrible, we are putting distance between who we claim to be *now* and the other awful person of the same name who acted, or failed to act, in the past. A passage from X's journal illustrates this maneuver:

> *I lie awake, unable to sleep, filled with shame for something I did, or failed to do, maybe yesterday, maybe many years ago. I tell myself there's nothing I can do about it right now, and I will be better off in the morning if I stop punishing myself, relax, and go to sleep. But I resist this advice: How do I dare to care for myself, to be at peace or enjoy life, while this offense goes unpunished!*[14]

By castigating and humiliating himself for failing to be what the big Other demands, X is trying to enjoy the power of the bully. In his position of accuser, he becomes a different *I*, an *over-I*. (In Freud's German, this is the *über-Ich*, usually translated as "superego".)

As we denounce ourselves for our sins and errors, taking the part of the accuser rather than the accused, we create ourselves *also* as the victim, the object of our attack. The sentence handed to me by a judge in court drafts me into the position of criminal, a status I will have to live with. In the same way, my self-accusation as, say,

---

14 In X's mind, the wrong he has done, and that it must be punished (indeed, that *he* must punish it), are objective facts, not mere "attitudes" of his that could be set aside. He does not believe in God—and yet he continues to act and feel as if God's commandments were fully in force with all their power to make us guilty. God may be dead, but his ghost still haunts us.

incompetent bungler creates me *as* that bungler, a sense of myself I will have to live with. Indeed, it establishes, or maintains, my feeling of being a guilty child scolded by a parent. Our souls oscillate between the attitudes of the judge and the condemned, the punitive parent and the reprimanded child. (We will have more to say about the over-I and the child in a later chapter.)

In Chapter 7, X asked, *"Who are these hectoring voices in my head that badger me, how did they get there, and why do they have such a hold on me?"* This chapter has now begun to answer the first of these questions. We began by calling the big Other out of the shadows, taking note of our shared sense that we are always in the presence of a higher authority, and we named this presence the big Other. The big Other is real in the way that a nation or corporation is real: we all agree to talk, think, and act as if it were. This agreement is not, however, freely undertaken: we could hardly live in the world as it is unless we internalized the social imperatives of the big Other. These imperatives, ranging from the basic rules of logic and grammar to the most subtle rules of etiquette, constitute the Symbolic, the structure that makes what we experience into a more or less coherent world. When we lie awake at night rehearsing all the terrible and embarrassing things we have done, we are split into two opposing camps, accuser and accused. We ally ourselves with the big Other to condemn what we have done and failed to do, yet at the same time we suffer from that condemnation. We are both bully and bullied, parent and child. The over-I calls forth an *under-*I who is cowering, apologetic, and eager to please.[15]

---

15 As we will see in later chapters, this under-I can flip into resentment and rage.

Looking Back and Moving On

The big Other appears, at this point, to be an unavoidable consequence of social life; social life "secretes" the Other.[16] The Other
is the force, as invisible as gravity or magnetism, that holds individuals in their (imperfect) social orbits, creating the (virtual)
human community that the word "we" refers to in its broadest
sense. Conversely, none of us could be the self-conscious individuals we are, capable of identifying ourselves as "I" and being
identified by others as "you" and "he" or "she", without having
been inducted into the symbolic system under the authority of
the big Other.

The big Other becomes a part of us, a co-possessor of our souls,
as we become recognizable and responsible persons. I learn to
answer to my name and to recognize that when someone uses the
word 'you' in my direction, that means me. I become part of the
dynamic, cooperative system for exchanging and sharing words,
acts, and responsibilities. I become part of the Other and the
Other part of me. The Other is the virtual author or impresario of
the social script and the social scenarios in which we live out our
lives together.

Just because the big Other demands so much and punishes so
vindictively, it is also an object of resentment, and thus the
real target of nihilistic and self-destructive behavior, the drift
into insensibility and death through drugs, alcohol, and outright
suicide. Our ability to live well depends on our implicit feelings
about the Other.

Our relationship with the big Other began during our earliest
initiation into social life. So in coming chapters, we will be exploring

---

16 "*So ideology is as such an organic part of every social totality*. It is as if human societies
could not survive without these *specific formations*, these systems of representations
(at various levels), their ideologies. Human societies *secrete ideology* as the very ele-
ment and atmosphere indispensable to their historical respiration and life."Louis
Althusser, "Marxism and Humanism," p. 232 (final emphasis added). The big
Other is the anchor of ideology in each of us.

what it was like for us as infants and small children being introduced to the Other and trained up into symbolic social life. We will find the answers to X's questions about the origins of the big Other and the hold it has on us, and whether we might be able to mitigate or moderate that grip, in the chapters to come.

9

The Underground Soul

Holy the mysterious river of tears under the streets!

ALLAN GINSBERG[1]

Introduction

IT'S TIME NOW to begin lighting up the darker corners of our souls where the demons thrive. The line from Alan Ginsberg's poem "Howl" gives us an image of the flow of strong feeling contained beneath the orderly façades of everyday life. We can think of the big Other as the virtual authority that maintains the order of the streets, keeping our disruptive feelings out of sight, relegated to sewers and drains below the surface, where in darkness they become more resentful, vicious and powerful—demonic, in fact. The order of the streets—their grid-like pattern, their lines, signs, and signals—is what we have been calling *the Symbolic*: the vast web of subtle and deeply engrained norms and expectations and habits that make us intelligible to each other when we act and talk.

---

1 Allen Ginsberg, *Howl and Other Poems*.

The thicker the pavement, the more violent those transgressive impulses become.[2] The further out of sight and out of mind they are, the more mysterious and the more demonic they are, and the more they appear as alien monsters threatening our very hold on who we think we are.

Emotional Undertows

Experience is always emotional. There are no thoughts or perceptions that do nothing more than register information or state a fact. To put it in more technical terms, consciousness is never purely cognitive, but always affective.

To see this, let's think for a moment about what we know about human beings as biological organisms—organisms that have developed complex symbolic communications systems for arranging their lives together. As we move through the world engaged in our various activities, our bodies are constantly responding to what is going on around us and within us. These responses of our bodies are at one and the same time perceptual, emotional, and interpretative. They add up to what we might call our "take" on a situation. For example, I see someone I know at the coffee shop; I take him to be a friend who likes me, I feel glad to see him, I greet him and join him at his table. Our interpretative and emotional response gets underway well before we take conscious notice of what's going on and how we are reacting.

Our immediate and pre-conscious responses to what goes on around us can be described neurologically. When, for example, we perceive an object coming towards us,

---

2 A high school friend of mine giving the Valedictorian address to several hundred people including parents, teachers, and fellow graduates, feeling the pressure to be a high-minded example of good citizenship, confessed to me afterwards that he had had to restrain the impulse to break out into a string of obscenities.

depending on the object, there may be different proportions of musculoskeletal and emotional accompaniment, but both are always present. The presence of all these signals …, from retinal images, from muscular-postural adjustments, and from muscular-visceral-endocrine adjustments—describes both the object as it looms *toward the organism* and part of the reaction of the organism *toward the object* as the organism regulates itself to maintain a satisfactory processing of the object.[3]

In other words, our bodies are constantly receiving, processing, and reacting to signals that come not only through our eyes and ears and other external senses, but also from our bodies' impulses to approach or flee from something. We do not just perceive and think about the world: we are constantly *feeling* it, and feeling initiates action ("muscular adjustments"). The flow or surge of emotion is a constant stream:

> …even when we "merely" think about an object, we tend to reconstruct memories not just of a shape or color but also of the perceptual engagement the object required and of the accompanying emotional reactions, regardless of how slight. Whether you are immobile… or quietly daydreaming in the darkness, the images you form in your mind *always* signal to the organism its own engagement with the business of making images and evoke some emotional reactions. You simply cannot escape the *affectation* of your organism, motor and emotional most of all, that is part and parcel of having a mind [or, I would say, soul].[4]

---

3 Damasio, *The Feeling of What Happens*, p. 147.
4 Ibid, p. 148.

The constant flow of feelings in our bodies as they sense and react to the world around us is much wider and deeper than our conscious minds can accommodate: most of it is never explicitly formulated in symbolic terms—that is, we do not consciously spell out what we are experiencing. And yet our immediate reactions of interpretation and emotion are not the work of a primitive, or untrained, gut. They make use of our complex symbolic grasp of situations and relationships. For example, without conscious attention or intention, we read complex social situations and react to them with complex judgments and emotions. For example, jealousy may rise up within you when you see someone you love involved in conversation with a stranger at a party across the room. You may have taken yourself to be losing your special place in her feelings while being entirely unaware of this thought and of the emotional response you are having. Others, however, may notice it in your irritability with your beloved. You may notice feeling angry at her but attribute it to something else. And if you do realize that you feel jealous, you may be mystified by its intensity.

Besides emotions like jealousy or anger or joy that rise and fall within us, there are also background emotions[5], or "existential feelings"[6] that are more pervasive and yet harder to focus on or admit. These are feelings of life in general and our place in it; they flavor our experience and lead us to interpret and respond to situations in certain ways. For example, the people for whom this book is being written suffer from deep, usually unspoken, existential doubts about whether they really exist, have the right to exist, or matter in the lives of others. Since these doubts persist regardless of whether they are, or can be, articulated, they can properly be called *feelings* –– feelings of *being*. They are not reactions to particular events; rather, they characterize our "background

---

5 Ibid pp. 51-53.
6 Ratcliffe, *Feelings of Being*, pp. 1-4.

orientations through which experience as a whole is structured.[7]
For a concrete example, we once again intrude into Mr. X's journal:

> *I have always the feeling that I'm running behind, or I'm unpre-*
> *pared, no matter what the task or how well I'm really doing. It even*
> *includes getting to bed "on time," so that I feel guilty whenever I stay*
> *up later than about ten. My mother nagged me about homework,*
> *chores, and bedtime—but she is no longer part of my life and I'm*
> *a grown man. Somehow I have taken over and even amplified her*
> *worries.*

X felt this way long before he was aware of it, and many feelings that
move us, especially existential feelings, can remain forever in the
background.

There are, of course, positive existential feelings, for example
the feeling that all is right with the world, that your place in it is
secure. This was the feeling expressed in the Paul Simon song "Born
at the Right Time" quoted wistfully by Mr. X in Chapter 7. But our
concern is with our *demonic* existential feelings, our inner demons.
Let's look at these: self-loathing, guilt, anxiety, the sense that one
is not real, and rage.[8] We will take them up in more detail in later
chapters.

First Demon: Self-Loathing

In the most literal sense, self-loathing can be a primal dislike for
oneself like that felt by a character in Edmund White's novel *A
Married Man*: "Austin strove to like himself, but the very familiarity

---

7 Ibid, p. 2.

8 It might seem surprising that I do not include depression in this list, even
though it is experienced as a pervasive background, or existential, feeling. But I
take depression to be the feeling of hopelessness coming from being trapped in
guilt, self-loathing, and the others.

of his habits of mind, the perfect attendance pin his eternal physical presence had won, revolted him or, worse, bored him so much
he was repelled."[9] It can also be the conviction that one's life is a history of failure owing to stupidity, incompetence, or some mysterious
inability to meet the demands of life. Here's a relatively mild case in
point—the thoughts of a writer as he's trying to fall asleep at night
after receiving a letter of rejection from a publisher:

> He applied thought like a painful tourniquet to a bleeding
> wound: anyway, this was just another failure. He had had
> plenty.` This was their time to visit. All you had to do was
> wait and out of the blackness would float the shapes of fail-
> ure. They were never far away, the night whisperers. They
> kept their distance until they could get you on your own,
> conspirators who plotted endlessly to persuade you that you
> were not who you might have been.[10]

Even when someone like this does have a success, he or she is likely
to feel undeserving —as if somehow others had been deceived or
were not paying attention.

Second Demon: Guilt

Then there is *guilt*—a general sense of having committed some terrible but unremembered crime for which we could never be sufficiently punished, as in this prose poem by Vern Rutsala:

> We sense a criticism, possibly overhearing it as we walk, and
> immediately begin rearranging our past to fit the crime we
> suspect we are suspected of. By the time we reach home we
> have altered our history, discredited all alibis, documented

---

9 White, *The Married Man*, pp. 92-93.
10 McIlvanney, *Weekend*, p. 105.

and labeled evidence, and, opening the door, we begin to serve our sentence.[11]

Third Demon: Feeling Unreal

Next, we have the sense of *unreality*, the feeling that I am not real, that I am only pretending to be someone, that no one really lives at my address. *I don't know who I am* easily becomes the doubt that I really exist at all. I feel invisible to others, but also to the big Other who authorizes all my perceptions. Thus my perceptions of myself are exposed as the flimsy fantasies they are. I am beset with existential loneliness. R.D. Laing calls this state of the soul *ontological insecurity*.[12]

Fourth Demon: Rage

Many people have an abiding and unacknowledged *rage* at the world in general—at the way things are, at the big Other. They feel that somehow they are expected to do the impossible and are condemned for failing at it. With no clear idea of whom to blame for this injustice, many people lash out at one or another bunch of politicians, at government in general, or at some convenient minority group. Some of us direct this rage back at ourselves, taking the role of the above-I to rake our miserable child-like self over the coals.

Fifth Demon: Free-Floating Anxiety

Finally, there is a generalized, free-floating *anxiety* or dread, a sense that something terrible (if only I knew what!) is going to happen

---

11 Rutsala, *A Handbook for Writers,* p. 95. This poem does not describe something we do deliberately, or by conscious choice. It just *happens* in us.
12 Laing, *The Divided Self,* pp. 39ff.

or is happening. This is the feeling the hare must have in Kafka's parable:

> The hunting dogs are still playing in the courtyard, but the hare will not escape them, no matter how fast it may be flying through the woods.

The hare flees because it is afraid, even though there is (as yet) nothing to be afraid of.

Anxiety is attached to all these demonic feelings because they all threaten to expose the hollowness of our lives. Self-loathing provokes the fear of being exposed as a fake person, as an imposter, of having to admit the shameful fact of a failed life. What makes this exposure so threatening is that we take it to mean that we have no right to the recognition of others and so would be left utterly alone—which feels like death.

But this anxiety has another side: we are afraid of facing up to the possibility that there is a life we have *not* lived, a life of love and desire that we let pass us by in our sweat to be what we were supposed to be. So we are afraid of two things: that we have *not* been what we were supposed to be, *and* that we have been *nothing more* than what we were supposed to be.

> ...and she is beginning to feel twinges of the old panic, the knot in her throat, the blood rushing too quickly through her veins, the clenched heart and frantic rhythms of her pulse. Fear without an object, as Dr. Burnham once described it to her. No, she says to herself now: fear of dying without having lived.[13]

---

13 Auster, *Sunset Park*, p. 106.

We fear that we will not ever be recognized for, or be able to enact, or even know ourselves as, the passionate, overflowing, loving, experiencing beings we sense, or hope, that we really are. In order not to have to admit the reality of this terrible loss, we maintain our ignorance of it. This only makes the fear worse because we are now beset by another demon hiding in the dark.

This doubled anxiety can be illustrated by a moment in the life of Mr. X: Well into the second year of his first job in a career in which he felt he was hopelessly failing (though no one had the guts to tell him or to help him), one December evening in a crowded, noisy Sears Roebuck cafeteria on a Christmas shopping expedition accompanied by his wife and two small children who were dependent on his meager salary, he found himself struggling to breathe, his heart racing. He said, "We have to leave, I can't be here any more," and they drove home, where he made his first call for help from a therapist. Only looking back on it many years later, can X see that the source of the panic in which he was drowning was not just his sense of failure, but the dreadful knowledge that he was condemned for life to a narrow path of joyless responsibilities, one (but *only* one!) of which was to meet demands for Christmas gifts he couldn't afford and didn't believe in.

Guilt has the same double-sidedness. In alliance with the big Other, we humiliate ourselves with charges of moral failure and incompetence. Yet ironically we hate ourselves for submitting to the Procrustean bed of conventional norms and expectations. We can even feel guilty for feeling guilty.

Ontological insecurity, the sense of not really existing, of being hollow inside is, on the one hand, the fearful conviction that I am unrecognizable because I don't play my part well enough to deserve recognition. But it is also the feeling that I have lived my life entirely in an empty and artificial symbolic realm.

What I have been describing here so far is a complex of largely inarticulate, and often unnoticed, feelings about what social existence and language demand of us. These feelings are pervasive and over-whelming, especially for the people we are trying to address and comfort in this book. But however tongue-tied we might be about our feelings, most of us are sensitive to the gulf between what we are and what is expected of us. It's a fault line of which we do not normally speak, but along which we know we could crack up.

Transgression

No matter how dedicated we may feel to being perfectly intelligible signifiers in the symbolic system, no one is *really* able to live up to the demands of the established order of things all the time. Most of the responses to this pressure we have discussed so far, except for rage, are submissive. But any of our demonic feelings can seek relief in angry action. Most people are not willing or able to live only on their knees: they demand some escape for the energy of the human body and its desires. This brings us to the problem of *transgression*.[14]

Our energies are simply too large to be restricted to what we are supposed to do. For example, sexual desire, as we all know from our private fantasies and daydreams, as well as from what people actu-ally do (not to mention a great deal of the world's literature), refuses to remain within the approved boundaries of polite social life. The same is true of our hostile impulses. But the issue of transgression is more complex. There is actually *a will to transgress*: we desire trans-gression for its own sake. Why is this?

The prohibition of something *stimulates* the desire for it. The fruit of the forbidden is desire itself. Lust is fueled and burnished by a ban; the condemned object, place, person, or course of action takes on a mesmeric eroticism.[15] After all, if the authorities are

---

14 I draw heavily in this section on Chris Jenks and the sources he cites. Jenks, *Transgression*.

15 Ibid, p. 45.

trying to keep me away from something, it must be because it's really worth having. If they don't want me even to think about it, it must be because if I knew about it, I would really want it! And if others are willing to risk punishment to get it, it must be worth having. And then there is the *pleasure* of transgression itself, of flouting and making fun of authority, which shows that you are your own person and not controlled by "should's" and "ought-to-be's". For people who have felt marginalized or excluded by the ways of the world, transgression is often ramped up by resentment and even hatred for the forces that have humiliated them. Mass murderers and serial killers are generally isolated and lonely men who feel betrayed or scorned by others.

Then, too, there is the *excitement* of risky behavior, of gambling against being caught, ruined or killed. Transgression can be what one writer (Stephen Lyng[16]) has called "edgework"—living, and possibly dying, on the edge, as in "rock and ice climbing, bungee jumping, downhill skiing"—as well as "stock trading, vandalism, unprotected sex, and sado-masochism."[17] Edgework is transgressive in the sense that it "violates the sense of purposive control over one's life."[18] We live, after all, in a society that puts pressure on us in a myriad of ways, through government, the mainstream media, doctors, lawyers, and insurance companies, to be careful, to plan ahead, to avoid risk. So risk taking becomes an exciting form of transgression.

The symbolic order is able to remain in place by offering a variety of loop-holes and escape hatches through which people can, in practice and in fantasy, violate that order. Violent movies and stories of crime—both fact and fiction—enable us to identify vicariously with transgressors.

The attractions of transgression, which many of us work hard to deny but often give into in various ways, help us to understand crime,

---

16 Lyng, *Edgework*, 2004.
17 According to the blurb on Google Books for Lyng's book. (http://books.google.co.uk/books/about/Edgework.html?id=PTIEMrpebzIC)
18 Lyng, "Edgework," 1990. Cited in Jenks, *Transgression*, p. 179.

from petty thievery to mass murder. But we shouldn't overlook the ways in which transgressive impulses give rise to everyday nasty behavior: aggressive reckless driving, bullying of vulnerable individuals whether on the playground or in the workplace or in the military, and the vicious verbal tirades launched at others in the on-line comment sections everywhere on the internet, not only on opinion sites but even on entertainment venues like YouTube. In medieval Europe, the institution of Carnival, the week before the piety and sobriety of Lent, was a time when social conventions and lines of authority were turned upside down, when transgression was the rule. The Symbolic order became an object of ridicule, and the human body and imagination were encouraged to do what they're normally supposed not to do:

> defecation, dissociation, deconstruction. We are enabled to flatulate, to move from the center to the periphery, to break the relation between the signifier and the signified and choose another meaning..... 'Carnival releases us from the terrorism of excessive significance, multiplying and so leveling meanings'.[19]

However, as all human activity got swept up into the cash nexus controlled by the principle of productivity and profit, meaning that "time is money," the profitless time of Carnival ceased to exist. As a result, the need for transgression that was once harmlessly discharged at a special time is instead gratified in "places of fun and naughtiness" (casinos, strip joints, on-line porn sites). "We no longer anticipate the joys of carnival, we go to places where its manifestations can be routinely guaranteed."[20] But, as already remarked, transgression leaks out into the "normal" world. "To ban carnival is to release the specter of transgression upon the full span of everyday

---

19 Eagleton, Terry, "Bakhtin, Schopenhaur, Kundera". Quoted in Jenks, *Transgression*, p 168.
20 Jenks, *Transgression*, p. 169.

life, to render it invisible, to pathologize it and, perhaps worst of all, to add to the piquancy of such excess now covert."[21]

But in the everyday life of work and family, the people whose souls we are trying to illuminate here try to keep their most vulnerable and transgressive thoughts and impulses silenced and out of sight, even when they are alone. Our concern for being acceptable and recognizable is so compelling that no disaster could be worse than being unmasked. (This is why people often commit suicide rather than face the world when some shameful side of their lives has been exposed.) Yet aggressive feelings and thoughts do insist on happening, things we feel that we must not (cannot) report. So we learn not to represent them, or to *mis-represent* them, even to ourselves. We let a narrow version of the Symbolic be the measure of what is real.[22] So our souls go dark and our all-too-real emotions grow ever more restive in their invisibility.

Obstacles to Understanding

We are working to understand, so far as possible, how and why our emotions go dark on us and take on the aspect of demons. There are two things about these surges of dread that arise within our bodies, that make them difficult to grasp clearly.

One is that we simply do not *want* to think about them. So we pretend not to have such feelings, which means we avoid displaying them or even admitting to ourselves that we have them. We do not want to know, or anyone else to know, that we are not in full control of ourselves, for that would mean we are unpredictable, untrustworthy, and not fully responsible. But being responsible is the main requirement for being taken seriously by others. To be besieged by

---

21 Ibid, p. 166.

22 We live our lives in a double fantasy system—a public fantasy, or ideology, that we largely share with each other; and intersecting with that one, we each have our own private fantasy that we construct without knowing that we do. In the next chapter we will ask, How is it possible to do all this work without knowing that we are?

intense anxiety or guilt or self-loathing is to feel in danger of coming apart like a child who is crying or screaming without being able to say why. As adults, we have crossed into a territory where we *must* not become helpless in the grip of our unspeakable emotions. There is nothing more terrifying than being an adult on the verge of a flood of childish tears; we should remember that some people live much of their lives in that state of fear.

It takes a lot of work to keep our most terrible feelings about ourselves out of sight, but we do it because the alternative seems to be annihilation—being left all alone in an empty universe. When we are trying to get things done, we need to believe in our own competence. Guilt, self-loathing, anxiety, and invisibility do not belong in the story we want to be enacting as we engage in the challenges of social life. So we learn how to live, to present ourselves, *as if* we felt ok without admitting that we are frantically hiding the fact that we are *not* ok.[23]

It's not easy to override this fear and to think and write about one's demonic fears, even privately. It takes more courage to seek out a therapist with whom you can speak of these matters. It seems easier to ignore them, creating a divide between the outer, public self and the anguished inner, private self.[24] In the next chapter, we will see in more detail how and why we flee from emotions, thereby

---

23 Of course we all know people who make sure we know they are *not* OK, but they usually hide their self-hatred or guilt by blaming others for their anguish.

24 Such a divided soul may either be quiet and reticent, too preoccupied with keeping the demons under control to fully engage with the other people in his life; or she may be able to use a flamboyant or aggressive style of engagement with others as way of keeping her demons at bay. Drugs and alcohol, or staying resolutely, or frantically, occupied with work or sports or politics or sex are other strategies. Sleep can also be an escape: a character in Iris Murdoch's novel *Nuns and Soldiers*,

... knew that if he did not tend himself he could fall into a pit of crippling misery. Sleeplessness and night terrors were then greatly to be feared. He wanted the darkness of death-like sleep, even the hurly-burly of bad dreams, anything rather than an active idle consciousness. Murdoch, *Nuns and Soldiers*, p. 36.

It's the idleness of the active consciousness, like that of the writer in McIlvanney's novel a few paragraphs ago, that lets the demons in.

creating demons and losing sight of our past and the reasons we do and feel what we do.

The second reason our emotions are hard to grasp is that the language we use to make the world clear to ourselves is not well-suited to describing our emotions. Emotional life is too ephemeral and indistinct to be nailed down by the categories of our thinking. We will see that there are poetic and expressive ways of thinking that come closer to the nuances of our feelings, but unfortunately these ways of thinking are not welcome in the precincts of the big Other.

10

The Mystery of the Unconscious

Introduction

WE HAVE EXPLORED some limits of our default understanding of ourselves as unified, transparent, and fundamentally self-conscious creatures. We can be angry or fearful without knowing it, and we can have desires and attitudes we will not admit even to ourselves. Behind our own backs, as it were, we punish ourselves for sins we cannot name. In the preceding chapter, we took note of how hard we work to keep our most terrible feelings about ourselves out of our minds. All this seems to point to a lot of unconscious, and yet purposeful, activity, including the activity of deciding what to be conscious of.

Because we are under pressure to present, and to see, ourselves as responsible adults who know, and can control, what we are doing, we resist being told that we are not what we think. As patients in therapy, for example, we may find it hard to accept the therapist's suggestion that some uncomfortable anger or fear could be the result of a belief or attitude we don't know, and don't believe, we have. How can therapists claim to know more about what's in our minds than we do?[1] If we are philosophically inclined, we might

_____

1 For example, a therapist might suggest that your distrust of a teacher has something to do with how your father treated you, even though you are sure that you

wonder how we could work to keep unpleasant thoughts out of our minds. If I am going to keep myself from being conscious of, say, my anger, would I not first have to be conscious of it in order to keep it out? I can't bar the door to certain people unless I know who they are. I will deal with this puzzle at the end of this chapter

These doubts about whether it even makes sense to speak of unconscious activity can close our minds to the kind of self-reflection we are trying to do in this book. So this chapter will try to unravel the confusion and make sense of the unconscious.

The Conscious and the Unconscious

The reason we find it so hard to wrap our minds around the unconscious is that we begin with a conception of ourselves as fundamentally conscious beings. We identify ourselves with ourselves at our most focused and alert, aware of all that is going on within us. We imagine ourselves as operating in a clear field all the way to the horizon—the *I* as a perfectly functioning "eye". So from that perspective, it is impossible to conceive of oneself doing, or experiencing, anything without being aware of it. How could the eye /I avoid seeing something unless it could already see it? In a mind so conceived, how could there even be anything in the mind that the mind did not know?

But what if consciousness is not our baseline, or default, condition, but rather an achievement from within a fundamentally unconscious state? There is nothing essentially conscious about what goes on in our souls—our feelings, perceptions, and thoughts. We become conscious of what we are feeling or thinking when we articulate it, when we bring it into the Symbolic, when we put it into a

---

have nothing but the greatest respect for your father and have completely forgiven him for deserting the family when you were a child. And you might well be puzzled not only by the idea that you resent your father, but also by the suggestion that you connect (identify) your teacher with your father.

communicable and recordable form that is potentially accessible to others.[2] For any state of our souls, we may have reasons to express it symbolically, *and* we may also have reasons *not* to do so.

Moving through our everyday lives, we are constantly, but unconsciously, responding perceptually and emotionally to situations as they unfold, interpreting and reacting to what is going on. Every emotional response is the beginning of an action: to begin to respond interpretively and emotionally to something is to *begin to act*, to initiate a sequence of behavior. Impulse, emotion, and action are parts of one integrated, unfolding process. Anger, for example, is not just a feeling in one's body and a turmoil in one's mind; it is an interpretation of a situation as *wrong* and a gathering of one's muscular energy to act aggressively. If the aggression is limited to a look or a raised voice, that is because we know how to contain ourselves within more or less acceptable bounds.

We are usually unaware of the flow between feeling and action because we have learned to interrupt that flow by inserting a moment of hesitation between impulse and action. This moment gives us time to moderate the action or to make up an acceptable story about it.[3] We are rarely allowed (or rarely allow ourselves) to simply let our impulses flow directly into action. Before—or after—we act, we must find an acceptable symbolic form with which to represent what we are doing—to ourselves as well as to others.[4] That is how we make ourselves conscious of what we are doing.

---

2 See the Appendix to Chapter 13 for more about the relationship between consciousness and the Symbolic.

3 In this pause for conscious thought, we put the emotion on hold, as it were, and so we experience the emotion in the form of blocked impulse. The result is that emotions are mistaken for an inner turmoil isolated from action. This is why emotions seem so foreign to us: in the act of conscious thought we have fenced them off from their full expression.

4 There are some forms of cultural activity which encourage the free flow of some emotion into symbolic expression: spontaneous dancing, improvisational jazz, sex with someone you know and trust. All artistic expression is to one degree or another the flow of what we know practically into symbolic representation. Or better,

Consciousness and How to Avoid It

When we find a way to represent symbolically our take on a situation, we make it available to the big Other. We stand with the fictive community and thereby *take responsibility* for what we are doing and feeling. We make ourselves answerable for the feeling, action or perception; we acknowledge the right of others (or at least the big Other) to engage in conversation about what's going on.

The *decision* to become conscious of something—or not—is taken without consciousness. To suppose otherwise would lead to what philosophers call an "infinite regress." If I had to consciously decide to become conscious of how I feel, then I would have to first consciously decide to decide whether to do so, and so on.[5] So our beliefs, emotions, and actions are grounded in spontaneity. They are not guided from the start by conscious thought. Consciousness of what we are doing, thinking and feeling is always after the fact.[6]

So the choice *not* to become conscious of something we are doing, thinking, or feeling (to remain *un*conscious of it) is the

---

we are extending and elaborating what we know practically by learning how to expand the scope of its symbolic expression.

5 If this argument seems too abstract, there is also empirical evidence: psychologists have shown that the neurons that move our muscles into action begin firing before we are conscious of the decision to act. Research suggests "that the experience of conscious will kicks in at some point after the brain has already started preparing for the action." (Wegner, Daniel, *The Illusion of Conscious Will* p. 54.) Our choices result from processes we are not aware of working on a mass of environmental and psychic material beyond our ken. Guiding our attention away from taboo or shameful topics is just more thing we have learned to do without thinking about it.

Wegner argues in his concluding chapter that our sense of agency, our feeling that we have freely chosen, helps us to keep track of what we have done and what we will be held responsible for. But just as a ship's compass follows, but does not steer the ship, so our sense of agency monitors and records, but does not determine our actions.

6 We may be moved by events or by someone's intervention to consciously ponder our lives and to resolve to live more consciously, more intentionally. Sometimes this works. But whether we are so moved, as well as whether we actually do it, depends on forces within us of which we are not the masters, as our many lapsed New Years resolutions demonstrate.

choice to avoid taking responsibility for it, avoiding the public gaze, *and this is precisely why we do it—to avoid being answerable*. When we put the matter beyond the reach of symbolic expression, it is unavailable for reflection or discussion. We have lost our grip on it, and are effectively in *its* grip.[7]

It might seem strange to speak, as I just have, of *unconscious choices*. We are often told sternly that we are responsible for our own choices, making the assumption that choices are always conscious. For how could we be held responsible, and therefore punished, for what we do if we did not know we were doing it? What psychologist Daniel Wegner calls "The Illusion of Conscious Will"[8] is used to justify unsparing retribution such as long prison sentences for people whose choices flowed from conditions of their lives and of their souls which they did not choose. People in trouble—homeless or unemployed or in prison, for example—are said to have nothing and no one to blame but themselves for the bad choices that got them where they are, so they deserve no mercy or compassion or help from the rest of us. Moreover, this attitude of condemnation, applied to ourselves, locks us into our ongoing sense of guilt and self-loathing. *There must be something*, we feel, *that makes me do these stupid things—if only I could see it clearly!* There are indeed unconscious choices, including the choices about whether to be conscious of what we feel.[9]

---

7 At least it puts it out of our reach insofar as we are who we *think* –pretend—we are. There is still something we (really) are that continues to work with the issue, but in other ways for which we are unable to answer.

8 Wegner, Daniel, *The Illusion of Conscious Will.*

9 Philosophers generally assume that to say I chose to do something implies that I could have done otherwise. But this implicit claim refers only to the external circumstances that left it open to me to choose either way. The claim does not extend to everything going on in my soul. I might think now that I could, and should, have taken piano lessons as a child when my mother offered them to me, but thinking back to that time, I can feel the resistance that I experienced then, even though I can't clearly see the reasons for it.

Because we automatically monitor and regulate the emergence of impulse into action, we always experience a lot of blocked, delayed and frustrated impulse. Moreover, this frustration, felt only as stress, is also blocked from direct expression, and the resulting cauldron of denied impulses is what makes our emotions seem so enigmatic and chaotic.

Let's try out this account of our inner demons with a concrete example. Here is another entry from Mr. X's journal:

Out for a walk, I passed a father and two small boys playing basket-ball in their yard. The Dad was enthusiastically encouraging them, shouting at one point, "Great shot, buddy!" I found myself shrinking from the scene, wanting to turn my gaze away, walk quickly by, and erase it from my memory. Why? The man was being a good father, trying to raise self-confident sons; why shouldn't I rejoice? If someone walking with me had remarked on what a good father that man was, I would have agreed, and sincerely—even as I struggled to hide my aversion. Why all these fearsome emotions?

X does not know. But he is willing to speculate about how he might be interpreting the scene:

Perhaps I take that man's whole-hearted playing with his kids to be a model, a norm that I as a man should also follow; and yet the thought of playing enthusiastically with children and shouting "Great shot, Buddy!" gives me the heebie jeebies—of which I am ashamed. Why? What's wrong with me?

Unlike many, X does recognize that he has emotions he doesn't understand. He does not construe his reaction as the perception of an objective fact, saying, for example, "That guy is behaving child-ishly," or "wasting his time with kid-stuff." Moreover, X is willing to admit that there is more to say about his reaction than merely "I just don't like children." He knows that an aversion to being or seeming childish just rises up in him. He even has an aversion to that aversion—he is ashamed of it. He might just walk away and try to think no more about it, but he knows that the feeling of shame would continue to nag at him as he tries to immerse himself in other thoughts and activities. So he goes home and writes about it in his journal.

Where should X look to understand these rogue feelings? What is the real situation he is interpreting and reacting to, and from which he has been cut off? Since there is nothing in his conscious beliefs and memories that could explain how he feels, the explanation must lie in his *unarticulated take* on the situation. But what would explain that "take"? Perhaps he is responding to something from his childhood and responding as if he were *still* a small child.

We can imagine the following plot in his personal "Garden of Infantile Catastrophe"[10]: his parents, especially his mother, maintained an orderly household in which emotions were never openly expressed and confronted. Yet there was considerable stress going on in the household, resulting in a separation and divorce when X was five. After the divorce, X, who was the older of two children, was told that he was now the "man of the family," and to take good care of his mother. To X, that meant, implicitly, that he should no longer be a child, that all things child-like, including emotions, should be kept under control, that he must not cause problems for his mother by being a child.

Obviously this is only the "stub" of a story, one that needs to be filled out by much reflection and digging through memories. The details vary with each individual, and there is no substitute for thinking and talking through the events of one's childhood using all the resources one can gather (conversations with relatives, letters, photographs, and psychotherapy).

---

10 James Grotstein. See Chapter 3, n. 20.

X did not consciously choose his interpretation of his situation or his emotional response to it (his fear of being childish), nor is he conscious of them when he flees from the scene of a father acting "childishly." It was not X as he represents himself, X as defined by what he is willing to take responsibility for, that does these things. It is the totality of X that is only dimly and partially aware of itself. This totality is X's soul, a soul anxious not to be sucked into the responsibilities of fatherhood that require child's play.

Knowing and Not Knowing: the Puzzle of the Unconscious

The idea that we think and feel and do so many things without *knowing* that we do can be very puzzling: How can we purposely *not* think of something without *knowing* what it is that we must not think of? It seems that we *must* know what we seem not to know. How can we keep secrets from ourselves unless we know the secrets? How can I lie to myself unless I know the truth?[11]

To explain this paradox, let's note that there are different kinds of knowing. Some philosophers have distinguished between *knowing how* and *knowing that*,[12] or between *practical* knowledge and *propositional* knowledge. The "Centipede's Dilemma" illustrates the difference: when a centipede was asked which leg moves after which, it could no longer walk. It knew how to walk, but did not know how it walks. Most of us are in this relation to tying our shoes.

---

11 Also, the idea that we might run so much of our lives without knowing what we're up to makes us seem deeply irresponsible. We seem to have no more control over our actions than a leaf in the wind—or a snake in the grass. So what good does it do to teach people moral principles? For an attempt to deal with this puzzle from which I learned a great deal but that differs from the one that follows, see Fingarette, *Self-Deception.*.

12 Ryle, *The Concept of Mind.* Chapter 5.

Propositional knowledge is what we can deliver in words, and we can get it by being told, or by reading about something. I can learn a lot about New York City or how chopsticks are used or how a harmonica is played from pictures, stories, and books. Propositional knowledge is expressed *symbolically* in sentences or diagrams or pictures with captions. I don't have to have been there to know that Grand Central Station is on 42d Street. But then there is the kind of knowledge we come to have by walking the streets of New York, learning to use chopsticks or play the harmonica. Having done these things, we can then, in imagination and memory, be sensuously and practically immersed in the living activity that involves these places and things.

Let's call this *practical* knowledge. Practical knowledge is "know-how"; it is embedded in our bodies as habits and skills, in our ways of reading and responding to familiar situations. The difference between propositional and practical knowledge is the difference between having studied marriage in sociology, anthropology, and psychology courses and having been married; or between having read about a war and having been *in* it as a combatant or journalist—or as a civilian. We make a similar distinction about memories: I remember being on a train from Chicago to Sacramento in 1945; but my younger brother only remembers *that* we took that train. He remembers the fact from having heard about it; I remember being there. If I have practical knowledge of a situation, then I know what it's like to be in that kind of situation and can more fully imagine what it's like for others to be in such situations. If you tell me about problems you are having as a college teacher or a father, I can empathize and identify with you more than if you are talking about issues that arise for you as a tax accountant or a mother.

So there is propositional knowledge without practical knowledge; we often know a lot about situations we have not lived, and so do not know "from the inside". Conversely, there is much that we know practically that we do *not* know propositionally. We are sensuously and practically immersed in situations far beyond our ability to speak of them. A native New Yorker knows the city in a way that people who have not lived there can not, no matter how many maps and guide books they study. The long-time user of chopsticks and the skillful harmonica player have practical knowledge that they could not formulate symbolically. Creative people, like song writers, rarely claim to know the principles by which they create; they know how to write or compose, but they don't know how to explain how they do it. The difference between being fluent in a language and being merely competent lies in having an intuitive and automatic grasp of vocabulary and grammar, unlike those who have to keep the rules in mind. In fact, the latter often have more propositional knowledge of the language and can explain the rules better than native speakers whose knowledge is mostly practical.

Our practical understanding of our world and how to live our lives plays a much larger role than what we know propositionally. Most of what we do and think and feel is done, not as the result of conscious deliberation and conscious choice, but automatically— out of habit, instinct, or intuition, and we give our conscious attention to such things only when something goes wrong. For example, I find I'm playing the wrong note in a song on the harmonica, so I have to stop and figure out where that note is on the instrument. We know how to make grammatical sentences in our own language without thinking about grammar. Similarly, while we are thinking or talking, we know when to speak and when to be silent, when to let the big Other see what we are doing and feeling, and when not to do so. We are careful about what we want to be responsible for—to be conscious of.[13]

---

13 I am here discussing the kind of consciousness that we take pains to avoid in the act of repression, the consciousness that takes place in the implicit presence of an other. This is the same as becoming conscious of it (con scire = knowing with). It is what Mead (Mead, *Mind, Self & Society*) specifies as "self-consciousness," which he says "refers to the ability to call out in ourselves a set of definite responses which belong to the others of the group" (p.163). This is central to the kind of

We choose unconsciously, then, what to be conscious of. Recall that the way we make what we are doing public, if only to the big Other, is by naming it, using the public resources of language to signal our activity. But I do not need to, and in fact could not, name, or spell out in symbols, my decision to go, or *not* to go, public with (to symbolize) my action. So the choice to be conscious or not is always itself unconscious. I am not fully responsible for my choice to take or avoid responsibility for my actions and attitudes. I know what I am doing practically, but not propositionally. Like everyone else, I am a master of the complex technique of evading consciousness selectively.[14]

Why would I (unconsciously) choose not to know something propositionally? To know something symbolically, consciously, is to invoke our common language, and therefore to expose it to the perspective and judgment of others—more precisely, the big Other. This means that to know something propositionally is to take responsibility for it, and we may well have reasons not to do that. So practically we avoid facing up to, becoming conscious of, what we would be ashamed to have the big Other see. Nevertheless, a soul that would know itself must learn to let at least one other soul in on its secrets.

---

consciousness that supports human social life. A mature person "becomes a self in so far as he can take the attitude of another and act toward himself as others act" (p. 171). This is *not* the notion of consciousness as subjective experience that philosophers of mind debate when they ask, for example, whether a complete physical (neurophysiological) explanation can be given, for example, of the sensation of red or of pain.

14 Herbert Fingarette asks us to think of "explicit consciousness as a form of telling [oneself] something," bringing out the "banal truth that what a person tells himself is highly selective, highly purposeful, namely, that he may at times purposely tell himself what is not so." (Fingarette, *Self-Deception.*, p. 54) But we might ask, how can he *purposely* tell himself what is not so unless he "knows" what is, and is not, so. My answer is that he knows *practically*, but not *propositionally*, what is and is not so; and he knows practically how to *avoid* knowing it propositionally, i.e. how to avoid telling himself the truth.

Conclusion

In this chapter, we have looked at how and why we split off large parts of our souls from who we think we are. It's as if we disown much of what belongs to every human being so that we can pass ourselves off as something we feel the big Other can accept. As long as we refrain from representing—putting into symbolic form—our renegade impulses, we do not have to judge those impulses from the point of view of others—or as the big Other would see them.

To rephrase this in terms of consciousness: we are not automatically, or by default, conscious of what we think, feel, and perceive. Our experience becomes conscious when we, as it were, put it on the table for consideration by others, when we bring it into the network of symbolic action, when we respond to it as a person connected in the symbolic web with other persons.[15] We may or not do this; we do it selectively, in light of the judgments that others and the big Other would make. Becoming conscious of something is something we do, or refrain from doing, according to how we feel about how the big Other would judge us. The more we fear the judgments of the big Other, the more likely we are to repress our impulses and existential feelings, which is what keeps them unconscious and demonic.

However, at this point, the dark places in our souls from which our inner demons arise should be a little less mysterious. The darkness is something we produce by our fearful self-monitoring and self-control. We split ourselves into reputable and disreputable domains—into what is *admissible* and what is *inadmissible*.

---

15 This is not to say that we only become conscious of something when we actually name it. The claim is rather that what makes something conscious is the posing of the question how it shall be represented or otherwise emplaced in the symbolic order. Something that cannot be named can nevertheless be brought into the symbolic order by pointing or referring to it. Put otherwise, I become conscious of something when I engage with it as a responsible member of the discursive community, asking in effect, "How shall we think, feel, react to, this?" See the Appendix to Chapter 13.

In the next two chapters, we will see that there is an even deeper reason for the gulf between what we say and how we feel. It is a gulf that would persist no matter how good our relations with the Other might be.

Appendix: More on Unconscious Emotions

Our emotions and immediate interpretations of situations are gut reactions, and they become demonic when the reactions occur but we have no idea of what we are reacting to. We react, but refuse to look squarely at the objects of our reaction or at the reaction itself. We refuse, that is, to aim our field of representation at what is bothering us. We also refuse to represent ourselves as having those reactions, for only certain kinds of reactions are acceptable in the face of the big Other. Unable to bear the thought of myself as angry, I angrily pretend, even to myself, not to be angry. So we either pretend we are not reacting at all, or we tailor our reaction to be more acceptable (I am indignant, not angry), and that may lead us to represent the situation to which we react in a particular way (You lied to me—it wasn't an innocent oversight!). The result is that we have a distorted take on the situation and, and we misconstrue our own reaction to it.

We need to be clear that we do not pull this wool over our eyes consciously. Our reading of a situation and our intelligent gut reaction to it gets well underway before (and whether or not) we take conscious notice of how we are reacting. Emotions and the interpretations of situations that give rise to them, as well as the decision to articulate (acknowledge, confront) them, precedes their consciousness. Inner demons come from our unconscious refusal to articulate, to confess, what we are feeling, thinking, and doing.

11

Lost In Language

*"Inexpressible and nameless is that which gives my
soul agony and sweetness and is even the hunger of my
entrails."*

NIETZSCHE[1]

*I have much more experience than I have written there,
more than I will, more than I can write. In silence we must
wrap much of our life, because it is too fine for speech,
because also we cannot explain it to others, and because
somewhat we cannot yet understand.*

RALPH WALDO EMERSON[2]

Introduction

IT SEEMS STRANGE that we all know, at least in a general way, that a
great deal of our experience cannot really be described or expressed

---

1 Nietzsche, *Thus Spoke Zarathustra*, First Part.
2 Quoted in Cross, *Sweet Death, Kind Death*.

in words—and yet we have to keep reminding ourselves of this, for we lose sight of it in daily life as we constantly and confidently give names to how we and other people feel. So we sometimes ask people to tell us exactly what they mean, as if what they thought or felt must have an exact name. Or we say to someone, "Either you want it or you don't—which is it?"

When we do this we assume that everything in us is identifiable and easily named, that "there is a perfect scheme of verbal expression for all the internal moods and meanings of [people], ... that [one] has a word for every reality in earth, or heaven, or hell....". And yet we know "that there are in the soul tints more bewildering, more numberless, and more nameless than the colors of an autumn forest."[3] So the more our sense of who we are is limited to what we can clearly say and verbally communicate to others, the more blind we are to all that cannot be articulated in the words of our shared language, and that turns out to be a lot of what we are and what we know.

Reflect for a moment on what goes on in you as you listen to music, watch a movie, read a poem or a novel, engage in conversation, speak or sing in public, savor a meal, stand close to someone you're very attracted to, walk quietly in the forest or a garden, or recall a dream. Of course there is much you *can* say about these experiences: some of it can be named and told to others—the plot of the novel, the story of your life or of what happened yesterday, the names of the people and places you see. Even some of your emotions, like the colors and smells you find in the forest, have names.[4] But there is always, if you attend to it, more to these things than you can convey to another person—more, even, than you can

---

3 G.K. Chesterton, quoted in Borges, *Other Inquisitions, 1937-1952.*

4 But it isn't always obvious what to call the emotion we are feeling. "She had a quick vision of Blanco [a man who had sexually abused her], headless, hanging upside down. What did she feel about that? Pleasure? Pity? She couldn't tell."Atwood, *The Year of the Flood.* The same is often true of colors, sounds, tastes, smells, and other bodily sensations.

convey to yourself, as you discover when you read your notes about the dream you had last week. You can tell someone how high a mountain is and have a good chance of their understanding exactly what you mean. But you can't tell someone who has never tasted it what you like about a favorite food.[5] Nor can you use language, at least not the language of everyday life, to adequately communicate how you feel when you feel anxious and alone in the middle of the night.

The deepest feelings that are evoked by your world usually pass without notice, but if you do dwell on them (and *with* them), you find yourself aware of what cannot be said—"that which gives your soul agony and sweetness" and "the hunger of your entrails." No doubt we call them *deep* because they escape the reach and the illumination of articulate speech.[6] Among the deepest of our feelings are the existential feelings we have discussed: self-loathing, anxiety, guilt, rage, and ontological insecurity.

In the last chapter, we looked at why we refuse to give these emotions our attention: they contradict the act we put on to seem fully in control of ourselves. In this chapter, we will investigate the ways in which language itself is biased against the description of such hazy,

---

5 Wittgenstein asks us to
Compare *knowing* and *saying*:

> how many feet high Mont Blanc is
> how the word "game" is used—
> how a clarinet sounds.

If you are surprised that one can know something and not be able to say it, you are perhaps thinking of a case like the first. Certainly not of one like the third. Wittgenstein, *Philosophical Investigations*, §78.

6 "Would that disinclination bias her work? Well, sure. If not consciously, then deeper. Consciousness was just a thin lithosphere over a big hot core, after all." Robinson, *Red Mars*.

shape-shifting things as feelings. What is it about language that cuts us off from the fullness of our experience?[7]

Language at Work and at Play

What is language for? Let's begin with the idea that language is used to *coordinate the social actions of individuals* who cooperate in the activities that meet their needs.[8] In order for us to live and work together to create and maintain the complex activities and institutions that make up our complicated societies, we need to be able to communicate with one another about what needs to be done, the lay of the land in which it is to be done, who is to do what and with whom, and who is willing and able to do the things that need doing. So we have histories, scientific explanations, maps, and general ideas about what animals, vegetables and minerals, as well as people, institutions, and systems, are likely to do and where to find them. We also use language to make arrangements with each other about what to do and how we shall do it. We ask, or order, people to do things, and we agree or promise (or refuse) to do our part. Sometimes these arrangements are made cooperatively with give and take, and sometimes they are made by authorities (like bosses, teachers, judges, or police).

In all this coordinated social activity in which we depend on each other's cooperation, it is inevitable that we will make judgments about how reliable people are, to what extent they can be trusted to

---

7 The late David Foster Wallace once wrote, "What goes on inside is just too fast and huge and all interconnected for words to do more than barely sketch the outlines of at most one tiny little part of it at any given instant." ("Good Old Neon," quoted in Minor, Kyle, "Behind the David Foster Wallace Myth."). This is a different problem from the one I'll be discussing. Wallace is pointing out that what goes on in our complex system of responding to the world and what's going on inside our bodies is way too big for us to write it down in linear fashion. Our concern is rather with the incommensurability of feelings and words.

8 This idea has been forcefully and extensively developed by Jürgen Habermas in Habermas, *The Theory of Communicative Action, Volume 1.*

do what they say they will do or to fulfill the roles we assign to them. And each of us talks to others, as well as to ourselves, about what we are willing and unwilling to do, and the reasons we might or might not be able to follow through on our promises (excuses and explanations). And, as we have seen, we are concerned to be recognized as legitimate and valuable players in the institutions and activities going on around us, so we use language to defend and justify ourselves as worthy of recognition. All this that I have sketched out in a very general way makes up what I will call the *utilitarian* use of language. It is language used to get things done. Let's look at two requirements of this kind of language—objectivity and precision.

Objectivity

When we are sending and receiving utilitarian language, we want our words to be like money: the words that I write or speak should have the same value when they reach you as they do for me, and they should retain that value when you pass them on to others.[9] Otherwise, they will not serve as guides to what is going on in the world in which we are carrying out our cooperative activities. If I tell you to meet me at the Jonesville bus station at 4:30, we'll both be disappointed if the words "Jonesville" and "four thirty" don't have objective meanings in a language we share—if, for example, "Jonesville" is my private code name for some town in my imagination with no reference to any real place. Then the name would have only a *subjective* meaning.

Whether we are planning a tryst or doing theoretical physics, our cooperative activities require objective language. I learn something about your dog if you say she weighs twenty pounds, but if you say she is beautiful, I know something about your feelings, but not about the dog. She might seem ugly to me. "Ugly" is a *subjective* term,

---

9 The monetary system is part of, and can be a model of, the whole symbolic system. It works as a synecdoche.

while "weighs twenty pounds" is objective. "Ugly" and "beautiful" are words used to convey personal—even bodily—responses, even though we often express them with the expectation (or even the demand) that others will share them. Even if you have clear standards for what makes a dog beautiful (like those applied by a dog show judge), they are not necessarily my standards. So what we say is more useful for coordinating our activities when it is objective, rather than subjective.[10]

Precision

Since we make *use* of the things we say to each other, we prefer statements that are precise to those that are fuzzy or vague. If I tell you to bring me some apples, you are left uncertain about what to do, as compared with my giving you a number. It's harder to make use of fuzzy statements, harder to apply them. If I ask you to meet me downtown in the morning, you won't know exactly where and when to show up.[11]

Beyond Utility to Expression

Utilitarian language (discourse), striving always to portray the world objectively—independently of how we feel about it, and as if everything in the world comes with clear boundaries matching the most precise words we can find or invent, tends to blind us to, or make us forget, two things: First, we forget how much *all* our experience

---

10 Objectivity and subjectivity are opposite ends of a continuum, and there are probably no pure examples of either one.

11 Fuzzy, or "open-ended" statements can be appropriate when we want the person to whom they are addressed to think for him or herself. If you and I are going camping together, asking you to get "some apples" leaves you room to share in the decision about how many to get. Precision is favored by authoritarian and bureaucratic institutions so that they can draw a sharp line between compliance and noncompliance. Democratic and cooperative associations, built on trust, allow more open-ended, flexible, less precise guidelines.

of the world and of ourselves takes place within a welter of hope, desire, anger and fear. Reasoned thought rides on, or just under, the moving surfaces of deep rivers of urgent, and sometimes violent, emotion. Secondly, the pressure to conceive the world and our experience as made up of discrete items with exact boundaries conforming to precise words obscures from us how moving, fluctuating and unstable our perceptions and thoughts are. Utilitarian discourse alienates us from *subjective* life, from the full sensual and emotional response of our animal souls. Language imprisons our souls when the only language we know, or dare to use, is utilitarian.

But what other kind of language is there?

> ... there are two types of reality—the hard-nosed, general kind, which is "an unbearable burden," "fragmentary and without meaning," and *an internal realism*," composed of our own fragile, fluttering intentions, which can be both beautiful and truly affecting."[12]

This "internal realism" is what we aim at with *expressive* language. It expresses how we feel and how we are responding to a situation, and that makes it subjective, rather than objective. It issues forth from us experimentally, trying to find a way of talking (or singing or dancing or painting or ...) that does more than just transmit information. We want to put our audience, not just "in the picture", but in a shared emotional space.

Expressive discourse is *aesthetic*—driven by feelings rather than a commitment to truth or fact. And it is expressive more than descriptive: its function is to express, to be the vehicle for, what is going on in us, rather than to describe or map or picture the world as it is apart from our response to it. It's the difference between groaning in pain and telling a doctor that you are in pain, or laughing with

---

12 Kavenna, Joanna, "Things Fall Apart: A Spanish Master's Quizzical Unravelings. Review of *Dublinesque* by Enrique Vila-Matas."

joy and describing yourself as feeling joyful. (Of course these can be combined, as when we joyfully describe ourselves as feeling joyful.)[13]

Expressive language is not just groans and shouts. In poetry, music, art, and film, we use images and metaphor to convey experiences that go beyond the limits of strict and literal language. For example, this short poem by Philip Larkin[14] shows how (perhaps due to self-loathing) one small moment of failure can metastasize to defile one's very being.

As Bad as a Mile
Watching the shied core
Striking the basket, skidding across the floor,
Shows less and less of luck, and more and more

Of failure spreading back up the arm
Earlier and earlier, the unraised hand calm,
The apple unbitten in the palm.

Feelings like these are with us all the time, usually unnoticed in our rush to satisfy the utilitarian demands the world makes of us. Poets are always on the alert for ways of using words to bring these moments to our attention (though many people use poetic language from time to time).[15] Film makers are also good at addressing our emotions. Watch how a scene in a movie uses lighting, the angle of

---

13 Some works of art, including poetry, "are designed to evoke experiences defying verbal categorization....The paradox that language can evoke experience that transcends words is perhaps the highest tribute to the power of language. But those are words in poetic use. The words in our daily lives more often do the opposite and either fracture...experience or send it underground." Stern, *The Interpersonal World Of The Infant A View From Psychoanalysis And Developmental Psychology*, pp. 176-77.

14 Larkin, *Collected Poems*.

15 See the section "Forms of Vitality" in Chapter 13 for further discussion of this point with additional poetic examples.

the camera, music, and other cues to sweep you into a particular mood, whether it's comfort and cheer, foreboding, or terror.

When we share our feelings, we do more than merely *tell* how we feel: we *show* it. We use not just symbols like words, but facial and bodily postures and movements and dynamic tones of voice that are parts of the feelings themselves. Like the poem, and like a piece of music or film, we delineate, and invite our listeners into, a common space of *feeling*, not just *thinking* (assuming for the moment a clear distinction between feeling and thinking). Facial expressions and other body language are not symbols that we intellectually decode to derive their meanings; they act directly on our own emotional receptors and those of others.[16] In expressing how we feel to others, we rely upon their capacity for empathy, their ability to respond to feelings with feelings.

Words can convey our emotions to others when we describe our experience of situations that bring them about—falling on a cement playground or being lost at night in a strange city or having a good friend let you down. Here we use our descriptions to highlight what we reacted *to* in the expectation that it would lead the other person to react vicariously in a similar way. In a similar way, writing about a painting or a piece of music can help us to focus on features of the work that evoke a particular interpretation and emotional response. For example, "Listen to how the tempo picks up here after the long slow part," or "Notice how the jagged lines in this painting express anxiety."

---

16 The recent discovery of mirror neurons in the brain would seem to support this concept of emotional receptors. "A **mirror neuron** is a neuron that fires both when an animal acts and when the animal observes the same action performed by another. Thus, the neuron 'mirrors' the behaviour of the other, as though the observer were itself acting." "Mirror Neuron."

The Utility of Expression

If we are obsessed with being serious and responsible and doing what we are supposed to do, then we are probably locked into the utilitarian way of using language and following standards of objectivity and precision. We are likely to regard expressive language as dangerous or at least a waste of time. Words like "vague" and "subjective" are used mostly as reasons not to take expressive language seriously. Expression in the arts will seem unimportant, something we are allowed to do for relaxation in off hours—though for some folks, there are no "off" hours, we are always *on*. But expressive language—in fact, expressiveness in and beyond language—is necessary to knowing *and being* who we are.

The two kinds of discourse we have distinguished—utilitarian and expressive—are suited to two ways we try to account for and justify ourselves. We may feel that utilitarian language always overrides language that is emotional or subjective, in which case we dedicate our lives to clear demonstrations of our objective worth, whatever we may think these are (money, titles, fame, etc.). And this is a dominant attitude in our world. Yet we often turn to expressive language to reveal who we are when we can. What moves us to step away from the purely utilitarian way of speaking and to *express* ourselves—and to care about the expressive activity of others?

Let's face it: we want to be loved. We all share the desire to be understood in a way that does not involve judgment and assessment, to be seen, heard, comprehended, accepted without conditions. We exert ourselves to function in utilitarian discourse out of a desire to be recognized, to be called upon, to count as responsible and contributing members of the community that cooperates to get things done. But in expressive discourse, we want something "*beyond recognition.*"[17] We hope to find, or carve out, if only in imagination, a safe space in which we can feel accepted simply for being what we

---

17 Oliver, *Witnessing*, last two chapters.

are. In expressive activity, we can aspire to *showing* who we are. This is most obvious in conversations with people we are very close to like our parents might have been when we were young (if we were lucky). Part of the reason for making art and for seeing, reading, and hearing art is that it creates a space of shared emotions and emotional responsiveness.

The artist is typically concerned not only with getting a hearing for his or her personal emotional take on the world, but with opening up or defending cultural and/or political space for the expression of responses to the world that cannot be put into utilitarian language. As one critic has noted, "We feel, reading a great poem, that a small corner of the soul has for a moment become public property."[18] It may be that music is the most direct and effective way of communicating emotionally, and I will have more to say about that in Chapter 12.

It is worth mentioning that this book, while not a work of art, is also trying to break open the shutters of utilitarian discourse that try to restrict us to the rule of the big Other. We would like to draw a more generous picture of the soul that might enable us to understand and accept what utilitarian discourse censors.

The Coerciveness of Utilitarian Discourse

Why do we always feel that we are in court? Why are we afraid to expose ourselves? What would lead us to take the big Other so seriously that we cannot take a breath without fear of humiliating failure or of acting on murderous, resentful impulses? Let's remind ourselves of how threatening the big world is, the world in which we all grow up and learn how we have to act in order to be recognized.

As we grow up, we gradually become aware that we have been dropped into a social structure that hems us in with a vast

---

18 Longenbach, "A Music of Austerity."

multitude of complicated prohibitions and requirements backed up with a host of heavy sanctions. The criminal justice system has us under more or less constant surveillance, ready to punish or harass us for breaking, or seeming to break, any one of more laws than we can keep track of, quite possibly unjustly. Various agencies of government can prevent us from travelling or holding many jobs for reasons they may not disclose. Most of us need to spend most of our waking hours under the authority of employers who have the right to demote, penalize, or fire us for good or bad reasons. Financial institutions can refuse to loan us money, lower our credit ratings, evict us from our homes, or assess exorbitant interest or penalties for failing to fulfill their arcane conditions. Schools can expel us, refuse to certify us, and ruin our future with low marks or bad recommendations. Insurance companies can deny our claims, increase our premiums, or refuse to cover us. Media outlets, including internet service providers, can refuse to get our message out, as can museums, galleries, and publishers. Sports associations can penalize us or refuse to let us play. If we are in the military, we can be demoted or dishonorably discharged. And churches have a variety of formal and informal sanctions against heterodoxy. Of course any particular rule and its sanction can be defended by the officials in charge (that's their job), but the point is that everywhere we go, we feel the pressure to dedicate ourselves to living up to the image of a law-abiding citizen, a responsible credit risk, a productive worker, a patriot, and so on.

And these are just the rules and sanctions imposed by institutions in the *public* sphere of life—in government and the economy. But there are other social settings which produce their own pressures to conform and where transgression can be punished with humiliation and the withdrawal of recognition. The family is one, but informal social circles of friends and acquaintances and even strangers on the street can treat us with subtle or overt contempt according to norms that are variable and only implicit—for here we are dealing less with norms and rules and more with emotional reactions of our friends and relatives and even other drivers on the highway. Accordingly we are careful about how we dress and groom ourselves, how we speak or make eye contact with others, and so on. This is another source of anxiety about whether we are living up to the demands of the Other.

Conclusion

To recap this chapter: In our waking lives, we are always perceiving, interpreting, and reacting to what is going on in us and around us. If we reflect on all this activity in our souls, we realize that, although we often feel called upon to give an accurate account of ourselves both to others and to our own inner judge, what we can say describes it very imperfectly. The stronger our urge to give such an account, the more we find ourselves cut off from what does not fit the words we have at our disposal.

What is it about language that makes it unfit to represent us adequately? One reason is that in the business of daily life, we are compelled to keep what we say within the bounds of *utilitarian* discourse, the use of language that organizes practical and cooperative life. Such discourse hews to standards of accuracy, objectivity and precision; it rejects language that is subjective and vague, that is *expressive* discourse.

Yet we are moved to engage in expressive discourse because it invites others to share, to resonate, with our own "take" on the world, and because it tries to open up a space of shared subjectivity. This sharing of subjectivity can be broadly public, as in the arts; or it can be private among a few people, as in conversations among intimates and in psychotherapy. In sharing subjective space, we are looking for more than just recognition; we are looking for love.

What prompts us to feel that we are always in court—monitoring ourselves from the point of view of a punitive and judgmental

Other? Quite simply because we are deeply social beings living in a social order that maintains itself by a myriad of overt and covert, explicit and implicit, blatant and subtle, physically violent and psychologically stressful punishments and threats of punishment.[19] So it's no wonder we may feel compelled keep our souls hidden behind a wall of normalizing words.

In the next chapter, we will find a way to see behind that wall, to get around the censorship of utilitarian discourse.

---

19 Why does this social order require such punitive means to maintain itself? I will try to address this question in the concluding chapter.

12

Uncovering the Infant

...the infant psyche remains the basis of all psychic functioning.

HARRY GUNTRIP

...maturity is not an outgrowing, but a growing up: ... an adult is not a dead child, but a child who survived.

URSULA LEGUINN[1]

Childhood Lessons

THROUGH OUT THIS book, I have stressed that becoming an adult means learning to be an intelligible and responsible actor in the social world, treating everything we do as a symbolic act that will be "read" by others—and by the big Other. We become signifying creatures. Yet we have also seen that something in us cannot be contained in this structure. Something rebels against the discipline of

---

1 http://www.brainyquote.com/quotes/quotes/u/ursulakle132606.html

the social order, and it is this conflict between what we have called our "animal" souls and the demands of civilized life that generates our inner demons. In other words, there is a conflict between the requirements of adulthood and what we were before we were adults, i.e. when we were infants. In some way, we must *still* be the infants we once were.

So in order to understand more fully who we really are now, we need to know something about how we experienced the world as infants, before we learned to pretend that we were what we were supposed to be. In other words, before we learned to pretend not to be infants. Georges Perec writes,[2]

> My childhood belongs to those things which I know I don't know much about. It is behind me; yet it is the ground on which I grew, and *it once belonged to me, however obstinately I assert that it no longer does.*...I have no alternative but to conjure up ...the things that stopped, the things that were closed off—things that surely were and today are no longer, but *things that also were so that I may still be.*

We cannot use the words we now have at our command to conjure up our first few months and years of life as clearly as we can remember our later years. We have grown so far apart from the babies we once were that we can only know them from a distance—by hearsay, as it were. Nevertheless, we can learn enough about our infant selves to care for them and maybe even love something in us that we might now loathe.

As responsible adults, we operate on the assumption that we have left childhood behind. As the Bible tells us, "When I was a child, I spoke and thought as a child; when I became a man, I put away childish things."[3] (But childish things do not *stay* away no

---

2 Perec, *W, or the Memory of Childhood*. Emphasis added.
3 First Corinthians, 13:11

matter how far away we put them.) To deserve the status of adult, we must be sober and independent, so we resist the very thought that we *really were* once tiny, vulnerable, and helpless. Yet, "…in the little world of the baby, tremendous things happen," as Donald Winnicott wrote[4], and those things are *still* tremendous in our souls whether or not we think about them. So let's think about them now.

Our aim in doing this is not to enter into and relive our past infantile experience, but rather to learn to appreciate the continuing infantile side of ourselves that is struggling to stay afloat in the "mysterious river of tears under the streets." This will help us accept that we are still powerfully affected by events in our infancy we can no longer remember or even imagine. Moreover, there is also a side of our adult experience that remains infantile, which means that even recent events we think we understand may have affected us in ways we do not know. We are made up of forces and processes beyond our grasp and our control. Understanding this much can open the door to therapy and other avenues for self-reflection by letting us see ourselves—our thoughts, feelings, impulses and actions—as requiring investigation and reflection.

What are some of the things that settled in our souls before we had any say in the matter? What did we come to wordlessly feel, expect, desire, and dread? The painful existential feelings we have already discussed are certainly among them:

- Guilt—the sense of having done some terrible thing for which we deserve to be punished;
- Self loathing—the feeling that one is horribly unattractive and incompetent;
- Free-floating anxiety—a fear of something (or nothing) one cannot name;

---

4 Winnicott, *Winnicott On The Child.*

- Ontological insecurity— a sense of emptiness, of not really existing;
- Rage—a free-floating resentment at the way the world is.

These feelings, for those of us beset with them, seem so deeply rooted and so permanent that it's hard to imagine ourselves without them. This indicates that they were laid down at our beginnings, soaked into the timbers of our souls.

Here are some additional attitudes that are similarly built in:

- Our sense of what can be shared and what must be held back;
- Our feelings about what people and situations can be trusted and what is to be feared;
- Whom (and whether) to love
- How to reach people—or avoid being reached.

In this chapter and the next, we are going to look at five features of the infantile experience that was ours as when we were babies, and that continues to course through us while we are busy pretending to be adults. Infantile experience is (1) not conscious of itself; (2) deeply social; (3) dynamic, never static; (4) amodal, that is, not divided into separate sensory channels; and (5) global, meaning that it does not divide what is being experienced into separate objects and qualities.

Consciousness Not Conscious of Itself

In our own adult consciousness of the world, the self seems always present. When I watch or think about what is going on around me or within me, I am always implicitly aware that it is *I* who is watching or thinking.[5] As I listen to the lawnmower outside or pay attention

_____

5 David Hume, writing in the 18th Century, famously denied this awareness of the self. Proust, however, makes it vivid. He notices this doubled consciousness when

to the pain in my back, I really have *two* concerns: one is to locate and assess the noise from outside or the pain in my back. The other is about *my performance* as I observe and respond to the noise or the pain. Am I right about what I am hearing or feeling? Is my response appropriate? Does it fit the image of myself I want to own and to project to others?

By contrast, an infant who has not yet heard or answered the call of language, who has not yet begun to move his name or personal pronoun around in the game of social life, feels the pain or hears the noise simply, without the presence of an *I* who is doing the listening or feeling.[6] We could describe the way that an infant, or an animal, is in the world by saying it is *conscious without being self-conscious.*[7]

This is hard for us to grasp because our own experience, whenever we reflect upon it, appears always to be self-conscious. Why? Simply because we have *made* it so by reflecting upon it. We cannot imagine our consciousness to be other than self-conscious, because when we try to imagine any piece of our experience, we necessarily

---

he thinks back to sitting in the garden reading in a "little hooded chair...in the depths of which I would sit and think I was hidden from the eyes of [others]. And wasn't my mind also like another crib in the depths of which I felt I remained ensconced, even in order to watch what was happening outside? When I saw an external object, my awareness that I was seeing it would remain between me and it, lining it with a thin spiritual border that prevented me from ever directly touching its substance; it would volatize in some way before I could make contact with it, just as an incandescent body brought near a wet object never touches its moisture because it is always preceded by a zone of evaporation. [There was a] sort of screen dappled with different states of mind which my consciousness would simultaneously unfold while I read, and which ranged from the aspirations hidden deepest within me to the completely exterior vision of the horizon which I had, at the bottom of the garden, before my eyes..." Proust, *Swann's Way.*

6 This direct experience of things is something we can aspire to in, for example, Zen meditation, but rarely and only fleetingly achieve.

7 Philosophical discussions of consciousness generally do not recognize the possibility of consciousness that is not conscious of itself (for the reasons given in the following paragraph of the text), and thus assimilate all consciousness to self-consciousness. This can lead some to deny that infants or animals are conscious at all, or else to ascribe full, articulate self-consciousness to animals.

bring our own activity back into it. This means, too, that we have a hard time admitting that any of our own experience is not self-conscious since we can bring it into view only by its becoming self-conscious. As children, we may have been puzzled by the question, What does the stuff in the refrigerator look like when the door is closed and the light is off? Vivid color illustrations of the inner organs of the human body seem to show what they "look like," even though they don't normally *look* like anything since they exist and carry on their activities "where the sun doesn't shine".[8] This dilemma has been compared to that faced by a flashlight asked to show us an object in a dark room as it "really" is—that is, what it's like with no light shining on it[9]. Similarly, it makes no sense to ask ourselves what our consciousness is like when we are not paying attention to it, because to ask the question is to direct our attention to it.[10]

To say that adults are always self-conscious is not to say they are always thinking explicitly about themselves—as if we were always egotistical. But it is to say that in everything we do that has a social meaning—in other words, in everything we do—we act in the light of what others, or at least the big Other, desires of us. For example, we talk to another person to communicate a particular piece of information, but in doing so, we also monitor what we say and how we say it to be sure that it makes sense and is true and appropriate—*not* just from the point of view of the one we are talking with, but from the wide perspective of the big Other. We look to the standards of

---

8 Related to this is the difficulty of understanding, or accepting, the fact of death—our own death. We try to imagine what it will be like not to exist when, of course, there is no such experience to imagine. So we have to imagine death as a form of existence and therefore to suppose that the soul must be immortal. The alternative is to accept that not everything we know to be true can be imagined.

9 Jaynes, *The Origin of Consciousness in the Breakdown of the Bicameral Mind*, p. 23.

10 Philosopher Matthew Ratcliffe cites S. Gallegher who warns that, "any experimental situation that places the subject in a reflective attitude in order to ascertain something about prereflective experience is questionable" Ratcliffe, *Feelings of Being*..

grammar, logic, politeness, and accuracy which we *take* to be (treat as) universal (even if we know they are not).[11]

Again, it is simply *expected* of us that we know what we are doing and that we believe we are justified. It is a mandatory assumption that we are, or make every effort to be, deliberative, conscious and rational. This is the position into which we are coerced by our desire to be what the big Other desires us to be, and it is from this position that we are loathe to admit that the unconscious infant lives on within us and that we don't have complete knowledge or control of what we think and feel and do.

So the first thing that is different about the way babies experience the world in the first few months before they swear allegiance to the big Other and fidelity to the symbolic is that they are conscious *without* being self-conscious. They take in and respond to what goes on around them and in their bodies without the socialized egos that automatically oversee everything adults do.[12] This makes babies innocent; they are free of the knowledge of good and evil. We can also see now why it is so difficult to recognize how much we are still the infants we once were: this side of us is in violation of our pact

---

11 This description overlooks, or abstracts from, the more flexible, or even transgressive, attitude most people have towards the obligations imposed by the big Other. (See Chapter 9, "Transgression") The point is that the more determined I am to live up to the impossible demands of the Other, the more cut off I am likely to feel from other real people, and the more self-loathing, anxiety, guilt, and insecurity I will feel.

12 Describing a dream-memory of childhood, Julio Cortázar writes that to speak of it, he would have to "locate himself rather in that zone where once more his childhood house would be suggested, the living room and the garden in a clear present time, with the colors as they were seen at the age of ten, reds so red, blues of tinted glass shades, green of leaves, green of fragrance, smell and color, *a single presence at the level of nose and eyes and mouth*." *Hopscotch*, p. 490, emphasis added. "A single presence at the level of nose and eyes and mouth" means the absence of the monitoring gaze of the big Other.

with the big Other. As a responsible adult, I *must* maintain that I know what I am doing and why I do it.[13]

Most importantly, though, this difference between the *we* who are *now* thinking about these things and the infants we once were makes it impossible for us to imagine what it was like to be as we were. Infants do not monitor their experience through the eyes of another; their consciousness is not self-conscious. We, on the other hand, cannot help but experience our own consciousness through the perspective of an other (the big Other). This makes for an unbridgeable difference between us and them. It is a barrier of language (not a barrier between languages, but the barrier *of* language) standing between adults and babies. This same barrier exists also within our souls—between what we say and think, and the raging river of our unspeakable feelings.

We now turn to a second feature of infant experience: that it is deeply social. Even though they have not taken on the Symbolic, babies engage viscerally with their mothers (or other primary caretakers) in ways that do not depend on language.[14]

The Society of Mother and Baby

There really is no such thing as *a baby*, only the *baby-mother pair*—as Winnicott has pointed out. As infants we can not live without the kind of constant care a mother provides. This means that our experience of ourselves—our feelings, perceptions, and gradually forming awareness of things—all occurs in the course of intimate immersion in the life of our mother. With her bodily presence and contact, she satisfies our intensely felt desires to be warm, nourished, and held close and

---

13 We also feel obligated, as representatives of the big Other, to hold others responsible for what they are doing, and that often leads us to insist that malefactors were conscious of what they were doing regardless of what they themselves say.

14 See the appendix at the end of this chapter for reflections on how our individualistic ideology denies to us our social connectedness.

away from danger. But it is also in the intimate circle of her presence that our *active* desires to play, to have fun, to experiment, and to move into the world under our own steam are either encouraged or discouraged, liberated or confined. So a mother's personality—the tempo, warmth, eagerness, flexibility, optimism/pessimism, fear/confidence with which she engages with her baby—has a lot to do with whether we go forth into each day with confidence or with fear and trembling. Every thought and perception is highly saturated with untold emotional meaning from the earliest days of our lives beyond the reach of memory and words. (I will say more about how this interaction shapes us in the next chapter.)

We all know that time passes more quickly as we get older, so consider the timeless time of the first year or two of life. We have not yet begun to foresee the future in terms of tomorrow, next week, or next year. We have not yet undertaken the major task of learning to organize all experience by knowing the names of things. We have not yet learned to live symbolically, organizing our perceptions and feelings according to the rules of a common language. So in that time of earliest childhood, our main preoccupation, beyond getting fed and staying warm, is *play*—having wordless fun with the person who was always there. Even in the midst of feeding, bathing, and being put to bed, mothers and their infants play. Mothers elicit smiles and laughter from their babies with funny or "scary" faces, vocalizations, tickles, and tossings in the air; and babies reciprocate within the limits of their growing abilities.[15]

This intimate communion with our mothers –- or *the lack* of it — is a foundational experience in itself; it is not just the condition or the setting for our early experiences. The experience of sharing the world with others is one that permeates everything we think and do and feel, from infancy all through our lives. Whenever we do things with other people, in addition to whatever practical task we

---

15 My mother once told me that my baby brother when nursing would bite her nipple and then grin up at her.

are trying to accomplish, there is always the question of how well or badly we are *connecting*. We are likely to be aware of connecting well or not so well in a conversation with others that has no particular agenda—just chatting or getting to know each other. But communion, or its absence, is part of every social experience—in a classroom, a committee meeting, at a family dinner, in bed with a lover, and, of course, in therapy. We want to "be on the same wave length," "dance to the same (or complementary) beat," or just have fun with others. Having fun with others is not just each of us having fun in the same space. It is enjoying the enjoyment of others, and enjoying the awareness that my enjoyment is part of what you are enjoying and vice-versa. This sense of solidarity, of communion, is a crucial part of feeling that you belong in the world, that you really exist. Nothing affects our day-to-day happiness more than how much we feel in tune with the others in our lives.

Our capacity to feel this way begins—or is thwarted—in the intimacy of the mother-baby pairing.

Mothering does not have to be perfect in order for a child to grow up with the ability to connect well with others, only just "good enough." Speaking to reassure middle class British mothers, Winnicott says, "it is the luck of most babies to be held [i.e. cared for] well most of the time."[16]

In reality, few of us are so lucky. A "good enough" mother, for Winnicott, is one who "can adapt to the baby's needs at this early stage *because she has no other interest for the time being.*"[17] Mothers in our world (as in Winnicott's) are often unable to put aside everything else for their babies. This is not to blame mothers. Just as there is no such thing as a baby abstracted from its mother, so there is no such thing as a mother and baby apart from the wider conditions of their lives.

---

16 Winnicott, *Winnicott On The Child* p. 51.
17 Ibid.

Being a "good enough mother," at least for the first couple of years, is a full-time occupation. That doesn't mean it *has* to be the responsibility of just one individual; it can be parceled out among childcare workers, older siblings, spouses, relatives, friends and neighbors, which means that there are several personalities shaping the development of the infant's soul. Nevertheless, the mother is usually the center of the network of caregivers.

But the center can fail to hold. Just as the baby is dependent on its mother, mother and baby both depend on a network of social institutions, friends and family members for support of her and her baby. This network often comes apart: Husbands or boyfriends can be partners, but they can also be abusive or absent. The mother's older children can get sick or in trouble, as she herself can. Neighborhoods can be violent. Jobs that pay the bills can be lost and homes can be taken by foreclosure or eviction. Disruptions like divorce, death of a parent, and various kinds of chaos and violence can affect the baby directly, as well as distracting the mother from her baby. And if her own childhood left her with a fragile sense of her own existence, she may be unable to give over her own concerns for those of the baby even when the surrounding conditions are peaceful. All this makes it seem unlikely that "good-enough mothering" is typical.

In the "Garden of Infantile Catastrophe[18]

No matter how willing we are to call up memories of childhood, our earliest weeks and months are beyond our power to recall them. Nevertheless, events that terrified us in those early days are still alive in us.

Winnicott writes

---

18 See Chapter 3, n. 20

...[B]abies are liable to the most severe anxieties that can be imagined. If left for too long (hours, minutes) without familiar and human contact, they have experiences which we can only describe by such words as:

going to pieces

falling forever

dying and dying and dying

losing all vestige of hope of the renewal of contacts[19]

Experiences like these—of abandonment and eternal isolation—can surge wordlessly back upon us as adults. They are all the more frightening because we cannot name them or explain them. They seem to arise out of nowhere from some dark place within us, with no evidence that they come from the past. They are memories that are not experienced *as* memories, but as demons.

A few pages back, I listed five features of our ongoing infantile experience. We have considered two of them—that it is unconscious of itself and that it is deeply social. We have seen how our souls can be roiled with deep fears of abandonment and isolation that we cannot explain and are loath to admit. In the next chapter, we will look more closely at the "vocabulary" of infantile experience and how it is shaped and preserved.

Appendix: The Paradox of Being Alone Together

The philosophy of individualism—the notion that individuals begin as separate and unconnected atoms and must somehow forge their ties with others as they *become* (for better or worse) socialized—pervades Western philosophy and common sense. Rousseau begins his book *The Social Contract* in 1761 by writing, "Man is born free; and everywhere he is in chains."

---

19 Ibid, p. 67.

But there is a flip side to this remark that seems truer in the modern age of alienation: "We are born enmeshed with each other; and everywhere we are lonely." Daniel Stern's book *The Interpersonal World of the Infant*[20] shows in detail that our development, beginning at birth and continuing through to the more or less self-conscious beings we are now, is deeply immersed in the lives of those around us. We are social from the start.

And yet, we are lonely. Too many of us feel terribly alone and find ourselves, like this character in *The Gallery* by John Horne Burns, seeking some mechanism for making contact with others:

> This reaching out in vain was only felt when he tried to mesh himself with the gears of other people. When he was drinking alone, he was aware of certain untapped potentialities in himself. But when he talked to others, something in him went limp and kept sneering at him that he was alone alone alone and wrapped in some inaccessible womb, that nobody else really cared, or that they were doubled up with secret laughter at the sight of him.[21]

The feeling that one is alone and that no one cares comes naturally in a capitalist and individualistic social order where recognition and dignity come to us only as individuals competing against each other for money and social position.[22] Most of us lack the emotional and material resources to care for many people outside our immediate families. We could not get on with the business of everyday life if we tried to provide every suffering person we came across the care we know they need. Even social workers whose job it is to provide services for people in need are forced to harden their hearts against those who do not meet certain bureaucratic standards. A social order that goes by the principle that only those who can pay

---

20 Stern, *The Interpersonal World Of The Infant A View From Psychoanalysis And Developmental Psychology.*
21 Burns, *The Gallery.*
22 "In a society where competition for the basic cultural goods is a pivot of action people cannot be taught to love one another, for those who do not compete with one another except in play" Henry, Jules, "Golden Rule Days: American Schoolrooms.".

for the goods of life shall have them, and that charity for those who cannot pay shall be doled out according to narrowly defined rules, must of necessity establish a regime of moral feeling that stifles the general love of our fellow human beings.

This is why utilitarian discourse and bureaucratized procedures are standard in our public[23] dealings with each other: that discourse and those procedures are tools for plowing ahead through life as if it did not matter how isolated or connected people feel. But of course the isolation and loneliness felt by so many has real and terrible consequences, including suicide and mass murder, from which we mostly avert our eyes or come to take for granted as inevitable.

However, the alienating structure of capitalist society does not explain the particulars of your soul or mine. That structure is the background condition for all of us, but how each of us grows up within this society depends on how our families are situated within the social structure and on the unique dynamics within our families. So our task now is to try to understand the nature of infantile experience—how babies take in and react to what goes on in their small worlds and how the demons of our souls are established there.

---

23 Public in the sense of relationships outside our families and circles of close friends: dealings with employers, businesses, governments and strangers.

13

Vitality: The Raw Material of the Soul

Our first way of experiencing the world is largely what psychoanalysts have called fantasy. This modality has its own validity, its own rationality. Infantile fantasy may become a closed enclave, a dissociated undeveloped "unconscious" but this need not be so. This eventuality is another form of alienation. Fantasy as encountered in many people today is split off from what the person regards as his mature, sane, rational, adult experience. We do not then see fantasy in its true function but experienced merely as an intrusive, sabotaging infantile nuisance.

R.D. LAING[1]

Our wishes and our endeavors arise from certain needs of our nervous system that we find difficult to put into words.

THOMAS MANN[2]

---

1 Laing, *The Politics of Experience*, pp. 30-31.
2 Mann, *Buddenbrooks*, p. 411.

Childhood is measured out by sounds and smells and
sights, before the dark hour of reason grows.

JOHN BETJEMAN[3]

Language as soul splitter

LANGUAGE HAS THE great advantage of making possible ways of relating to each other that are not available to other animals or to infants before the onset of language. Words enable us to share much more complex experiences with each other, and to construct a narrative of our lives. It creates the common world in which the cooperative activities that make up culture and civilization (for better and worse) are possible.

Yet language also splits our souls in two. As Daniel Stern says of language,

> It drives a wedge between two *simultaneous* forms of interpersonal experience: as it is *lived* and as it is verbally *represented*.... And to the extent that events in the domain of verbal relatedness are held to be what has really happened, experiences in these other domains suffer an alienation (they can become nether domains of experience).[4]

---

3 Cited in Stein, "Childish Things."

4 *Stern, The Interpersonal World Of The Infant A View From Psychoanalysis And Developmental Psychology, pp. 162-63, emphasis added.* Here's more extended and evocative reflection on linguified experience:

If one could only establish a direct mode of communion with another being, instead of undergoing this pitiful struggle of conversation? Extraordinary the way conversation, even the most intimate... concealed or *refracted* the two personalities engaged. Impossible to present, all at once in a phrase, a sentence, a careful paragraph—even in a book, copious and disheveled—all that one meant or all that one was. To speak is to simplify, to simplify is to change, to change is to falsify.... The experience of an individual is co-extensive with the world and therefore infinite?—he is, in epitome, the history of the world, a history still being lived. But this 'language'—by which one such epitome seeks to make himself understood

We regard what is said in strictly utilitarian language as *objective*, as aiming to describe something real in a way that anyone else who knows our language should be able to understand. We take what we *say* more seriously than what we *feel* but cannot say, or can say only in expressive language. We think of what is expressed poetically, or in art or music, as merely *subjective*, and therefore not valid when it comes to governing our lives—except in the special preserves of the arts.[5]

In the table below, I have laid out several ways in which our lives as we represent them are split off from our lives as fully experienced. I have made the right column larger to indicate that it contains the dominant movers and shakers of our lives, the left side being mostly a performance for the sake of others. And the right column is shaded to represent the darkness we cast over that side of ourselves by our pretending to be what we think we ought to be.

The persona, the social self	The animal soul
The grownup	The infantile
Who we say we are or pretend to be; how we represent ourselves	Feelings and attitudes that don't fit the way we represent ourselves; the minds of their own that our minds have.
The responsible adult – responsible to the Other	The angry, resentful source of transgression
Objective, utilitarian language	Expressive language, including the arts without words (music, dance, painting and sculpture)
Self-conscious consciousness, living in the gaze of the Other	Consciousness not conscious of itself, immersion in the moment

or felt by another (felt, rather than understood!)—this meager affair of signs and sounds, this tiny boxful of shabby, worn trinkets, few in number, dim in colour and crude of shape—how much, of one's infinitude, could one express by an earnest stringing together of these? Little or nothing. *Conrad Aiken, Blue Voyage,* pp. 99-100.

5 There are, of course, people who do organize their lives around artistic or spiritual or religious values, but the organization of our society around money makes this quite difficult for people who are not born rich or recognized very early for special talents in, for example, music.

Language—everyday utilitarian language—empowers our heads but weakens our hearts. What can we do with our words and our heads to help us know our hearts?

We might say that the demonic and respectable parts of our soul speak a radically different and untranslatable language. But it's not really a difference in language: it's a different way of being engaged with the world, with different forms of perception and feeling. In trying to control the recalcitrant or transgressive sides of ourselves we are like the parent telling a one-year old having a tantrum to behave: they are, as it were, in different worlds. Yet you and I, in spite of appearances, are still babies with deep roots in the baby's world, a world with which we are now unable to communicate. By growing up and becoming responsible adults, we have become foreigners in our own souls. We will always have to manage our lives with that emotionally fragile baby within us. It is especially cantankerous when we pretend it isn't there. So let's see what we can do to become better acquainted with it.

Infantile "Vocabulary"

Now although the infantile way of responding to and learning about the world does not involve the soul-splitting symbolic language that ties us to the big Other, babies and other animals do learn things about their world and themselves. They acquire, store, and process information. So even though they do not record what they learn in words, we may still wonder what form that information takes. How shall we understand its "vocabulary" and its "grammar"? Again, this is just not a question about babies. It is also about the deepest currents that flow within us—that mysterious (unconscious) river of tears under the streets (of consciousness).

Infantile experience is radically different from our own in two ways, as we saw in the last chapter. First, infants do not monitor their experience through the eyes of an other; their consciousness is not self-conscious. Since we cannot help but experience our own consciousness through the perspective of an other, there is an incommensurable difference between us and them. Language is a barrier standing between adults and babies—including the babies we still are.

We have also seen that babies have a wordless, "direct mode of communion with another being"—namely, or especially, their mothers. Mothers and their babies commune by sharing their feelings, by evoking and provoking each others' feelings.[6] We all learned a great deal about social life in our first months of life before we learned to harness our expression to words—to place our souls in the yoke of the Symbolic. So what we learned then was not precepts or principles, but habits of feeling and reaction. Our earliest life lessons are *practical,* not propositional, knowledge.[7]

Now we turn to three features of the elements—or "vocabulary"—of lived experience that utilitarian language does not capture: it is dynamic, amodal, and global.

First, lived experience is *dynamic.* When we record and communicate what's going on in sentences, we freeze a moment in time. We state, as philosophers put it, what *is* the case. A sentence is like a snapshot or a diagram[8] of how things are at a moment: once written or uttered, the sentence just sits there, finished, while the action it tried to "capture" moves on. Even if we name actions or processes— like the moves in a game or a battle, or the beating of someone's

---

6 So obviously adults who are mothers or otherwise bonded to infants are able to participate in infantile experience—relaxing the symbolic imperative. The ability to do this—to play with children—is part of what makes a good parent, and not everyone can do it.

7 See Chapter 10.

8 Wittgenstein's *Tractatus* Wittgenstein, *Tractatus Logico-Philosophicus.* articulates this conception of language: "The world is everything that is the case. The world is the totality of facts, not of things." "We make to ourselves pictures of facts. The picture is a model of reality. The elements of the picture correspond to the objects [in the fact]." §§1, 1.1, 2.1, 2.12, and 2.13. (The last of these I have rephrased for clarity.)

heart—the real events are always ahead of what we are saying, constantly falsifying our words.

What goes on in us, then, is not a sequence of such discrete items as images, perceptions, thoughts, or sensations, but is rather a continuous motion and flux in which nothing remains the same from one instant to the next. Indeed, the very notion of an "instant" is a fiction—an abstraction from real time.

To come as close as we can to describing infantile experience, we need dynamic concepts that apply to *processes*. Think of the feelings "involved with all the vital processes of life, such as breathing, getting hungry, eliminating, falling asleep and emerging out of sleep, or ... the coming and going of emotions and thoughts ".[9] Think also of becoming gradually, and often imperceptibly, sexually aroused by your interaction with someone. These ebbs and flows of little noticed feelings need to be foremost in our minds as we try to grasp the way we took in the world as infants and the way we still, unconsciously, take it in today.[10]

Next, lived experience is more unified, more whole, than we represent it in language in two interconnected ways. To begin with, it is not divided into separate channels (or sensory modalities) coming from different organs of the body, such as eyes, ears, nose, skin, and so on. We do not have to be taught by experience that, for example, the distinctive shape of something we see is the same as the shape of something we touch. Studies cited by Stern show that

---

9 Stern, *The Interpersonal World Of The Infant A View From Psychoanalysis And Developmental Psychology*, p. 54, drawing on Suzanne Langer's book *MIND: An essay on human feeling* (Langer, *Mind.*). It's useful to extend these examples: the pleasurable, unpleasurable, and mixed feelings that accompany such activities as eating, taking a psycho-active drug, falling down (or watching someone else fall), and so on and on.

10 The language I am using to refer to these dynamic experiences does not describe them or represent them but rather leads us to recall and imagine them for ourselves. This is the most that words can do to convey sensory experience. The idea of perfect communication comes from supposing that the kind of description that can be given of, for example, a geometrical figure or the dimensions of something like a house, can be given of the smell of coffee or how to ride a bicycle.

the infant brain already does that combining automatically.[11] It is language that pulls our experience apart to be accounted for in separate columns. The experience itself is *amodal.*

Further, in order to communicate with each other about situations and events, we have to separate the total shape of our experience into distinct, and therefore nameable, objects and their qualities, relationships, actions, and changes. Thus we structure a world corresponding to the contents of our available words—our tool kit of nouns, adjectives, verbs, adverbs and prepositions. But every moment of our lived experience is *global*, a gestalt, that includes everything going on around us and within us. If you ask me what I'm experiencing right now, I have to make a list of objects and what they are like and what they're doing: I'm looking at these words coming onto the screen, I feel the keys under my fingers and my fingers moving and pressing them, I hear the hum of the air conditioner and feel the faint cool breeze as it comes across the warm room; I'm aware of the rest of the room with all its furniture and books and papers lying about; and I can feel the pressure of the chair on my back and buttocks, as well as the vague uncertain state of my stomach that is neither full nor empty. But my experience is segmented into separate things in this way by my activity of recording it in words—or even in images for the purpose of later description. In itself, it is one whole—a *gestalt.*

---

11 "Infants thus appear to have an innate general capacity, which can be called *amodal perception*, to take information received in one sensory modality and somehow translate it into another sensory modality. We do not know how they accomplish this task. The information is probably not experienced as belonging to any one particular sensory mode. More likely it transcends mode or channel and exists in some unknown supra-modal form. It is not, then a simple issue of a direct translation across modalities. Rather, it involves an encoding into a still mysterious amodal *representation*, which can then be recognized in any of the sensory modes." (Stern, p. 51)

To illustrate how language takes what begins as a unity and divides it into categories, Stern[12] asks us to consider a child having the global experience of a room filled with sunlight, an experience that is all at once warm, bright, pleasurable and much more besides. The child is "feeling-perceiving" the scene. Then consider what happens when someone appears and says, "Oh, *look* at the *yellow* sun*light!*"

> Words in this case separate out precisely those properties that anchor the experience to a single modality of sensation. By binding it to words, they isolate the experience from the amodal flux in which it was originally experienced. Language can thus fracture amodal global experience. A discontinuity in experience is introduced.

The adult's intervention in the child's experience not only isolates the *visual experience* from the larger "feeling-perception," but it separates the patch of sunlight as an *object* outside the perceiver and separate from the rest of the scene felt and perceived by the child. Words fracture the amodal into the modal, and the global into the particular.

As we learn to talk about what we experience, the "language version" of these experiences "becomes the official version, and the amodal version goes underground...." The amodal experience can be brought to light in certain mental and emotional states and by works of art that "are designed to evoke experiences defying verbal categorization"—for example, music, poetry, and film.[13]

---

12 Stern, *The Interpersonal World Of The Infant A View From Psychoanalysis And Developmental Psychology,* p. 176.

13 Stern remarks on the "paradox that language [poetry] can evoke experience that transcends words," and adds, "But those are words in poetic use. The words in our daily lives more often do the opposite and either fracture amodal global experience or send it underground." (Stern, 2000, pp.176-77) The "words in our daily lives" belong to the utilitarian language discussed in Chapter 10.

Forms of Vitality

So the "feeling-perceiving" of what's going on in us and around us, including our "gut reactions" to all of it, is a vast current of ever-changing feeling, or *affect* moving through us. Let's call this current of life *vitality*, following Daniel Stern in his book *Forms of Vitality*.

The first thing to say about vitality is that it is not merely the *taking-in*, or the passive recording, of events going on around us. It is our active engagement with the world we are in. In seeing the world, we are already getting set to deal with it. When you see a tool, for example, your nervous system gets ready to deploy your muscles and limbs to use that tool.[14] As its name implies (*vita* = life), to have vitality is to be alive, and to be alive is to be engaged with the world.

In our official view of ourselves as responsible and rational individuals, we tend to suppose that our feelings about what is going on are separate and distinct from our thoughts and intentions. How we *feel* only distracts us from the real business at hand. The assumption is that the real substance of life is found in what we say and do and take responsibility for, while how we feel is either an unfortunate obstacle to our projects, or, in the case of pleasure or pride, a side benefit—frosting on the cake, as it were.

But this picture has things upside down: when we understand our feelings to be shapes of our vitality, we can see that what we feel, consciously or not, is the driving, or motivating, force of our lives. What we *say* and *think*, like the documents we sign, are the superficial representations worked up for public consumption—for the benefit of the big Other. Stern's claim is "that dynamic forms of

---

14 "If one approaches a distant object, he approaches it with reference to what he is going to do when he arrives there. If one is approaching a hammer he is muscularly all ready to seize the handle of the hammer. The later stages of the act are present in the early stages—not simply in the sense that they are all ready to go off, but in the sense that they serve to control the process itself. They determine how we are going to approach the object, and the steps in our early manipulation of it." Mead, *Mind, Self & Society*, p. 11.

vitality are the most fundamental of all felt experience when dealing with other humans in motion".[15]

We can become partly conscious of the shapes our vitality can take if we focus on those moments when our vitality is most lively. Music is a good place to start. When we listen to music, with full appreciation—not just grasping the patterns of sound, but enjoying them—letting the rhythms and melodies play through our bodies— we ourselves become part of the music, which by itself, apart from our feeling it, is nothing.

John Dewey points out that because we hear it, rather than see it, music affects our emotions directly. "Sounds *come* from outside the body, but sound itself is near, intimate; it is an excitation of the organism; we feel the clash of vibration throughout our whole body....What is *seen* stirs emotion indirectly, through interpretation and idea. Sound agitates directly, as a commotion of the organism itself." The boundary fades away between the object of our experience, and the experience itself. "Sounds," Dewey writes, "have the power of direct emotional expression. A sound is itself threatening, whining, soothing, depressing, fierce, tender, soporific, in its own qualities."[16]

Take a few minutes right now to listen to some very different pieces of music.[17] Notice how and where you feel a military march, a sad ballad, a piece of Dixieland or ragtime jazz, or the different movements of a Beethoven symphony. Notice also how these affects literally move you—inclining you to sing, dance, tap your foot, or to assume a posture or facial expression of sadness or of peace. Forms of vitality are activations of our muscles.

---

15 Stern, *Forms of Vitality*, p. 8.

16 Dewey, *Art as Experience*, pp. 237-38. In a dream, I told a friend that the changing qualities of a sustained vocal tone track the changing, modulating line of vitality in the singer, and evoke similar changes in the vitality of listeners.

17 Look for the following on YouTube: Pan's Lullaby; Dick Hyman plays Fats Waller's "Handful of Keys"; Colonel Bogey March; and Beethoven Symphony No. 7, Adagio.

Music can serve as a model for how *everything* we see, hear, smell, taste, and feel—not only on the surfaces of our skin but in the workings of our bodies—resonates throughout our amazingly complex nervous systems including our brains with their trillions of neural connections, setting off waves of vitality. Again, little of this rises into consciousness, and when it does, it is often pared down to fit our stock of words and phrases. In the next chapter, it will become clear that this onrushing stream of vitality, with all of its rapids, eddies, undertows, and deep shady pools, mostly unnoticed and scarcely comprehensible in our utilitarian form of consciousness, is the "mysterious river of tears under the streets," also called "the unconscious."

Our vitality noticeably rises and falls, surges and recedes in other situations, like seeing a particularly intense movie, taking drugs, sexual arousal and activity, or the excitement of a new idea. We can also look at the dynamics "of the very small events, lasting seconds" that happen when we're with others: "the force, speed, and flow of a gesture; the timing and stress of a spoken phrase or even a word; the way one breaks into a smile or the time course of decomposing the smile; the manner of shifting position in a chair; the time course of lifting the eyebrows when interested and the duration of their lift; the shift and flight of a gaze; and the rush or tumble of thoughts."[18]

We can see now that the standard words we use to name our feelings are inadequate, whether we are thinking of such basic emotions as fear, surprise, anger, sadness, joy, disgust, and affection; or much longer lists that include, for example, such variations on *sad* as *dejected, despair, despondent, forlorn*, etc.. These are all names of states that one *is*, or that one *has become*.[19] Feelings of vitality are processes that, like

---

18 Stern, *Forms of Vitality*, p. 6.

19 Adjectives say what we *are*; past participles, what we *have become*. Vitality must be approached with verbs and adverbs—or with nouns (derived from verbs) that name *events*.

musical phrases, take place over time. They can be indicated by verbs like *rushing, falling,* or *surging.* Stern points to a variety of "rushes".

> For example, a rush of anger or of joy, a perceived flooding of light, and accelerating sequence of thoughts, an unmeasurable wave of feeling evoked by music, and a shot of narcotics [or coffee] can all feel like "rushes."[20]

Our usual words about feelings fail us in another way: they suggest to us that to each word in our vocabulary of feelings there is one state of mind corresponding to it. Just as it might seem that a really good color chart would enable us to describe with perfect accuracy the color of any real object, so we might think that there could be a complete list of emotions and feelings that could in principle describe any stretch of our experience. But if you put the best color chart you can find next to the palm of your hand or a tree trunk, you will be hard pressed to say what color the thing is. Each real thing in each moment is unique. The same is true of our vitality. The rush of feeling I had when I drank a cup of strong coffee an hour ago, or the gnawing in my stomach now as lunch time approaches, are not repeatable types. They are, as it were, dissolved into (in solution with) the total experience of the moment and my whole sense of who I am and what I am doing. Our ordinary vocabulary of emotions and feelings cannot chart the oceanic currents of vitality that ultimately drive what we do and say.

Novelists and poets are good at creating situations in which we can partially share the experience of another. This happens, not because they correctly name that experience, but because they

---

20 Stern, *The Interpersonal World Of The Infant A View From Psychoanalysis And Developmental Psychology,* p. 55.

put us imaginatively into the situation that evokes the experience. Consider Emily Dickinson's familiar lines[21] about the snake:

> Several of Nature's People
> I know, and they know me—
> I feel for them a transport
> Of cordiality—
>
> But never met this Fellow,
> Attended or alone
> Without a tighter breathing
> And Zero at the Bone—

Dickinson here evokes two contrasting moments of feeling: "a transport of cordiality" such as one might experience when meeting a friendly dog; and the "tighter breathing and Zero at the Bone" that comes over one on seeing even a small snake. Neither of these experiences has been named, but we have been invited to imagine a situation and to see if Dickinson's words fit it.

Here's another example from a novel by Conrad Aiken. The narrator is responding to a performance of "Morgen," a song by Richard Strauss.

> Extraordinary sorrow in that song. That queer feeling that comes over me when something moves me too much—a kind of ache that seems to begin in the upper part of the mouth and throat, and yet it isn't an ache so much as an unhappy consciousness which seems to be localized there and to spread downward through the whole aching body, a

---

21 Emily Dickinson, "Poems of Emily Dickinson: Series Two; Nature, Poem 24: The Snake."

slowly-flowering sort of echo in a hollow darkness, opening out with painful tentacles . . . [22]

Stern remarks that these moments of vitality "are experienced as dynamic shifts or patterned changes within ourselves." It is also important that this is how events are remembered. Proust writes of a melody

...you happen to hear during the warm season [and] afterwards reminds you of it; it is connected to the summer by a ... necessary bond: born of the fine days, born again only with them, containing a little of their essence, it not only awakens their image in our memory, it guarantees their return, their presence, actual, ambient, immediately accessible.[23]

Social Vitality

Although our words can partially connect us with each other by evoking similar emotions, there are ways in which our forms of vitality interact directly and wordlessly with each other. We are tuned into each other—to the smallest gestures and tics—without conscious attention or memory. We may come away from a meeting, a conversation, or even a brief wordless encounter, with a vague feeling that is either good or bad—a sense, for example, of having been liked and accepted, or else a sense of being scorned and shut out. The impact we have on each other in this way is enormously important in shaping our souls—our deepest sense of what we are worth

---

22 Conrad Aiken, *Blue Voyage*, p. 174. The narrator first describes the performance itself: "That girl ... singing *Morgen*, waiting for the beautiful melody as given first by the piano to reach the downward curve, and then coming in so deeply and sorrowfully with the slow rich voice. O God, O God that strange mixture of the soaring melody, so perfect in its pure algebra, and the sad, persistent meditative voice—there were tears in her eyes when she finished, and she had to turn away."
23 Proust, *Swann's Way*, p. 85.

in the world. And as we shall see, this impact is especially profound and long-lasting upon us when we are very young.

As we work or play together, focusing on the task or the game, we may have little or no awareness of the communion that is nevertheless going on between us, of the waves of feeling that wash through us. Besides whatever work is getting done or information conveyed, we are also adjusting to each other's rhythms and tempos. We might try to get into a groove with each other like improvising jazz musicians, encouraging each other to play their best. If we join in with others in some ongoing activity—playing a game or cooking a meal, for example, we tend to pick up and match the movement patterns of the others. Similarly, in a conversation, we can't help but adjust our ways of speaking to the prevailing one, or to the patterns of those who seem most influential. These are examples of what Stern calls *affect attunement*, or the "matching of vitality forms."[24]

When adults interact in these ways, they are usually focused on the content of their activities—what they are trying to accomplish—not on the form of vitality that is going on within.[25] And they are enacting the roles that are called for by the social scenario they are involved in. But consider someone who has not yet developed the capacity to use and respond to symbolic language, and yet is in an intensely social relationship with someone he or she depends on for survival and love—a baby with its mother. In their relationship, the matching and mismatching of vitality forms—affect attunement—will be the only form of social interaction, and it will be the medium in which the infant acquires its first, and most foundational, habits, attitudes,

---

24 Stern, *Forms of Vitality*, p. 43.

25 By contrast, Diane Keaton, writing about her father's visit to her dressing room after an unexpectedly (to him) brilliant performance in a high school play, took note of and was transformed by his vitality: "Dad had tears in his eyes. I'd never seen him so excited....I could tell he was startled by his awkward daughter—the one who'd flunked algebra, smashed into his new Ford station wagon…. For one thrilling moment…I was his heroine…There were no words. It was all—every timeless second—encapsulated in his piercing blue eyes…. There was no going back." From Keaton, *Let's Just Say It Wasn't Pretty*, quoted in Als, "The Good-Bye Girl."

and expectations about how to be with others. Here is where our basic structures of feeling, including anxiety, rage, self-loathing, ontological insecurity, and guilt, are laid down.

We will turn to this forgotten period of our lives in the next chapter.

Appendix: Wordless Consciousness

Philosophically minded readers may wonder if this chapter is not trying to do something that I have implied was impossible. I said in Chapter 10 that we become conscious of something when we bring it into the realm of the Symbolic where it is accessible to others. In other words, we become conscious of something by bringing language to bear on it. But I have also said that ordinary language cannot do justice to forms of vitality that are always far richer than words can tell; there are no adequate names for forms of vitality in all their global and amodal richness. This is all true. But these ineffable experiences can be brought into the Symbolic without any attempt to adequately describe them. When I point out something to you (a flower, a painting, someone suffering), I am inviting you, as one who shares our language and culture, to respond in communion with me to this thing. I have zoomed in on a moment of our experience and brought it into the network of our common symbolic activity.[26] It has become a reference point for further communication. We may use poetic language to evoke and sharpen the experience. Even if all we do is shake our heads in amazement or sorrow, we have brought our language to bear on the experience. Poets like Dickinson and Larkin, without trying to give an exact description of their feelings are nevertheless able to evoke similar feeling in their readers, and thereby make those feelings public property. In this chapter, I am trying to provide some focus that will enable us to recognize and understand the obscure and complex feelings we call our "inner demons," while at the same time acknowledging that there can be no fully adequate description of them.

---

26 A.K. Bierman proposes that we think of names, pronouns, and demonstratives (referring terms) as empty spaces in our sentences into which we *emplace* the things being referred to. For example, if I tell you "This cigar has gone out", I am emplacing the cigar in the sentence I have spoken. The cigar is brought into the Symbolic. In Emily Dickinson's poem, the shared form of vitality produced by a snake in the grass is emplaced in our discourse. (Bierman, *Logic: A Dialogue*, pp. 183-85)

14

Soul Sculpture

Introduction

OUR SOULS ARE the activities of our bodies, bodies that have learned to live and communicate with each other; souls are not immaterial, ghostly things that float free of our earthly bodies. This means that human souls are at least as complex as human bodies with their multitudes of chemical interactions and some trillions of neural connections. Then they take on the additional, multidimensional complexity of the languages and cultures in which we are embedded. This is why we are so hard to know—why it is impossible to fully explain why we do what we do. What we know of how the human body works is far from complete, and we have never been able to understand what we do *collectively*––as cultures, nations, or as a civilization.

When philosophers take inventory of the mind, their lists include thoughts, beliefs, perceptions, intentions, memories, volitions (or acts of will), sensations, and emotions. But, as we saw in the last chapter, underneath, and carrying all this along, is the vitality of the human body, without which these "mental acts" would lack what our real experience has: excitement, pizzazz, élan, drive, or energy. "Only when the contents of our minds are yoked to *arousal*," to the vitality of our living, breathing bodies, "do they take on a dynamic form of vitality. This is what gives them the feel of flowing and aliveness—of being human."[1] (Of course, vitality is felt not only when it is going up, but also when it's going down. There are rushes of anxiety, fear, and depression as well as rushes of joy and exultation.)

Our embodied souls register every big and little motion of our constantly moving bodies, reacting to what is going on around us and within us, and that every such motion has some particular multi-modal shape of vitality—that is, a pattern of rhythm, tempo, and intensity that may be felt (and not only on the skin), heard, seen, smelled, and tasted. This always-changing flow of vitality is the real substance, the real power, of experience.

These dynamic patterns are intrinsic and necessary to memory; our memories would be nothing more than fragmented and lifeless words and images unless their content (*what* we remember) were wrapped around, and powered by, the dynamic vitality of the remembered experience, a vitality that comes back to us as we remember.[2] Think of some intense, frightening or joyful moment in your past, and consider the difference between just knowing *that* it happened and remembering the moment as you *lived* it. It is the gestalt of the moment's vitality that brings the memory back to you spontaneously—that causes us to remember things without meaning to.

There are events in our lives that we remember with little or no vitality, but only as bare facts. I remember that I started high school in the fall of 1952, yet I have no conscious memory of what I saw and felt that first day. This memory has little vitality. But what if some events left powerful forms of vitality but no memories of *what* happened? Such unmoored feelings could be what's behind the soul shaking waves of guilt, self-loathing, rage, ontological insecurity, and objectless anxiety we are trying to understand. Joy, excitement,

---

1 Stern, *Forms of Vitality*, p. 23.
2 Ibid, p. 11.

or a feeling of well-being can also come over us in the same way—for no apparent reason. The real events that gave rise to them happened before we were old enough to form lasting memories of who did what to whom. After all, there are for each of us some three child-years of concentrated, mostly pre-verbal experience that are beyond the reach of memory. Moreover, much of our experience in the next couple of decades—into our twenties—consists of social exchanges of vitality that can also lay down vitality habits for better or worse.[3]

In the last chapter, we compared a form of vitality to a musical phrase: it moves us, or we move along with it, dancing to its beat, our hearts rising and falling with the melody. Obsessive feelings like guilt are like tunes stuck in our heads—except that they go on in our hearts and guts, not just our heads. Our inner demons are *vitality habits*, patterns, or chains, of vitality that can be set off by events in daily life or by thoughts that occur to us for whatever reason. We perform them in our lives and in our relations with others. They just kick in and take us with them when they are called out in us by circumstances. Guilt is a song of myself I can't help singing—and living. For example, something I am doing, or a word from someone, reminds me of a person I feel I have treated badly, and then the cascade of guilt and self-loathing washes through me. It doesn't just stay inside me, but gets enacted in my face, posture, and in what I think and say about myself.

How did these "tunes" get into us in the first place? How did the stream of our vitality get shaped at the beginnings of our lives? This is the question I will try to answer in this chapter—the question Thomas Wolfe is asking about his protagonist Eugene when he writes in *Look Homeward, Angel*:

---

3 Even after we begin thinking and acting symbolically, our vitality is always engaged by our interactions with each other, and vitality habits can be shaped and reshaped. Think post traumatic stress syndrome (PTSD) or falling in love.

Thus, the entire landscape, the whole physical background of his life, was now dappled by *powerful prejudices of liking and distaste* formed, God knows how, or by what intangible affinities of thought, feeling and connotation.[4]

Sculpting Minds from the Inside Out[5]

To see how vitality habits get established, we need to go back to that unremembered time, around the age of six months, when we began to develop a real non-verbal, social relationship with our mothers (or other primary care-takers). Mothers and babies *play*—out of a mutual desire to enjoy each other, to have fun. But more than this, they strive to know, and be known by, each other, to share experiences. This requires more than just imitating what the other does. The mother takes the lead by matching the *form* of the infant's vitality, which is different from mere imitation. Here is an example from Stern:

> A nine-month old girl becomes very excited about a toy and reaches for it. As she grabs it, she lets out an exuberant "aaah!" and looks at her mother. Her mother looks back, scrunches up her shoulders, and performs a terrific shimmy with her upper body, like a go-go dancer. The shimmy lasts only about as long as her daughter's "aah!" but is equally excited, joyful, and intense.[6]

---

4 Wolfe, *Thomas Wolfe's Look Homeward, Angel*, p. 202. (Emphasis added)

5 "...the matching/mismatching of vitality forms can shape what the infant does and how he feels about doing it. It is like sculpting his mind from the inside out. It is a powerful tool in the parent's ongoing socialization of the infant into the family and wider culture." Stern, *Forms of Vitality*, p. 115.

6 Stern, *The Interpersonal World Of The Infant A View From Psychoanalysis And Developmental Psychology*, p. 140.

What the mother has done is to match "the dynamic features [the rhythm, tempo, and intensity] of how the baby acted," thereby assuring the baby that her mother saw what she did. But Mother did it in her own way, with her own choice of movements, her own "signature," showing her daughter that she felt the same way.[7] We can also say that the mother *attuned* to the baby's vitality.

Most mothers do this instinctively; they do it "to be with" the baby, or to "join in" or "participate."[8] We might think of vitality matching as a mother's way of welcoming, or enfolding, her child into the human community.[9] It can establish the vitality habit of getting on the same wave length with others, of communing or sharing feelings with them. Good friends *attune* to each other. A good therapist attunes to the client. Attunement, or vitality matching, creates an unconscious understanding that others have feelings and

---

7 Stern, *Forms of Vitality*, p. 114. An excellent video has been made of this kind of mother-baby interaction which I suggest you watch if you can (search on YouTube for "Forms of Vitality Dynamic in the Arts and Therapy"). In addition to illustrating the beautiful matching of vitality, the video also shows the unhappiness of the baby if the mother goes "still-faced"—refusing to respond at all to the baby's invitations to play. It makes it quite clear that our need to *be with* each other is fundamental.

8 Stern, *The Interpersonal World Of The Infant A View From Psychoanalysis And Developmental Psychology*, p. 148.

9 In fact, this interaction can be called "communing"—as contrasted with "communicating," which consists of passing on information or trying to teach a lesson. Communing aims at establishing matching, or isomorphic, forms of vitality. This is what we aim for as adults when we go beyond communicating to get work done to engage, for example, in games or playful conversation. This is the deep understanding we adults often seek and rarely find with each other.

Political philosopher Jerry Boime (Boime, *Violence and Utopia)* claimed that war is a way to establish a communal meeting of minds and feelings among soldiers, for in battle, soldiers rely on more than each others' words, but on their willingness to die for each other. There are other things we do in order to break through the wall of language to meet each other directly: team sports, fandom—not only of teams but of musicians and political leaders, where what binds people together is not *what* they believe—an ideology or belief in the superiority of one's team or leader—but the need *to believe*, to be bound together with ties that transcend (or subtend) words. The unfortunate thing is that such passionate bonds seem to require an opposing other, or enemy, at least implicitly.

that feelings can be communal and not just walled up inside one's body. It creates the possibility for empathy and solidarity, the psychic foundations of community. Moreover, it lets the infant know that she exists, that *she* has been understood. She has seen (and heard) her feelings reflected in the mirror of her mother's face—and voice and gestures.

If they have learned to do this as infants, adults also interact with each other at the level of vitality, although their vitality matching is typically in a symbolic and cultural context that infants have no access to. Here is an example of two adults attuning to each others' feelings.

> The epiphanies in [Colin Toibin's novel] "Nora Webster" accrue slyly, in offhand moments: Nora's sudden pleasure at listening to the easy talk between her sister and brother-in-law, or her understanding, during a shared glance with her older daughter, that they both find her daughter's boyfriend humorless. The absence of melodrama brings these discoveries into relief, and the sense of life flowing around them, by turns meandering and rushing, gives the illusion that Toibin's ... novel is unfolding with the same erratic rhythms as actual life.[10]

Babies, however, connect with their mothers in the realm of vitality, unmediated by the symbolic. "In the earliest stages of life, the infant is first or predominantly sensible to vitality forms."[11] So it is at this vulnerable stage that our deepest sense of who we are and how we stand with others is established, at a stage beyond any power to remember—and in a form that exceeds the power of words to express.

---

10 Egan, Jennifer, "Finding a Voice, a Review of *Norah Webster* by Colin Toibin."
11 Stern, *Forms of Vitality*, p 111.

So let's look more closely at some of what goes on between babies and their mothers in these early days of social life. (By "mother," I mean whoever is *mothering*.[12]) First, we need to appreciate the intensity of the relationship between mother and baby. With our adult bodies and skills and well-established social positions, most of us can take for granted our moment-to-moment survival and our ability to understand the world for all practical purposes. Not so the baby, who depends directly on its mother for its most basic and most strongly felt needs—for food, warmth, and safety, and for guidance in learning about the world and how to be with people. The baby's dependence on its mother is not cushioned (as it implicitly is for us) by any grasp of a larger network of possible support, and this makes the *intensity* of the connection with the mother, extremely powerful. This is what Winnicott is getting at when he writes, "tremendous things" happen "in the little world of the baby." We saw at the end of the previous chapter some of what can go wrong when the mother's presence is missing or unreliable and basic needs go unmet, even briefly: the baby can experience terrifying feelings of isolation and abandonment that can continue to silently threaten us as adults.

Let's look now at how our vitality habits could have been formed in the play of feelings that go on between mother and baby as the baby is fed, dressed and undressed, bathed, held, carried, put to bed and picked up, and engaged in play. A few paragraphs ago, we saw an example of *vitality matching*, the mother's "shimmy" responding to the baby's "aaah!" This kind of play can accompany almost any activity the two of them engage in, and, as we saw, it can establish

---

12 There is no reason here to blame our mothers for what has gone wrong in our souls. Not only are there other family members who handle babies, but mothers themselves are shaped by and subject to an enormous range of conflicts. Moreover, our social arrangements unfortunately put almost all the work of "mothering" on the mother, especially during the first few years of life—though that is changing to some extent. Anyway, no one's life and actions belong to them alone; we are all caught up in the vast social web. See Chapter 12, Appendix. This whole book is an argument against moral condemnation of individuals. The buck never stops.

the vitality habit of engaging affectively with others and the feeling of being at home, being welcome, in the human world. What might happen if there was little or no such play in a baby's life, where there was no attempt to share in the play of vitality in the baby? Stern describes the interaction between a baby and a mother who had been diagnosed with schizophrenia, though she was not overtly psychotic at the time. The mother was concerned with the baby's physical needs in an exaggerated way, but had no response at all to her daughter's emotional expression. Stern anticipates for the child "a pervasive feeling of aloneness." "It would be hard," he writes

> for such a child at an older age not to get some hint that things were going on between other people about which she had only a glimpse but no real experience. Then she would truly experience an ego-alien aloneness and would probably fear the possibility of such a form of intimacy.[13]

The inability to affectively attune with others, to interact at the level of vitality, would make it impossible to love—to deeply care for someone else or to take in the love of others. A great deal of what moved and motivated other people would be meaningless. Imagine having no sense of rhythm and being tone deaf in a world where everyone was dancing and singing: a lot of what people did would seem senseless.

Much more common, of course, would be a pattern of very little, or inconsistent, sharing of vitality by an infant's parents, or by others in the child's life, leading to a fragile, insecure sense of belonging. What better foundation could there be for ontological insecurity– a deep uncertainty of one's own reality—than having little or no sense of being welcome in the world because no one welcomed you? Or because you were rejected or ignored as often as you were welcomed?

---

13 Stern, *The Interpersonal World Of The Infant A View From Psychoanalysis And Developmental Psychology*, p. 207.

Having a name and a social position, as discussed in Part I, means little without the vitality habit of expecting that others will be glad to see you. (Or better, worldly success comes to mean *too* much when you lack the deep sense of belonging.)

Beyond the question of how much vitality matching goes on, we need to think about what kinds, or forms, of vitality are matched. Parents naturally attune to their children selectively, according to their own personalities. Just as we adults respond with different degrees of interest, enthusiasm, boredom, or even disgust, to what other people around us are doing and saying, so mothers naturally react to what their babies are doing out of their own attitudes and moods. Thereby they shape their children's vitality habits. In particular, "they create a template for the infant's shareable interpersonal world."[14]

Babies are "full of beans." Their ever shape-shifting vitality is always on display, giving their parents plenty of opportunity to attune to it—or not. Mothers engage in *selective* attunement, responding to some kinds of behavior and forms of vitality and not to others—or to some more than, or differently from, others. Since what the baby wants, most of the time, is the *sharing* of an experience, what she learns from her mother's attunement or lack of attunement is *which* kinds of vitality can be shared and which are unshareable—or just insignificant.[15]

---

14 Ibid, p. 209.

15 An obvious, and important, example of a form of vitality that goes unmatched and unshared is masturbation. Even if parents do not punish or shame small children playing with themselves, they certainly don't attune to it. This non-attunement leaves children with the sense that this behavior, and these feelings, are not to be shared with others. This no doubt contributes to the transgressive excitement of sharing them when the opportunity arises later.

Keep in mind that these prohibitions and permissions about sharing are not learned as principles, but as habits of vitality. The baby learns to steer away from expressing forms of vitality that have been unattuned, and towards expressing those that have been attuned.

In some families and in some cultures, the sharing of feelings in general is discouraged. Thus parents *under*-attune the vitality affects of their children, and, as they grow older, re-tune their reactions into reasonable words. Such children would be likely to develop a distaste and fear of intimacy and a strongly felt preference for coolly rational ways of describing situations. They would favor unsentimental procedures for resolving disputes, and give no weight to feelings that can't be formulated. Mr. Wilcox in E.M. Forster's novel *Howard's End* is a classic illustration of this kind of character.[16]

Here are two mother-baby pairs, reported by Stern, in which the mothers attune differently to their infants' levels of enthusiasm.[17] Molly's mother attunes most to the highest levels of her daughter's enthusiasm, with the result that in her effort to get the most recognition from her mother, Molly comes to exaggerate her enthusiasm, to become slightly phony, and to let another person guide her feelings. Annie's mother, on the other hand, is more inclined to attune to her daughter's moments of *deflating* enthusiasm. As a result, Molly's more depressed feelings are likely to be disturbing to her, beyond the pale of shareable human experience. Annie, however, is more likely to back away from rising high enthusiasm. She may, as an adult, blame herself for being uncomfortable with such feelings since, of course, she has no concept of what her mother simply ignored. She might, for example, watch a scene from an episode of David Lynch's TV series "Twin Peaks" in which a woman dances sinuously in a dark room illuminating herself with a flashlight to entertain some children she is baby sitting, and be overcome with a strange and unwanted discomfort that comes with the impossibility of doing such a thing herself.

---

16 Wilcox is perfectly played in this regard by Anthony Hopkins in the film directed by James Ivory.

17 Stern, *The Interpersonal World Of The Infant A View From Psychoanalysis And Developmental Psychology*, pp. 208-09.

Another way of sculpting a mind from the inside is by getting the infant's attention and then expressing a very different feeling. One mother showed great disgust whenever her baby looked at her while pleasurably teething on some inedible object. Before long, the baby began to show similar disgust at his own behavior. Stern remarks that in this way "The mother had successfully introduced a 'badness'-tinged feeling quality into the infant's total affective experience of mouthing." Another mother would show in her voice and body great disappointment whenever her son would do something clumsy, and soon the child became more restrained in his movements; his own feelings—his "exuberant exploratory freedom"—were taken from him and replaced, at least in part, with his mother's feelings.[18]

Children are not just shaped or molded by their parents' matching and mismatching of their vitality; they can also, as it were, ricochet against, or out of, the bond with their families. Events or circumstances that threaten or frustrate a small child's developing sense of self can result in powerful feelings of rage. Rage can be a momentary state of mind, as we see expressed in a tantrum; or it can become a deeply engrained form of vitality, an habitual response towards frustrations. It can even take the form of constant, seething resentment at the world in general. We will revisit the issue of rage in Chapter 16.

What Can We See from Here?

We have now reached a point where we should be able to start to make good on the promise made at the start of this book: to illuminate the dark places in our souls and reveal the demons for what they are, expecting that, whatever they turn out to be under the light of day, they could never be as scary as they were in the dark of night.

---

18 Stern, *The Interpersonal World Of The Infant A View From Psychoanalysis And Developmental Psychology*, pp. 222-23.

Before we go further, though, we need to understand why this can be done only within certain limits.

We have traced our inner demons to vitality habits which were shaped in the intimacy of our homes by the continuous attuning and misattuning of the people who took care of us in the first years of our lives. But our ability to connect how we feel, think and act today with the events of the past is limited, most obviously, by the difficulty of retrieving, through memory or in others ways (photos, diaries, interviews) what really happened. Our understanding is also limited by the language we must use to talk and write about these phenomena.

What we are feeling and doing at any given moment arises out of the moving vitality of that moment, and that vitality in turn is the surging of the whole body as represented and enacted by the whole nervous system. To call one such moment "enthusiasm," for example, would be like calling a hurricane…well, "a hurricane". It's not that it's wrong, and it works fine for ordinary purposes. But no matter how rich our concepts of "hurricane" or "enthusiasm" might be, they are not going enable us to understand the origins or the path of a particular hurricane or burst of enthusiasm. So far, neither meteorology nor psychology have been able to reduce the weather or our living bodies to parameters that permit complete explanations (let alone predictions) of what happens. In the case of the many shifting forms human vitality can take, the roots of any one event are spread throughout the whole system indicated at the beginning of this chapter—not only each individual's buried past, but how that individual is connected with the surrounding social system and the history of that system as well.

The goal of the work we are doing here is to make clear that our souls are created by forces and events much older and bigger than we are, and so to reduce the guilty self-loathing that so many of us are afflicted with. These larger forces are impressed upon us, or installed within us, in the first few years of life in our immediate families, and these families are themselves produced by circumstances much older and bigger than they are. We have seen that the "language" in which we learn the first lessons of life is the language of vitality, a language that cannot be translated into the symbolic languages we speak as adults. And while the interactions between mother, father, and baby of attuning and misattuning can bring us into the human community, they can also make us enemies of each other and even of ourselves.

As I have just said, knowing exactly how your or my particular inner demons were established is beyond us—certainly beyond me. The most we can hope is to understand how inner demons in general arise, and some ways to think fruitfully about how one's own rage, guilt, self-loathing, ontological insecurity, and chronic anxiety might have come about. Again, not with the aim of pinning the blame on our parents (who, after all, grew up in their own particular gardens of infantile catastrophe), but with the aim of removing, or at least mitigating, the blame from ourselves. Blame is not where we're going.

15

Taking On the Other

*None of us can endure being our own sun. We must erect
a god-ideal outside ourselves in order to live at all, and
to avoid this being perceived as our own creation we must
forget we have erected it.*

DAVID LOY[1]

Introduction

AT THE END of Chapter 8, I said that our relationship with the big
Other determines whether we shall live well or badly, whether we feel
at home in the world or find ourselves drawn into one or another
form of self-destruction. I said, too, that this relationship is formed
in early childhood, for that is when the Other becomes part of us—
takes a controlling, if contested, interest in our souls.

Exactly how does that happen? How does the Other—and its
thuggish enforcer, the over-I—get installed within us? What we
have learned in the last chapter about vitality and the formation

---

1 Loy, *Lack and Transcendence*, p. 19.

of vitality habits should help us to answer this question. What are the vitality habits that lie behind our allegiance to the Other, and how are these habits formed?

The Other is the virtual author-director-impresario of the social scenarios we perform in our daily lives with each other. It does not direct us from the wings, but from within our very souls. The sum of its content is the Symbolic, the totality of all our musts, oughts and obligations. It is what is required and expected of us as responsible persons worthy of recognition, from the rules of our language and codes of etiquette to the highest principles of law and morality.

But all these norms and principles in the abstract do not justify themselves. Their claim on us does not happen from the mere saying or thinking of them. What is the source of their vitality? If the Other is part of us, if it plants itself within us, it does so by rooting itself in our guts, in our vitality. A system of beliefs and attitudes must rest upon a complex of vitality habits. We cannot understand the power of the Other without understanding how and why we acquire the patterns of vitality that flow through and move us no matter how much or how little we are aware of them.

The big Other comes with a darker companion, or over-I, very much as the Law comes with all the institutions of law enforcement—the police, courts and prisons. Laws are legislated with a view to some conception of social order: legislators expect most people (the "law-abiding citizens") to follow the law just because it is the law—the way most drivers stop at red lights even when there are no police in sight. In addition, laws usually establish what sanctions shall be applied if the law is violated—a schedule of fines and/or prison time. But the actual work of enforcement is done by institutions distinct from the legislature: police, courts, and prisons. And how these agencies operate—with what degree of cruelty and degradation towards those who are arrested, tried, and imprisoned—is often forgotten in discussing what the law should be. But in daily life, what we know of the law comes from our experience and fears of what happens if we are caught breaking the law. Law enforcement is the visible face of the law for the average citizen. Similarly, the over-I tells us what we will suffer if we don't do what we are supposed to do. The law and the Symbolic announce to us, "Thou shalt…, and thou shalt not….." Law enforcement and the over-I add the kicker phrase, "or else…".

It is out of our hope for some relief from the demons of guilt, self-loathing, anxiety, rage, and ontological insecurity that we are trying to bring the Other and the over-I into the light. What *is* there within us that attacks us from its hidden lair? Or does the Other somehow seduce us into attacking ourselves? Is it just me? Is it my mother? My father? Is it society? If only we could really understand how the Other operates and how it gets into us! Might not that alone reduce its grip upon us and ease our nameless fears?

Not everyone is so haunted by the big Other. Some people experience the injunctions of the Symbolic as if they were rules of a game that they feel free to stop playing if it starts interfering with more pressing, or pleasurable, pursuits. And they understand the rules as agreements that the players may alter by negotiation. They do not assume that there is some source of rightness transcending them that must also agree with them.

This book, of course, is written for those who do not feel that way, who need to see through and to overcome the Other and the over-I. For them, the Other needs debunking. *Maybe* that's not completely possible or desirable; some form of the Other may be a permanent and necessary feature of the social life of social beings. But by understanding its power, by grasping how it masquerades as real, understanding its "reality" as *virtual,* we can get some distance from it. If we understood how the over-I becomes as sadistic as T.S. Eliot's judge ("who can terrorize us/ And urge us on to futile activity,/ And in the end, judge us still more severely"), it might terrorize us less.

The big Other and the over-I work hand-in-hand in our souls. But in thinking about how they come to dwell within us, we need to take them in order, beginning with the Other.

Internalization and Identification[2]

The Other becomes a part of us; that is, we see things as the Other does, and we often act in the world as agents for the Other.[3] Another way of putting this is to say that we *internalize* the Other, or that we *identify* with the Other. To understand concretely what this means, let's set aside the Other for a moment and just think about internalizing and identifying with an other—a teacher or a parent, for example.

We obviously do not internalize someone in any literal sense—by eating them, say, or by implanting their souls or brains into our own. Nor do I literally identify with another person—a favorite teacher, say—by pretending to be her, or by stealing her identity so I can buy expensive items on her credit card.

Suppose I learn something from you—how to make an omelet or play a tune on the ukulele. Now we might suppose that when I do so, I simply take note, step by step, of what you do and resolve to follow that procedure myself. And sometimes that might be all that happens—I learn from you as I would learn from a textbook or a recipe.

What is typical and more likely is that I allow what you do to be contagious for me: seeing you pouring the eggs into the pan, or moving from one chord to another, begins to lay down the paths in my nervous system that will enable my body to do as I have seen yours do. For what I have seen is more than just what I could write down as step one and step two: I have seen and taken in a *sequence of vitality forms*, and this sequence, thanks to mirror neurons, is infectious. Mirror neurons respond to the perception of someone else's action by stimulating our own muscles to prepare to do likewise. As Stern puts it, "When

---

2 In this section, I will be drawing on, but going beyond Stern, *Forms of Vitality*. especially pages 141-46.

3 We are agents for the Other as parents, teachers, and anytime we handle money. A vivid example of this for me is my memory of working as a clerk in a Walgreen Drug Store in Chicago in 1957 and having to confiscate from an eight or nine-year old African-American boy a rubber ball he had stolen. At least I didn't call the police.

someone imagines a movement with its vitality form, something happens in the cortex that then sends a signal to the appropriate motor areas to activate the musculature of the body that would have been used if the imagined event were enacted".[4] Seeing people dance can make us feel like dancing.

So what we internalize from others is not a system of principle or rules intellectually grasped. Rather, we internalize forms of vitality that we "catch" from others. The forms of vitality we internalize include not only the right moves, but also some *attitudes*. As I learn from you how to make an omelet, you may express in what you say and how you say it some contempt for poorly made omelets and for cooks who, for example, overcook the eggs, or use too much salt. Then as I begin to make omelets myself, I will probably monitor my actions with those same (internalized) attitudes. As a cook, I have identified with you; I take your point of view, not only when I'm making omelets, but also when I comment on and react emotionally to the omelet skills of others.

We most readily internalize the attitudes of, people who are important to us in various ways—parents, teachers, older sisters or brothers, charismatic political or religious leaders. We can also identify with certain cultural or occupational groups whose practices and attitudes we share. We certainly do not automatically internalize all the forms of vitality we meet, in spite of our busy mirror neurons. We internalize the vitality of people who are close to us or whom we admire or love, or upon whom we depend for love or recognition. And the stronger these bonds are, the more likely we are to absorb patterns of vitality from them. Most important among these, for our purposes, are what we might call forms of recognition, approval, and love, as well as disdain, scorn, or disinterest.

---

4 Stern, *Forms of Vitality*, p. 133. Stern adds, "However, although some activation is recorded electrophysiologically in the muscles involved, it is not enough to release a movement."

We identify not only with people we love or admire, but often with our fiercest critics, even with those who treat us badly if they bulk large in our lives. Many people never stop trying to win the respect and love of a mother or father who scorned them, demonstrating their loyalty to their parent by scorning themselves even more than the parent did. This is one way we become divided against ourselves: we identify with, and so must always be confronting, a hostile other. How do these attitudes of other people coalesce into an absolute authority, the big Other?

Arrival of the big Other

So we have seen what it means to identify with others: it amounts to internalizing a cluster of forms of vitality which then enact themselves through us. Sometimes we know that what we are feeling or saying comes to us from others ("As my father used to say..."). Sometimes we assume that we are simply seeing what is obviously true and right. A moment in Ben H. Winters's novel *World of Trouble* illustrates a transition from the first to the second perspective. A detective who is fairly new in the job checks out a crime scene, and hears in his head the voice of his mentor reminding him to look for how the perpetrator entered and exited the scene. But he suddenly realizes that "it's not he who is right, it's me, *I'm* the one who is recalling" what must be done.

> It's him I'm hearing, but it's really me—anytime I hear a voice telling me to do something, Detective Culverson's mild voice, or my mom's or my dad's.... *At a certain point you have to concede to yourself that it's just you out here.*[5]

---

5 Winters, *World of Trouble*. Emphasis added.

But of course it's never really "just you out here." Or rather, the "you" that is out there is a complex of vitality habits acquired from others *and* from your own unpredictable responses to the stream of circumstances in your life. At some point in our lives, the plural voices of the others take on a weird sort of unity, for they seem to be not only *my* voice but they are also vested with an authority that transcends me.

The Other *begins* in the nursery, not in what our mothers say to us, but in the rhythms, tempos, and intensities with which they match and mismatch our vitality. Vitality, after all, is the medium of our first lessons in reality. And there is an enormous amount to learn—to internalize as habits of vitality:

> ...what you do with your eyes when with another, how long to hold a mutual gaze, what turn-off head movements work, and with whom, how close you should let the other come to you and at what speeds (or you to them, and what distance for whom), what you do with your face (and with whom), how to kiss, how to read body positions, how to solicit another for food, for physical contact or to play, ...how to enter into turn taking when vocalizing with another, how to greet or not greet your mother for a reunion when she returns after a separation, and how to joke around, negotiate, escalate, back off, and express affection, make friends, and so on.[6]

We did not learn all these *lessons of being* by formulating rules, or by conceptualizing what we do in terms of formal acts called "smiling", "asking for food", "playing", "greeting", "joking", and so on. In the course of our daily interactions with our mothers and our other caretakers, we learned "the forms of dynamic flow that carry social

---

6 Stern, *Forms of Vitality*, pp. 110-11.

behaviors."[7] We learned how to be with other people *by being with other people*, people who shared their forms of vitality by attuning or misattuning to us. Of course, when we begin to use and understand language, we can be told how to act and we can ask "why." We can learn what the rules are. But even then, a great deal of what we learn happens at the level of vitality, in what is not, and mostly cannot be, spoken.

This is where the big Other begins: in the social and natural world in which we find ourselves. We arrive in a world of already-written and ongoing social scenarios, as if we were dropped into a long story in which we are expected to play a part even though we have not heard what went before and do not even speak the language of the story. We arrive, as Simone deBeauvoir puts it, in a *serious* world.

> In [the child's] eyes, human inventions, words, customs, and
> values are given facts, as inevitable as the sky and the trees.
> This means that the world in which he lives is a serious world,
> since the characteristic of the spirit of seriousness is to con-
> sider values as ready-made things.[8]

The big Other begins with the realization that *this* is how things are, *this* is how things are done, *regardless* of my desire. The big Other begins with the negation of desire—and the acceptance of this negation as part of the world, and not merely the fiat of one's parents.

When we arrive in this world, however, we generally land in the arms of a mother who, if she can, is willing to provide orientation and support in a dynamic language of vitality, a language of rhythm, intensity and tempo that we quickly pick up.

---

7 Ibid, 110-11. In *The Interpersonal World of the Infant*, Stern writes, "Like dance for the adult, the social world experienced by the infant is primarily one of vitality affects before it is one of formal acts" (p. 57).

8 Beauvoir, *The Ethics Of Ambiguity* p. 35.

Nevertheless, even with a mother to cushion us from the "serious" world, the Other is *other*, that is, it stands over against us, against our desires, many of which the world—including our mothers—does not fulfill. In the passage just quoted from Beauvoir, she also writes that the child finds "himself cast into a universe which he has not helped to establish, which has been fashioned without him, and which appears to him as an absolute *to which he can only submit*."

But quite often the child does *not* submit. She or he *rages* against being hungry or cold, and against being left alone. However well adjusted we might be to the ways of the world, there is always some suspicion, some resentment of the Other in all of us, and therefore a lot of transgressive behavior, from everyday minor slights and insults to mass murder. But now we must turn to the over-I, and particularly its darker side, the inner bully.

The Over-I as Inner Bully

Having internalized the Other and become agents of the Symbolic, what could lead us to take on the role of inner bully so well described by Žižek as "the superego":

> Superego is not an ethical agency proper, but a sadistic agent that bombards the subject with impossible demands obscenely enjoying the subject's failure to comply with them; the paradox of the superego is that, as Freud saw it clearly, the more we obey its demands, the more we feel guilty. Imagine a vicious teacher who gives to his pupils impossible tasks and then sadistically jeers when he sees their anxiety and panic.[9]

---

9 Žižek, *Event*, p.162.

In thinking about how we become this "sadistic agent," we must, with Nietzsche, own up to the fact that cruelty is highly pleasurable. In modern society, Nietzsche writes, our "delicacy... resists a really vivid comprehension of the degree to which cruelty constituted the great festival pleasure of more primitive men and was indeed an ingredient of almost every one of their pleasures; and how naively, how innocently their thirst for cruelty manifested itself, how as a matter of principle, they posited 'disinterested malice'...as a *normal* quality of man—and thus something to which the conscience cordially *says Yes!*" "To see others suffer does one good, to make others suffer even more: this is a hard saying but an ancient, mighty, human, all-too-human principle....".[10]

We do not need to take Nietzsche's word for it. A review of the horrors of history should be enough to convince us that cruelty is pleasing not just to a few twisted monsters. Children often take pleasure in torturing animals and harassing younger children. Military and para-military personnel from ancient times to contemporary warfare in the Middle East, are universally found to have engaged enthusiastically in systematic torture and in orgies of rape, mutilation and slaughter of men, women, children and infants. Police in many countries do similar things on a smaller scale. So it shouldn't surprise us that everyone, or nearly everyone, is capable of enjoying, and even causing, the suffering of others, though, as Nietzsche points out, with less honesty about it than our ancestors.

We will see in a later chapter that the desire to see and to cause others to suffer is a universal human capacity, but one that becomes active only under certain, but unfortunately very common, conditions. A world that is less cruel depends on a change in those conditions. But in history so far, Nietzsche seems to be right: there is intense pleasure in cruelty—though guilt may keep us from admitting it. We should not forget, as Stephen Mitchell says, "how exciting,

---

10 Nietzsche, *On the Genealogy of Morals and Ecce Homo*, pp. 66-67, original emphasis.

how stimulating aggression can be.... Aggression, like sexuality, often provides the juice that potentiates and embellishes experience."[11]

What does the bully in us look for in a victim? As we noted in Chapter 8, it looks for a creature who is weaker, and this weakness is a matter of having fewer or weaker allies. The victim is unprotected, or less protected than we are. When we meet a person who belongs to a group that is less powerful than our own, a group that our group is known to often bully, then the temptation to abuse that person is likely to arise. We may well be ashamed of it, but we feel the "right" to feel superior to the other, even the "right" to hate and to hurt him or her. We know that among our own group, that sense of superiority is normal and expected. We may welcome the opportunity to feel this way, especially if in other contexts we feel weak and inconsequential. Hating the weaker gives us the rush of vitality that comes with being in solidarity with the more powerful group that has the right (always exercised and always denied) to rule the weaker.[12] This complex of vitality forms survives our conscious and collective understanding that it is wrong to have such feelings, let alone to act on them.

Now how does it happen that we turn our bullying impulse against ourselves? Recall that we are self-conscious beings: we are always monitoring and evaluating ourselves through the categories of the big Other. As bullies, however, we are also eager to find weaknesses to excoriate whenever and wherever possible so that we can cement our alliance with the powerful Other. Therefore it gives me a kind of pleasure to seize upon the sins and errors of my recent and distant past and to inflict shame upon myself, thereby declaring myself at one with the big Other. I bully myself as a self-appointed

---

11 Mitchell, *Hope And Dread In Pychoanalysis* p. 165.

12 Political and economic factors are usually what create groups of lower social status. Black Africans were enslaved to profit tobacco, sugar and cotton industries, and their status as slaves made them targets for cruelty on the part of everyone who was not a slave, while in turn, the habit of cruelty towards them partially blocked sympathies for them that could have undermined their exploitation as slaves. Of course it did not do so perfectly, as evidenced by the Abolitionist movement.

representative of the big Other. Sadly, the bully and the bullied inhabit the same nervous system and the same soul, so I experience not only the sadistic pleasure of the bully, but even more intensely the emotional distress of one who is bullied. In becoming the inner bully, I also become the guilty, scolded child, and it is in that position that I lie awake at night full of regrets and self-recriminations.

Ridiculous, isn't it? If we can begin to laugh at how comic is this very human predicament, we might take ourselves less seriously and stop taking the inner bully's accusations as moral truths.

Appendix: Some speculations about the souls of others

Whenever we interact with another person in more than a fleeting way, we absorb, via mirror neurons, a gestalt of that person's forms of vitality—a sense of who they are that goes much deeper than anything we could say about them. I might say that we have an "intuition" of the souls of others, because what we see-feel-think about them is much more than what we consciously know. Yet this intuition may be far from accurate, for it is shaped not only by the other person, but by our own prejudices and expectations. Think of what most middle-class people (regardless of their color) see, feel, think, and imagine when we see a young African American man. This is a particularly obvious example of a "take" on another person that often has fatal consequences when the perceiver is an armed cop or self-appointed vigilante.

The nearly universal impulse to internalize the vitality forms of others may help us to understand the violent aversion that some people have towards others who are different. A visceral dislike of gays, for example, may in fact be a horrified rejection of one's own impulse to be like them. And someone with a strong nose-to-the-grindstone work ethic may find him or herself drawn towards the vitality of an easy-going culture, a temptation that must then be violently rejected.

Identification, understood as internalizing a cluster of forms of vitality that constitutes our intuition of a person, helps us to understand why it's difficult to accept the finality of death, why it seems that a person we knew well must still exist somewhere after death. For some people, a loved one who has died can seem very close.

> As a child I learned to fall asleep talking to my [deceased] mother in the darkness of my bedroom, telling her about the day's events, my adventures at school, and the things I had been taught. I couldn't hear her voice or feel her touch, but her radiance and her warmth haunted every corner of our home, and I believed, with the innocence of those who can still count their age on their ten fingers, that if I closed my eyes and spoke to her, she would be able to hear me wherever she was.[13]

Significant people—members of our family, close friends, or heroic public figures—become, in the persistence within us of their distinctive forms of vitality, part of the fabric of the world for us. The result of this is that it becomes almost as difficult to imagine their deaths as it is to imagine our own—for they are always in us directing or pulling at our gaze and pushing our responses.

---

13 Zafón, *The Shadow of the Wind*, p. 4.

16

The Roots of Guilt and Self-Loathing

Introduction

I HAVE STRESSED that this is not a self-help book that will enable you to dispel your rogue feelings and unbidden thoughts and replace them with more wisely chosen ones. It's not a book about how to fix, but how to *think* about your soul. Nevertheless, being able to think more clearly about the soul might make what goes on in it less mysterious and therefore less frightening.

Being able to think more clearly about something, however, is not the same as having arrived at a complete and precise understanding of it. We have seen that the soul—everything that makes us who we are—is not something that can be plumbed to its depths. It is not like the engine in a car that no longer seems mysterious once its workings are diagrammed and explained. Each of us—everything we think, feel and do—is intertwined in ways that beggar description with a social order that is also impossible to think through entirely. And all of this—every soul and every social relationship—is powered by forms of vitality which are incommensurable with the resources of the language with which we try to describe and explain things.

But if we refrain from trying to nail ourselves down with exact language and remember that no story, no explanation, is ever complete and final, then we can embark on an endless voyage of discovery that always enriches but never completes our picture of ourselves. What we aim at is a plausible narrative about what could have happened to us as children, given what we know and can find out about the circumstances and personalities surrounding us in those days. What were the tremendous things that (may have) happened in the little worlds of our infancies that continue to haunt us now? How might we have reacted to them? Can we see how some of our more painful and dysfunctional habits of vitality could have been shaped by these events? My hope is that when we see, not *exactly* what happened, but the *kinds* of things that very well *could* have happened, we will find ourselves less inclined to beat ourselves up over events of the past and problems of the present, and consequently able to face the future with less fear. So let us see what we can say about how our inner demons came to dwell within us.

Guilt is the center piece, the place we need to start in order to see how it all hangs together. This is not the guilt we might feel for a particular act or failure to act—like forgetting to meet a friend for coffee or giving too little help to a friend in trouble. The guilt we are concerned with here is unconscious—or felt only as a kind of unease or malaise. It is best understood as the felt need to be punished for something we know not what. Self-loathing is the punishment we inflict upon ourselves to relieve the guilt. We turn our inner bully loose on our everyday missteps and failures in order to have reason to punish ourselves for the sin we cannot identify. Anxiety and ontological insecurity arise, as we will see, from our punishment and our fear of it. Rage plays a key role in all this. Our infantile fury at those we most love and depend upon is our "original sin"—for which we feel we must be punished. This, at least, is the story I will try to make plausible in this chapter and the next.

Let's begin by considering what we had to be angry about as babies.

Tremendous Things in a little world

It is difficult for adults not to minimize the fears of children, especially babies. The world of the baby may look little to us, but to the baby, it's everything there is. The baby itself is tiny and vulnerable in a world where other people and things are enormous. It is not only tiny, but helpless: its only recourse is to cry out for someone to come.[1] If no one comes, what would seem like a short time to an adult can feel like forever to the baby who has no way to know that help will *ever* arrive. It could well be that the baby cries, not because of something as simple as hunger, but in *terror* of being abandoned to an eternity of isolation.[2] For that matter, hunger is no small or simple matter for the infant; hunger may fill the horizon like a tsunami.

We are not pointing here to extreme neglect, but simply to the ordinary delays between a child's felt need—on waking in the night or from a nap, for example—and the parent's ability and willingness to attend to it. At least in a world where small children are put down to sleep in separate rooms, rather than being constantly in their

---

1 I use the pronoun 'it' not in order to objectify the infant, but because at this age, it has no subjective gender: it is neither boy nor girl to itself. In fact, using either 'he' or 'she' might prevent half my readers from identifying with the situation of the infant. Unfortunately, there is no genderless, third-person personal pronoun. Bettelheim points out that in German (the original language of psychoanalysis), children are referred to with the ungendered pronoun *es*—since the word for child *das Kind* is neuter. Bettelheim, *Freud and Man's Soul.*

2 I had a recurring nightmare as a child of four of being alone on a flat, empty, gray surface that extended as far as the eye could see, terrified that I would never be anywhere else.

mothers' presence, every child is going to experience these fears. Thus is a vitality habit established making the fear of abandonment and even death universal in nearly every heart.

Many of us were infants in the middle decades of the twentieth century when parents were widely advised to let their babies "cry it out," on the theory that picking them up and comforting them whenever they cried would make children grow up to be excessively demanding and dependent. Letting them cry themselves to sleep at night, and not feeding them until a scheduled time, was supposed to lead to independence and self-reliance. This advice from "experts" of the day was based on no valid experimental evidence.[3] The evidence today points in the opposite direction. Two Harvard psychiatrists

> ...examined childrearing practices here and in other cultures and say the widespread American practice of putting babies in separate beds—even separate rooms—and not responding quickly to their cries may lead to incidents of post-traumatic stress and panic disorders when these children reach adulthood.

The early stress resulting from separation causes changes in infant brains that make future adults more susceptible to stress in their lives...[4]

There are other things adults commonly do, or fail to do, that can terrify a baby.[5]

---

3 Narvaez et al., "The Evolved Development Niche."

4 Powell, Alvin, "Children Need Touching and Attention, Harvard Researchers Say."

5 I am guided here by Stephen Mitchell's summation of the threats and dangers of infancy. Mitchell, *Hope And Dread In Pychoanalysis*, pp. 161-62.

1. *Separation.* Being separated from mother is almost always frightening, and yet nearly inevitable for most small children, especially today when many mothers work outside the home.

2. *Failure of Attunement.* We have seen (Chapter 14) how important vitality matching, or attunement, is for the child's ability to be with others and for establishing a sense of belonging and existing. This activity of communing is often disrupted, either because mother is distracted or because she feels the need to replace what the baby is feeling with some other, more "appropriate" feeling. Either way, the infant's sense of belonging is threatened.

3. *Parental Anxiety.* Forms of vitality are both visible and contagious; babies register and internalize what their parents are feeling. For example, parents are often anxious about their children for many different reasons—because their child is ill, not eating, crying too much, or not developing as they think it should. This anxiety shows itself in the parents' vitality which is mirrored by children before they have any articulate idea of what the anxiety is about. Also, kids often pick up on parental anxiety about things not directly related to the child, like money or the parents' own relationship..

4. *Fright.* Babies are often frightened by something sudden and unexpected, like a door slamming, a dog barking, or a parent's sudden, and, to the baby, inexplicable anger. It is not unusual for parents to become furious even with very young children, raising their voices, spanking, or shaking them.

5. *Disruption.* We have all seen small children scream with frustration when interrupted while doing something they are intent on, either because an adult thinks what the child is doing is dangerous or dirty, or because of the parent's schedule—which may really be the schedule of the parent's employer or some other coercive institution.

The things a baby cries about seem small because for us they are manageable. We know where the food is. We know that the loud noise, or even the anger, is momentary. But the infant does not have a bigger picture to put these things into perspective.

My point here is not to criticize parents for neglecting or abusing their children. It is rather that, as Stephen Mitchell puts it, "some experiences of endangerment in infancy and early childhood" are universal, and "even with the best care, there are inevitable periods of distress, helplessness, and longing."[6] We all have *some* cause to feel ontologically insecure, unworthy, anxious—and even angry, as we will see in a moment.

If this is the case "even with the best care," think about the vast number of us who have suffered much more severe traumas——for whom the Garden of Infantile Catastrophe is more emphatically catastrophic. We don't need to consider the very worst cases of violence and sexual abuse, though God knows these are not uncommon.[7] A recent study of 9500 "middle class" Americans[8] finds that two-thirds reported at least one "adverse childhood experience" (ACE) and that one in five experienced three or more. ACEs are forms of physical or emotional abuse, neglect, or "household dysfunction" (like divorce or an alcoholic parent; for details, see Appendix 1 at the end of this chapter.) The study also finds that the more ACEs in one's childhood (before the age of 18), the more likely one is to have serious health or social problems later in life—including alcoholism, depression, smoking, suicide attempts and a variety of serious

---

6 Ibid.

7 These can be found, for example, in James Gilligan's book *Violence: Reflections on a National Epidemic* (Gilligan, 1997). Gilligan traces violent crime to horrifically violent childhoods. Or to see further into the life of one such man, read Mikal Gilmore's account of his brother Gary Gilmore in Gilmore, *Shot in the Heart.*

8 That people of lower income and social status were not included certainly leads to an undercount of ACEs, since poverty and low social status are stress factors contributing the other ACEs.

medical conditions.[9] The study does not distinguish between ACEs in the first year or two of life and those occurring in our teens. It seems clear that the former would be immensely more traumatic and more difficult to remember.

Adverse experiences in childhood vary from the serious and obvious (like being beaten, raped, or humiliated by name-calling) to the more common (like parental divorce or an alcoholic parent), to the still common but less obvious (like being ignored or always interrupted or not listened to). And these shade off into the inevitable "threats and dangers" experienced by every infant.

Stephen Mitchell argues that these universal experiences of feeling helpless and abandoned are what underlie the centrality of *aggression* in human life and history. He asks, "How does the infant understand why" no one is answering its crying, or holding it when it feels threatened? Because someone *wants* the baby to suffer. Or, alternately, its suffering is required by reality, by the way the world just is. Either way, "the baby feels persecuted…because this is the natural way for him to construe his situation."[10] When things go badly for them, adults often ask "Why me?"—as if God or the fates had it in for us. Grownups may be able to find a more cogent explanation, but the baby cannot. As a result, infants develop some degree of resentment and an inchoate wish for revenge.[11]

This, then, is the position of the infant who has been overtaken by blind fury against the people it loves and on whom it is utterly

---

9 The study was carried out by the Centers For Disease Control. You can find it on line by searching for "ACE study. I am grateful to Betsy Langston for bringing this work to my attention.

10 Mitchell, *Hope And Dread In Pychoanalysis*, p 162.

11 Mitchell connects this resentment to the destructive aggression that flares up within families and between rival groups and nations. "… [T]he pursuit of revenge generated by a need to redress past insults or humiliations often propels people into situations that are physically very dangerous. Much of the political aggression and violence in the world today is connected with nationalistic and ethnic identifications that are rooted in a collective sense of endangerment and past humiliations." Ibid, p. 163.

dependent. The baby becomes terrified that the force of its rage has broken the bond with its parent(s). This terror remains with us for life. It is the original of every fear we have of what will happen if we lose control, if we become angry or reveal our transgressive feelings. We live in fear that our emotional ties will be severed, and we keep this fear at bay by punishing ourselves. Our enthusiastic self-loathing is intended to assure those against whom we have sinned that we are on their side. We crave punishment, and this is what guilt is all about.

If in a child's life, emotional ties were in fact broken—by the divorce of its parents, for example, it may come to see emotional ties themselves as dangerous and try to avoid them. The fear of losing contact becomes the fear of contact.

Guilt and Self-loathing

I am conscious of guilt when I find myself replaying my past crimes and misdemeanors.[12] But why must I revisit the painful past in this way? It's not simply that I want to learn from my mistakes; I bring up the past in order to excoriate myself with invective, with insults ("Boy, that was stupid!"). I need to be punished, and I can (and *must*) do it myself. This is the core of guilt: *the subjective need to be punished*. Sadistically (that is, with pleasure), I seize the chance to inflict pain by punishing my weaker self, the sniveling child who sinned against the big Other. I become the over-I, or superego:

> ...[T]he superego is [the big Other] in its vengeful, sadistic, punishing aspect....[S]uperego is real, the cruel and insatiable agency that bombards me with impossible demands and

---

12 For Freud, what we consciously feel about the bad things we have done is *remorse*, rather than guilt. Guilt is the unconscious conviction that we deserve to be punished. If it enters consciousness at all, it is "as a sort of malaise." Freud, *Civilization and Its Discontents, pp. 78 and 82.* But I will not insist on this distinction in the text.

then mocks my botched attempts to meet them, the agency in whose eyes I am all the more guilty, the more I try to suppress my 'sinful' strivings and meet its demands.[13]

Yes, but what was my sin? What did I do? Maybe it wasn't anything I actually did. When I was seven or eight, I often dreamed I had hidden the body of someone I had murdered and could hear the sirens of the police as they were coming to arrest me. I had done no such thing in reality, so why would I have this dream? For what crime was I punishing myself by having it?

The answer lies in what we just discussed: the rage that arises in the helpless baby in the Garden of Infantile Catastrophe. Furious in the way that a red-faced, screaming infant obviously is, we lashed out in hatred at the people who seemed to have forgotten us. In Stephen Mitchell's words,

> ...All of us experience enough danger and threat in childhood, regardless of the balance of health or pathology in our caregivers, to have experienced at least a fair amount of destructive aggression. It is *universal* to hate, contemplate revenge against, and want to destroy those very caregivers we also love.[14]

Our anger at the big Other, at the way things are, usually becomes more circumspect as we grow into responsible adults, though it flares up when we and people we care about are treated badly. But in our infantile souls, we feel that our rage has offended the big Other—the gods, God, and the order of things that sustains us, and so we step in to punish ourselves to set things right.

---

13 Žižek, *How to Read Lacan, p. 80.*
14 Mitchell, *Hope And Dread In Pychoanalysis*, p. 170 (emphasis added).

Guilt "is a way of controlling ourselves and other people."[15] We use guilt to try to keep ourselves and each other in line, conforming to the authority of the big Other. Notice how you feel when you become indignant—annoyed or angry—at someone doing what they shouldn't do, like playing loud music late at night or running a red light. Your tone of voice accuses or even condemns; it tries to call out the other's inner bully to do its job of punishing the other's inner child, to make it feel like the small child being thrown to the wolves.

(If you feel that my writing here is over-wrought and exaggerated, I put it to you that you are taking the adult perspective—understandably, since you are an adult—from which you cannot appreciate the enormity of these things as they look and feel to a child. Hyperbolic language aims to magnify these events so that they will look to us the size they really are to the child—and even to ourselves at the level of vitality that we hide by pretending to have "grown up".)

The superego is the bad cop alter-ego of the big Other. Its reality is "only" virtual, but knowing this does not reduce its power.[16] In some fleeting states of mind, its weight seems momentarily lifted—under the influence of marijuana, for example, as we see in this stoned entry from Mr. X's journal:

> *If one can slough off the overseer on the shoulder, that constant sense that there is exactly the right way to do whatever you're doing, then every* detail of the world around you changes—*loses its demands— making everything O.K.—just fine as it is.*

Much as we might like to believe otherwise, we cannot unilaterally "slough off the overseer" in our real relations with others. We can, at best, dream, and thus foresee, a world where that unnamed dread of failing the big Other has receded into a distant memory.

---

15 Phillips, *On Flirtation* p. 142.

16 Recall that virtual realities are social formations, like money and borders. They can be changed only as society changes.

In the meantime, though, the grounds for guilt are there for all of us. The big Other's norms and ideals, from the Ten Commandments to our local traffic laws and the promises we have made, demand more from us than our lives and bodies and souls can possibly manage. We know this even if we pretend otherwise—and we are, of course, under a lot of pressure to pretend otherwise. We pretend, in accordance with the big Other, to be willing and able to live up to its ideals, but of course we are only human, so we know we won't.[17] So we have reasons to feel guilty:

1. we cannot be what we are supposed to be,
2. we must *pretend* to be what we should be, and
3. we are angry about it.

When I speak authoritatively to myself, I also call into existence a *subjected* self, the child.[18] This creates two contrasting streams of vitality within me. One is the upsurge of domination or authority; the other is the shriveling sense of being a child or underling. The first (the inner bully) is dismissive, scornful, contemptuous. The other (the child) is resentful, victimized, oppressed, ashamed. It may also be apologetic, anxious to show contrition and willingness to do better. But this disempowering shame and resentment can provoke anger and aggression that leads me to take up the position of domination at the first opportunity. This aggression may be aimed at some other person or animal, or again at myself, thus repeating the cycle. My will to dominate, to be in charge, is a compensation for the powerlessness I feel when I am dominated by others or by my own inner bully.

---

17 Ernest Becker lays out the paradoxes of being a symbolic animal that must deny being animal in Becker, *The Denial of Death*.
18 This child is wonderfully portrayed in Charles Bukowski's poem "The Bluebird". See Appendix II.

Self-loathing is the punishment for our aggression against the big Other. The inner bully is bent on bringing me down in whatever way it (I) can devise, including disgust with my physical appearance and any failures and defects it can find or invent.

Using, abusing, and evading Guilt

Guilt is in the social air we breathe. It's always available to us as a way to get people, including ourselves, to do what we think they should, and to punish them when they don't. And it lies in wait on sleepless nights to bring back to our vivid imaginations a choice selection of things we wish we had done differently so we can be punished for them again and again. But the real crime for which we are being punished is our having wished, once upon a time, to destroy our parents.

We each have our own ways of handling the problem of guilt. Some of us do not do it well; they are afflicted with an active, persecuting guilty conscience (or over-I). Mr. X is one of these. So let's look at some of the different ways people handle guilt as well as at what can happen in childhood to increase the weight of guilt.

One common response to guilt is to put up with it. We are beset from time to time with fits of self-blame and self-abasement for something we did or failed to do. Or we lie awake at night reliving sins and errors of the past, punishing ourselves for them again. We reject any advice we get to let go of the past; to do so would be wrong, even dishonest. We do not deserve to live in peace.[19] The only thing we can imagine doing to lessen the guilt is to resolve to do better. However, even if we succeed in this, the existential guilt baked into our souls continues to look for excuses to blame and castigate us.

---

19 This attitude, projected outwards, can also be seen in those who complain about any improvement in the lives of prisoners: they deserve no release from our condemnation, which is signified by whatever degradation they must endure.

Another way of dealing with guilt is to become cynical. You distance yourself from the big Other, making use of it while denying that it has any authority over you. The norms of society and the mechanism of guilt are for other, fearful people. To be successful is to rise above the common herd and to manipulate the rules and feelings of others to make your own mark. It is natural to suspect that this is the philosophy of most people with wealth and power—that they serve their own interests first and claim to be serving the public only as a cover for their greed and drive for power. The character of Frank Underwood in the series "House of Cards" is a clear example.

The more radical path, though, is to pull (or at least dull) the teeth of the big Other, to rein in the superego, by connecting and cooperating with each other in voluntary associations held together through feelings of affection and mutual enjoyment. The voices and faces of these real other people in our lives can come to count more than the hectoring voice of the inner bully. The big Other may remain in the background, but it is no longer regarded with unquestioning respect and fear. What it would take to make this radical solution possible for most people, rather than just a very lucky few, will be discussed in the concluding chapter.

The Weight of Guilt

Probably most people, at least in our world, feel unconsciously guilty, but some feel it more than others. What would explain why some of us, more than others, are burdened by the feelings of worthlessness, failure, and incompetence with which we punish ourselves for the infantile rage we do not know we still feel? What would you look for in your past in order to understand the viciousness of your own inner bully?

Again, we can only point to a variety of factors that may be relevant. Our memories of our earliest days are nonexistent or incomplete, and what they might have meant to us lies beyond the reach of conscious thought in forms of vitality that are much too complex and subtle for language. We can ask ourselves, How much did I have to be angry about? How did my parents and other caretakers handle me? Perhaps I know something about what happened and how I reacted from what others tell me. I may be able to infer how my parents treated me from the way they now treat other children, or even from their attitudes towards me now. Like most infants, I was no doubt often furious at those I loved, and at some point turned that fury against myself— became guilty. But could I have been abused or neglected to the point that my ability to love at all was compromised? What impact would that have on my ability to feel guilty? Moreover, some children are quicker to anger than others, just as some are calm and others more excitable. It is enough to know that our self-loathing and guilt are our ongoing and understandable reactions to events and circumstances in early childhood. But these powerful feelings—or habits of vitality—are lies. We are not what our inner bullies say we are. We do not deserve to be punished.

Although guilt and self-loathing are born in the first years of our lives, they continue to be shaped, for better and worse, as we interact with each other symbolically—through language. The way parents and teachers talk to children has a profound emotional impact on them that adults often do not appreciate. It is by no means unusual for children to be told that they are stupid, clumsy, lazy, or careless. The tone of voice in which they are told to "clean up that mess," "wipe your nose," "finish your dinner," "hurry up" often conveys exasperation that can feel to children as if their parents would rather they didn't exist—unless they could somehow be somebody else. These slurs encourage the inner bully and provide it with additional ammunition for its attacks on the inner child. And so we begin to internalize a dark, judgmental side of the big Other and to grow an inner bully that exploits our vulnerability to guilt and self-loathing.

In the next chapter, we turn to the section of the Garden where we find ontological insecurity and anxiety—and more rage.

Appendix I: Adverse Childhood Experiences[20]

ACEs (adverse childhood experiences) come in three broad categories: Abuse, Neglect, and Household dysfunction.

1. Emotional abuse: did a parent or other adult in the household swear or insult you, or act in a way that you thought you might be hurt? Thirteen percent of women said yes, 10% of men.

2. Physical abuse: were you pushed, grabbed, slapped, or had something thrown at you? About 28% said yes.

3. Sexual abuse: Twenty four percent of women said yes, 16% of men.

4. Emotional neglect: did your family made you feel special and loved? Was your family a source of strength, livelihood, and protection? Sixteen percent of women and 12% of men said no.

5. Physical neglect: were there clean clothes, enough to eat, and medical care when you needed it? About 10% reported neglect of this kind.

There were five types of Household Dysfunction:

- Mother treated violently. Twelve percent said yes.
- Substance abuse: Was an adult in the family an alcoholic or problem drinker, or user of street drugs? About 27% said yes.
- Household mental illness: Was anyone in the family depressed, mentally ill, or did someone attempt suicide? Twenty-three percent of women said yes, but only 15% of men.[21]
- Parental separation or divorce: Twenty-three percent said yes.
- Incarcerated family member: Almost 5% said yes.

---

20 See above, note 9.

21 Perhaps women on average are more willing to recognize these conditions in their families—or to admit them.

Appendix II: the bluebird

the bluebird, by Charles Bukowski [22]

there's a bluebird in my heart that
wants to get out
but I'm too tough for him,
I say, stay in there, I'm not going
to let anybody see
you.

there's a bluebird in my heart that
wants to get out
but I pour whiskey on him and inhale
cigarette smoke
and the whores and the bartenders
and the grocery clerks
never know that
he's
in there.

...

there's a bluebird in my heart that
wants to get out
but I'm too clever, I only let him out
at night sometimes
when everybody's asleep.
I say, I know that you're there,
so don't be
sad.

then I put him back,
but he's singing a little
in there, I haven't quite let him
die
and we sleep together like
that
with our
secret pact
and it's nice enough to
make a man
weep, but I don't
weep, do
you?

---

22 Bukowski, *Run With the Hunted,* pp. 496-97.

17

Ontological Insecurity, Anger, and Anxiety

Introduction

WE NOW TAKE up the remaining demonic forms of vitality we have named—ontological insecurity, anger, and anxiety. Although anger (or rage) played a major role in the last chapter as the cause of guilt and self-loathing, we will visit it again since it is at the root of all our inner demons.

Ontological Insecurity

X's main complaint was that he felt "emotionally certain" that he did not exist, that the face he presented to other people was like a badly done counterfeit bill—easily detected and quickly rejected. Anyone could see that he was really nothing but the miserable child his inner bully insisted he was.

A first attempt to understand this feeling of being unreal is to link it to the guilt and self-loathing we discussed in the last chapter. X punishes himself with accusations of incompetence—"You're no good at doing anything well, so of course you don't pull off the act of performing the role of "X". Everyone can see you're nothing but a sniveling little boy! There is no X: X does not exist."

But this explanation assumes there is nothing for X to be but "X": that whatever it is that performs the role of X is in itself nothing, and that the only way X can have the sense of existing, of being ontologically secure, is to perform the act of being X competently. In other words, whether you become secure or insecure in your existence depends on how well you learn to act your social role, on how well you answer the call of the Symbolic and enter the social-discursive language game. But isn't it crazy to suppose that we can feel sure that we *really* exist by learning to play a role, in essence, to *fake* our identity?

We know now, from our reading of Stern in particular, that much of who we are, the forms of our vitality are shaped in the months of social interaction before we start learning to construct ourselves with names and pronouns and social roles. Couldn't it be there, in the realm of vitality, that we first achieve—or fail to achieve—a sense of being real that is prior to the social roles we learn to perform?

R.D. Laing[1], who first coined the term "ontological insecurity," describes this condition in ways that make it clear we are dealing with something felt very deeply—in, so to speak, our "vital" organs. First, the ontologically *secure* person

> ...may have a sense of his presence in the world as a real, alive, whole, and, in a temporal sense, a continuous person. As such, he can live out into the world and meet others: a world and others experienced as equally real, alive, whole, and continuous.
>
> Such a basically ontologically secure person will encounter all the hazards of life, social, ethical, spiritual, biological, from a centrally firm sense of his own and other people's reality and identity (39).

---

1 Laing, *The Divided Self,* cited in the text by page numbers in this chapter.

The ontologically *insecure* person, by contrast,

> ...may feel more unreal than real; in a literal sense, more dead than alive; precariously differentiated from the rest of the world, so that his identity and autonomy are always in question. ...[T]he ordinary circumstances of everyday life constitute a continual and deadly threat (p. 42).
>
> The [ontologically insecure] individual experiences himself as a man who is only saving himself from drowning by the most constant, strenuous, desperate activity (p. 44).

We feel ontologically insecure when we can't believe that we are really who we say we are and suspect that no one else really believes it either. But our security or insecurity goes back to our forgotten lives as babies; it was as babies, long before we began to put on a social mask, that we first developed, or failed to develop, a secure sense of existing.

> ...within an amazingly short time the infant *feels* real and alive and has a sense of being an entity, with continuity in time and a location in space. In short, physical birth and biological aliveness are followed by the baby becoming existentially born as real and alive (p. 41).

Unless, of course, the birth is followed by cruelty and indifference. Laing quotes a psychiatric patient who said in treatment,

> Everyone should be able to look back in their memory and be sure he had a mother who loved him, all of him; even his piss and shit. He should be sure his mother loved him just for being himself; not for what he could do. Otherwise he feels he has no right to exist. He feels he should never have been born (p. 172).

In chapters 9 and 12 of this book, we have seen how this kind of unconditional love may be established—but *also* many ways it can be poisoned—in the play, or clash, of vitality between mother and infant.

So although as adults, we blame our ontological insecurity on our failure to perform our social role, this insecurity begins in the thwarting of our early impulses to connect directly with others through the interchange of vitality. This may happen because the people caring for us were unresponsive or hostile to our cries for attention and our efforts to be playful. If this alone were not enough to lower our confidence about whether we are welcome in the world, the rage and guilt we discussed in the last chapter also play a role. Frightened of our own destructive feelings towards those we depend on, we shut down all our stronger feelings towards others.

When this early, vital sense of existing-and-belonging is missing, the only way to live in the social world that soon impinges on us is by putting on the social performances demanded by that world. So we fashion a defensive social identity. We grow up taking the demands of every social scenario with deadly seriousness.[2] We will lack the confidence to let our masks bend and shift, guided by the shifting currents of vitality underlying every social situation. The deeply secure person, on the other hand, can treat the big Other with a little distance, skepticism, and even humor. Being less bonded to a social identity, he or she is not desperate to defend it and so is not afraid of being exposed as a fake.

---

2 It seems probable that many people lack the sense of their secure existence at the level of vitality, yet understand in the symbolic dimension that they have the moral and legal *right* to exist. Their emotionally felt ontological insecurity makes them especially jealous of their rights, which forces them to take the Symbolic with deadly seriousness—as if their lives depended on it.

Anger and Aggression

Ontological insecurity, like guilt and self-loathing, are *inner* demons: creatures of the night that hide from the light of day. They attack us in the awful privacy of our own minds, rather than exploding and getting us into trouble in public places. In turning now to aggression, we are dealing with more than a feeling, but a way of acting. Aggression is hostile and destructive action; we pick out its subjective side by referring to *anger* or *rage*.

We first need to distinguish aggression from assertiveness. Stephen Mitchell describes assertiveness as arising from a joyful sense of living and engagement;[3] it's the affirmation of oneself and one's *vitality* in a conversation or other social situation. Sometimes we assert ourselves with hostile intent, but one can be assertive without hard feelings. Aggression, on the other hand, is essentially hostile and destructive; it arises from a desire to retaliate against someone or some situation one perceives as threatening.

Another useful distinction is between *core* emotions and *inhibitory* emotions. Core emotions push us out into the world to engage with others. These are anger, joy and sadness, which when *fully experienced* "lead to a sense of relief and clarity (even if they are initially unpleasant)." Inhibitory emotions include shame, guilt, and anxiety, as well as self-loathing and ontological insecurity. They inhibit the core emotions from being fully experienced, as when we are angry with someone but pretend, even to ourselves, that we are not.[4] Inhibited anger is still anger and it has real effects, including the anxiety that comes with the frequent failure of one's strenuous efforts to hold it in. This book has been somewhat inhibited in its focus on the inner struggles of inhibited people.

Some anger is probably an inevitable fact of life—a way of managing or adjusting our relations with others. A reasonable display

---

3 Mitchell, *Hope And Dread In Pychoanalysis*, p. 159.
4 Hendel, 2015.

of anger lets others know our limits. Aristotle remarks that even a gentle person is one who is angry sometimes but "only under such circumstances and for as long a time as reason may bid." A person who was never angry "at things that ought to arouse anger"—at character smears or insults to "those near and dear to him"—is rightly regarded as "servile."[5] When someone is justifiably, or at least excusably, angry, we say he or she is indignant, annoyed, or irritated. But anger that goes too far we may call "rage," implying that the angry person has lost control.

We all know people who become angry quite easily with very little provocation, at very small frustrations. This is reactive anger. We also know people who seem to have an established attitude or policy of aggressiveness. Without apparent provocation, they act destructively and with hostility towards others. They are not merely reactively aggressive, but proactively so—picking fights, bullying, insulting, fault-finding, and undermining others, often with an innocent air as if they were being entirely reasonable. In contrast with the reasonable anger described by Aristotle, we might call this *surplus* anger—anger in excess of what is needed to make a point or to warn others that they are crossing a line.

Where does this overflow of anger beyond necessity come from? In the last chapter, we saw that virtually every childhood has at least some, and often many, traumatic moments when the vital connections that support life seem, from the child's tiny perspective, lost. And the infant, lost in the dark and cut off from a grasp of the larger world, may well seethe with uncontrollable rage. This desperate anger is not sharply focused on one or two individuals, but boils over on to everything that is beyond the baby's control, to the way things are, to the big Other. We are thus left with an insatiable wish for what we suppose is lacking: power and recognition. Of course what we really want is love.

---

5 Aristotle, *Nicomachean Ethics*, Book IV, Chapter 5.

We can now understand the rage, the surplus anger, that riles up so many people, whether reactively or proactively. They are driven to seize power and command attention; they seek revenge for the feeling of powerlessness that eats away at their fragile sense of self-respect and surges up whenever they feel unrecognized or disrespected.

As we grow older, this pent up and nameless rage may cool as we learn our way around in the larger world and develop into more or less competent and respected persons. Nevertheless, in many of us, enough of this general resentment remains that many of the minor injustices and slights that come our way are interpreted as assaults on our dignity that require sharp retaliation. Those whose sense of powerlessness and abandonment continues to fuel their rage against the world may well embark on a permanent campaign of retribution against whatever sufficiently helpless targets they come across— small animals and children, subordinates, women, racial and ethnic others.

Letting Off Steam

Since we all have some rage, or at least resentment, against the way things are—against the big Other—transgression is inevitable. There need to be ways to vent. We have seen (in Chapter 10) that transgression is sometimes more or less condoned in certain locations or within certain circles of people. What many men say in the locker room or a barroom is not what they are comfortable saying in front of their children or their mothers. We can enact aggression vicariously, that is, in fantasy, by identifying with violent heroes or anti-heroes in movies or TV shows or novels. We can identify with athletes in violent sports like football and boxing. We can engage in competitive activities including business, sports, and formal or informal debate where we try to destroy the position of our opponents. The great chess player Bobby Fisher once told an interviewer that his favorite thing about the game was that moment when you "destroy the other man's ego." Then there is the common behavior that verges on the illegal or immoral, such as speeding and running traffic lights, vandalism, or political corruption. In the American TV series "House of Cards," Frank Underwood is told at one point that what he is proposing is "just shy of treasonous." He replies, "Just shy. So it's politics."

But aggression short of brutality does not satisfy the urge among some of us to retaliate against "the way things are." In his book *Transgression*, Christopher Jenks remarks

> Transgression is part of the social process, it is also part of the individual psyche. ...Practically this may mean that a defining feature of late-modern society is that our actions are organized through a stern paradox. Namely that people (sometimes 'monsters' but more often people like ourselves) who feel trapped, threatened or violently constrained by *external forces* beyond their control seek excessive and transgressive experiences which in some cases are even more threatening to their survival and, tragically in many cases, threatening to the survival of innocents also.[6]

Those external forces are the way things are, but the way things are, refracted through an internal lens cracked and warped by the way things *were*.

---

6 Jenks, *Transgression*. Emphasis added.

Anxiety

Dilemma of civilized man, body mobilized, but danger obscure.

Philip K. Dick[7]

Some degree of anxiety comes with the uncertainties of life; in moderate doses, it sharpens and energizes us to deal with challenges like tests, performances, and heavy traffic. But just as there is surplus anger, there is also surplus anxiety. It can be a constant fearful tension ("free-floating anxiety"), relating to nothing in particular or to everything in general. And it can rise to a blind and desperate panic, again with no real object in view.

I said earlier that anxiety is an inhibitory emotion, unlike anger that engages us forcefully with others. But anxiety is like anger in being more directly felt in the body than the more hidden feelings of guilt, self-loathing, and ontological insecurity. This makes sense, since both anger and anxiety move us to act: we want to attack when angry, and to flee or hide when anxious. But the trouble with free-floating anxiety is that its object is hidden from us, leaving us unable to act. We don't know where to run or what to hide from. So, like guilt, it assaults us mostly within, resulting in a wide variety of nervous and evasive behavior.

X feels the need to be always busy, always occupied, and he often feels overwhelmed by the number and difficulty of the tasks he has set for himself. The advice we are often given when we worry too much is to ask ourselves "What's the worst that could happen?" The idea is that the real consequences of not getting everything done on time could never be bad enough to justify the anxiety you feel. This focus on ordinary reality may distract us momentarily from the

---

7 Dick, *The Man in the High Castle*, Ch. 10.

nameless dread we are feeling, and we might go on to realize that our anxiety is surplus—unnecessary for our real situation.

What we really fear, though, is some indescribable terror out of our childhood imaginations. Free-floating anxiety taps into those preverbal networks of vitality that got set up when we were very little, at those moments when it seemed we had been left to die alone in our cribs.

X's need to be busy and always occupied, the feeling that there is always more to do than time to do it in, plus the anxiety that comes with not feeling useful, stems from being told (as we noted in Chapter 10) when he was six or so, that since his parents' divorce, he was now the "man of the family." Of course at that age, he had no idea of how to help his mother through the difficulties she faced as a single parent. He had been assigned an impossible task, including the task of *believing* that he could do it. So it was his duty to keep his mind at work always. X's mother was often anxious about money. X daydreamed often about ways he could save the family by, for example, winning or somehow finding a million dollars.

The underlying object of our anxiety is not the worst thing that could realistically happen, but a *fantasy* of the worst thing: something too dreadful to be adequately named or conceived. This makes us powerless before it. The only way to alleviate the infantile feeling of imminent catastrophe is with a gesture, like a hug, or, better, a secure relationship or circle of relationships that can reassure the infant we still are. In a word, love.

Anxiety attaches itself to *all* the disturbances of the soul we have been discussing. They render us unintelligible, unable to make sense, to explain ourselves to others in language authorized by the big Other. Even if we recognize, as we often do not, that what is going on in us is anger or insecurity or guilt, we don't know why we are insecure or what we are angry or guilty about. Being unable to explain ourselves makes us feel crazy, and that is frightening because the big world of other people and institutions has no room for crazy people except in confinement. We can't help telling ourselves, in the voice of the inner bully, that the big world is *right* to revile us, so we live in fear of standing inescapably condemned in our own eyes. It is this fear that we are trying to alleviate in this book by giving ourselves a perspective from which we can see how this condemnation arises.

So the most pervasive source of anxiety is not so much not knowing who we are; it is *knowing* that we are not really who we are supposed to say we are.

Moreover, each of the other disturbances includes anxiety in its makeup. R.D. Laing lists three forms of anxiety that erupt from ontological insecurity (43-48).

1. Having an insecure sense of identity, the ontologically insecure person fears *engulfment*: being swallowed up in other people, losing one's autonomy.
2. Feeling empty, one fears that one's soul will be wholly occupied by alien forces—by more powerful people in one's life or by dominant institutions like one's job or some political cause. Laing calls this *implosion*.
3. *Petrification*, or *depersonalization*. Not having a secure sense of oneself, one can fear being turned into a thing, an object. This is not an unrealistic fear in a highly commodified and bureaucratized social order where every thing we do and produce, every skill, talent, and activity has a price, and everyone can be located and tracked in social and physical space by commercial and government servers. A great many of us have a part in running this system; as a cop, landlord, teacher, or social worker, we are required to enforce rules that can throw people into the streets or into prison regardless of our sympathies. Because it is easier to deal with others as if they had no feelings, depersonalization becomes a universal social obligation that cuts against our capacity to care and be cared

for. Even most therapists must turn you away if you can't pay. Depersonalization is the normal way to treat people outside the circle of family and friends, and even for the latter, career and financial exigencies often prevail over caring for those close to us.[8]

It's easy to see why rage can provoke anxiety. Even ordinary, justifiable anger is confrontational and risks endangering our relationships with others. Arguments can spin out of control and lead us to do things we will regret and feel guilty for. If we become angry, for example, at someone who has insulted us, and then add to it our stored up resentment at the world that we feel has mistreated us since infancy, we become *enraged*. The consequence is that we not only make the immediate situation worse, but we reveal ourselves, to ourselves and to others, as irrational and irresponsible. When the anger cools, we will have to face punishment from the inner bully and the anxiety that arises, as we will see shortly, from guilt.

The Anxiety of Guilt and Self-Loathing

How can guilt provoke anxiety when guilt is about the past and anxiety is about the (unknown) future? The answer is that guilt is about something we have hidden out of fear of being caught, found out, exposed, and punished. Our anxiety is our fear of standing naked with our sins before the world, but even worse, to be punished by our own inner bully, the superego. We are concerned about the judgment of others insofar as it may lead them to treat us poorly, but what really matters is that their judgment makes it much more difficult to evade our own self-punishment by the inner bully. So we hide our guilt, from ourselves and from others, in order to silence, or at least muffle, the tongue-lashings from the bullying superego.

---

8 Magda Szabó's novel *The Door* is a powerful illustration of this.

But it is not easy to hide our sins;[9] we have a strong urge to confess. If I feel guilty about something that I have kept secret from others, it is natural to feel a lot of anxiety about others finding out and treating me with the contempt and rejection I already think I deserve (that's the inner bully talking). And what if I have kept my guilt a secret from *myself*? That is, I have not allowed myself to admit the enormity of what I have done. I give myself all kinds of justifications and excuses for it, and minimize the harm that was done, and I do my best to keep my mind busy with work or intense entertainment, and I quiet my searching mind with drugs and alcohol. To avoid the condemnation I will inflict upon myself if I face up to the full meaning and consequences of my sin, I work hard at shutting up about it. Surplus anxiety is the fear of the self-consciousness that keeps threatening to make us look.

Why is it so hard *not* to confess? First, we want to see ourselves as honest and responsible members of our social world, and that requires admitting and, as far as possible, making up for whatever sins we have committed. Even though it is more honored in the breech than in the observance, honesty is a fundamental principle of social life, a central norm of the big Other. So our urge to respect ourselves as responsible persons puts pressure on us to confess our sins.[10]

The darker motive that might drive us to own up to our moral failures is the demonic wish to punish ourselves. This is what the over-I lives for. Indeed, some of us are inclined to exaggerate our own faults and failings, and to ignore reasonable justifications and

---

9 As with the word 'soul', I use 'sin' with no theological implications. We use the word 'sin' to indicate things we have done for which we feel, or think we should feel, guilty.

10 Recall how much Jim needed to confess to Marlow in Lord Jim. The fourth and fifth steps of Twelve Step Programs for alcoholics and drug users are "Made a searching and fearless moral inventory of ourselves" and "Admitted to God, to ourselves, and to another human being the exact nature of our wrongs." *The Big Book of AA* makes it quite clear that unconfessed guilt can drive us to drink.

mitigating circumstances. Why would this be? Perhaps we feel like K. in Kafka's *The Trial:* we are guilty of something, but the crime we are accused of has been kept secret from us. Now where would we get such an idea? By now it should be clear: once upon a time, we wanted to destroy our parents who loved us and whose love we depended upon. But all that happened beyond the reach of adult memory and is utterly contrary to what we now think we believe about ourselves. And still we punish ourselves for it.

So we lie awake at night searching through our past for crimes and misdemeanors to admonish ourselves for, seizing on every little failure with accusations of incompetence and stupidity. This is why some of us have so much more anxiety than is necessary when we face the large and small challenges of life.[11]

We all wear a cloak of fiction to cover our shamefully naked bodies, so we live in fear of the child or the bully who will point out that our clothes are unreal and we are naked. Or could it be that we wish someone would see us as we are and love us anyway? Maybe that is why we dreamed as children that we went to school with no pants on.

Do we have the right to dream instead of a world where we would have no reason to fear exposure, where we could trust each other with our ordinary (and even extraordinary) human failings?

Appendix: The Fear of Death

There is a kind of anxiety that deserves special attention: the fear of death. There are, of course, many ordinary reasons I have for not wanting to die: unfinished projects (like this book), my family's need for my support, curiosity about what will

---

11 This sense of guilt can be momentarily relieved by vicariously identifying with and condemning other people who have done terrible things, in movies or novels or stories of criminals. These stories give us targets at which we can direct our moral condemnation, *and* the comforting feeling that we are not alone in our guilt.

happen next in the world—or just the pleasure I take in daily life. But sometimes the fear of death can strike such terror into our hearts that we desperately push the thought of it away. This is a surplus, or obsessive, fear of death. One reason for believing that the soul survives death is to allay this fear.

The fear of death becomes conscious, often at an early age, when we realize that our own lives will end while the world goes on without us. We imagine ourselves enduring an infinite time in the dark with no connection to the world and to other people. Poet Philip Larkin says that death is

> ...the total emptiness forever,
> The sure extinction that we travel to
> And shall be lost in always.[12]

Now it might seem that this idea of death could be dispelled by pointing out that we simply do not exist after we die, so there *is* no "we" to be "lost in" "the total emptiness forever." I will no more exist after my death than a candle flame somehow goes on existing after being blown out. There is no time for me beyond the time of my life.

Our own immortality is a natural illusion, rather like the illusion that all our experience is conscious that we discussed earlier. It is impossible for me to imagine my own death because when I try to imagine myself dead, I implicitly imagine myself there to imagine it. Margaret Atwood puts it this way: "...[T]he reason you can't really imagine yourself being dead [is] that as soon as you say, 'I'll be dead,' you've said the word 'I', and so you're still alive inside the sentence. And that's how people got the idea of the immortality of the soul - it was a consequence of grammar."[13]

We can also question whether immortality is even something to be desired. Wittgenstein points out that the belief in the immortality of the soul "will not do for us what we always tried to make it do. Is a riddle solved by the fact that I survive

---

12 "Aubade," Larkin, *Collected Poems*, p. 208.
13 Atwood, *The Year of the Flood*.

forever? Is this eternal life not as enigmatic as our present one? The solution of the riddle of life in space and time lies *outside* space and time."[14]

But while all this reasoning might make us feel that we *shouldn't* feel anxious about death, the fear keeps creeping back. And this suggests that what we really fear is something else, something we came to fear before we had any thoughts about death. There are two things death means at the level of vitality.

First, death in the infantile mind is isolation and abandonment—just what a baby feels, according to Winnicott, when left alone too long.

"Nothing to think with, / Nothing to *link* with" is what Larkin's poem says we fear.[15] Feeling unlinked, alone, or alienated is part of ontological insecurity: the feeling of being dead in the midst of life. It stems from the absence of vital connections in infancy. It is also a natural response of our souls to a social world in which each individual is supposed to depend only on him or herself for survival in competition with everyone else, a society whose attitude towards those who fail is scorn and indifference.

If we are not adequately created, if we do not feel our existence in our vitality, we are left on our own to create ourselves out of the resources of the Symbolic. So we adopt a persona, put on an act, and hope to make a mark in the world that will garner the world's recognition. But this is a project that often fails, and so we are beset with anxiety—especially about death since it would mean the end of our efforts to promote our existence.

We are not merely afraid of isolation and abandonment: we are enraged by the very fact that we must fear them. We *resent* being left to create ourselves by ourselves. This resentment merges with the anger and hatred we felt as infants when we seemed to be left to eternal loneliness in our cribs. But this resentment

---

14 Wittgenstein, *Tractatus Logico-Philosophicus* §6.4312. James Carse claims that
> If the future is opened indefinitely, the pressure is taken off the present. There is nothing that cannot wait.... What does it matter how the first several acts of the drama develop when there is an endless number to come?... Life would have no risk, nothing would be at stake....It is even quite likely that the personality itself would vanish into the vacuum, since its temporal structures would have become meaningless. A person's character is shaped by tragedy, suspense, hope, regret...—but in an indefinite existence all this would be meaningless. Carse, *Death and Existence*, cited in Loy, *Lack and Transcendence*, p. 40.

15 My emphasis.

and rage are terrifying because they threaten to destroy our ties to those who love and care for us. So this imposes on us, in addition to the task of self-creation, a second life-long and impossible project, which is to expiate our guilt, to atone for our original sin of wanting to destroy what we also love. That life comes to an end means we will never have atoned for the original sin of hating our parents for (what felt at the time like) their cruelty and neglect. We will die guilty: end of story. Facing up to death forces us to see that, for many of us, our lives are devoted to the impossible project of redemption, of expiating our guilt. We fear and deny death because it means our lives, so defined, must end in failure.

The best assurance that we exist is to feel *connected*, to be around those we can love and who love us. Being part of a community is also redemptive, for it provides the opportunity to replace, or at least overlay, our hostility to the world with active cooperation. More on this in the next and final chapter.

18

Love: Limits and Obstacles

What Have We Done?

WHERE DOES ALL this thinking about our souls leave us? What can we
do with it? In this final chapter, I'd like to reflect on where we are
with respect to our inner demons and what stands in the way of their
exorcism.

The central trouble for the troubled minds we have been working with is the bewilderment and helplessness we feel about our
guilt, self-loathing, insecurity, anxiety, and rage. We feel accused;
but who is accusing us? Sometime we find ourselves berating ourselves in what we take to be our own voice. Why do we do this? And
sometimes we identify with the accused: who, then, is the accuser?
And what exactly is it that we are being accused of? Why don't I
know? Similarly, what am I angry about? What am I afraid of? How
can I not know? Why is it not obvious to me that I exist and have a
place in the world?

Let's review some of the ground we have covered.

1. We have seen that we are embedded in the social world; we
   are deeply social beings. We enact our lives in a multitude

of relationships; everything we do involves others, directly or indirectly. We can also say that the social world is deeply embedded in each of us—in our language and our basic feelings about our place in the world.

2. It is fundamental to our souls that we are self-conscious. We can monitor, advise, reflect upon, and criticize ourselves. We can do this because language enables us speak to ourselves from another's perspective.

3. Nevertheless, we find the social order inside us and surrounding us a source of painful conflict. We are unable to live up to what the world seems to demand of us, including the demand that we should have a clear idea of why we do and say and feel what we do. In spite of this demand, we find that our understanding of our own souls is confused and fragmented; we are not transparent to ourselves.

4. Why do we take society's demands so seriously? How do they get under our skin? As we move out into the world where we must perform for those who don't love us as our mothers once did, we form and internalize a general conception of the world's demands—what we have called "the big Other." So these demands do not appear to us to come from outside; they have become part of our souls. Society is not just an external force.

5. The big Other is a *virtual* reality, just as money and borders are virtually real. We treat them as if they were as real as the stars, mountains and rivers even though they have no existence beyond our social practices.

6. The big Other's demands—which we can also call "the Symbolic"—do not exist within us like a book of rules. They have been absorbed into something much bigger and less articulate, namely the *vitality* of our bodies. Social categories shape our "gut reactions".

7. Our vitality was also shaped—contorted and bruised—by the ways we were handled and mishandled in early childhood. Our souls were sculpted from the inside by the way those closest to us matched and mismatched our vitality in social interactions before we acquired language, forming deeply entrenched habits of vitality. Traumatic events in later life can shape and reshape our vitality.

8. Self-consciousness begins when we enter the realm of the Symbolic. What we *say* about our experience becomes more important and valuable than the *living* of experience. So it is no wonder that we are only barely conscious of that vast organic realm of vitality that drives our emotional reactions, our basic attitudes, and our immediate takes on things.

9. Grounded in the inaccessible past are our fundamental attitudes about ourselves—whether we are lovable, competent, or worth anyone's attention. The big Other's impossible demands, as well as the injuries we suffered in the Garden of Infantile Catastrophe, make us angry—to the point, often, of blind rage against whatever target we can hit. One such target is ourselves as we enact a drama in which we play both parts: the bully punishing the child.

10. The history of our inner demons begins with infantile rage directed at those who care for us, and more generally, against the way things are. Fearing that this rage means we *deserve* to lose the recognition and love we need, we try to make amends by punishing ourselves. This need to punish ourselves is guilt, and the punishment takes the forms of self-loathing and ontological insecurity. Anxiety is the fear that the evil in our hearts and in our pasts will be exposed and we will no longer be able to pretend that we have any right to exist.

I hope that this story, painful as it seems, makes our souls and their demons less frighteningly mysterious. It does not turn on all the lights and make the soul transparent, but it does give us a rough idea of how our souls come to be in their present state—not from some original and continuing sin of our own, but as the result of quite understandable events that could, and do, happen to most of us to a greater or lesser extent.

Learning to picture ourselves as infants, as we did in Chapters 12 and 14, might give us a greater sense of continuity with the period of our lives that lies beyond the reach of conscious memory. It can help us to identify and sympathize with the infant we once were as well as the infant we still are below the thin level of consciousness. If we could appreciate the richness and complexity of every moment and every facet of our experience, how far it overflows the boundaries of language, and how much more there is to what we take in with our senses and in our bodies than we can name, then it might then be more natural and easy for us to enjoy the richness of sounds, colors, smells, and tastes—and the play of our vitality—without so much distraction from the labor of accounting for it all. The arts, including poetry with its allusive resources like metaphor, offer ways of responding to and sharing our experiences beyond the limits of the ordinary utilitarian language we use for getting things done.

Compassionate Reflection

We have been engaged in an exercise in self-reflection. I have asked you to join me in thinking about our souls and our lives, about how we feel, think, act and react. When we do this in a systematic way, we create for ourselves a new point of view. We build, as it were, a viewing platform outside ourselves from which to consider ourselves, and the one who is on that platform is, in an important sense, not the same person as the one who is being viewed. Instead of being simply immersed in our subjective world of feelings and attitudes, we now take that subjective world as the object of our thought. We get some distance from the torrent of feelings and can begin to see where they come from and where they are going. Instead of merely being angry or disgusted with ourselves, we can, try to see our anger or disgust as forms of vitality that respond to much more than what is going on in the moment. What we are feeling are currents of vitality that were set in motion in our infantile souls by events beyond memory. Our emotional repertoire—or more deeply, our habits of vitality—were shaped by events in the first, forgotten months of life. Moreover, events we do remember may well have left us with emotional disabilities we cannot see clearly. For example, you might remember much of what happened when your parents broke up when you were five or six, but never have wondered what that meant for your ability to love and trust people close to you. The stream of your vitality was roiled, but outside the scope of your conscious attention.

By trying to step out of the stream of immediate and subjective reactions, we are moving to a more "objective" view. But this is not to take up a "clinical" or "objectivist" position that reduces our souls to computable systems of definable physical (or mental) processes. The souls we are talking about are not, in the clinical sense, "subjects" or "patients" with "presenting symptoms." That kind of language puts too much distance between the "clinician" and the "subject", like the distance between, say, an entomologist and the insects he or she studies. The people we are talking about, troubled souls like X, *are us.* Let us consider them with compassion, understanding that we and they are all in the same boat, that their troubles are ours as well. Compassionate self-reflection can give us a position from which we can be someone other than the one who is caught up in demonic vitality habits of guilt, self-loathing and the rest of them. This alone helps us to feel less helpless against them. And the more we take that position from which we see ourselves with compassion, the less cause there is for guilt and self-loathing.

Mercy

We are all in the same boat, but it is a haphazardly jerry-built boat vulnerable to storms and currents we don't control. Among the things we share are the needs for love and solidarity—and for mercy. We are all wounded survivors of the Garden of Infantile Catastrophe; we are under siege from the impossible demands of the big Other and suffering from the insults of our inner bullies. If we understand this, then surely we should be merciful towards ourselves and each other. My own experience has been that the more I live with this picture of all human beings as damaged survivors of the traumas of childhood, the more I am able to override the scorn and contempt my inner bully would like to direct at people, including me, who do stupid or terrible things. This is not to say that judging what people do as evil or criminal is never justified and so every crime must simply be forgiven and forgotten. But it is to say that vindictive punishment aimed at individuals fails to understand that people who damage us are themselves part of the collateral damage that comes with human life, at least in the world as it is now. Vengeance against those who have harmed us does none of us any good; it only fuels the careening juggernaut of human catastrophe that is our history. We should now be able to recognize that the drive for vengeance is born of our own desire for an acceptable target of the cruelty we have accumulated in our own souls. It is also a way to stand with the big Other by enjoying the suffering of those who disobey it.

It's easy enough to see the values of mercy and compassion when we think about them in the abstract as we have just been doing, but not so easy to consistently *be* merciful and compassionate when we are in the throes of fear and anger at some dumb or awful thing someone (ourselves or someone else) has done, especially when we also have to contend with the daily problems of survival and self-defense in what is often a dog-eat-dog world.

Is there another way of being we could steer towards, a way of life with more backing for mercy and compassion?

How About Love?

Popular music, over and over, offers us *love*. We all know songs affirming that love is the answer, that all our problems could disappear if we could all just love more. In the 1960s, it seemed possible to believe the songs that urged us to love one another. Nothing, it seemed, stood between us and universal peace but making the simple resolution to love. The thought still beguiles us.

Our endless appetite for songs about love suggests that love may be our greatest lack in life. We seem to feel that if only our lives were filled with love, we would be happy. Perhaps the inner demons we have been thinking about all result from our incapacity to love and be loved. We see our failure to love in the stress and strain and breakups of our intimate relationships with our partners, children and parents, and in the cruelty and indifference demonstrated in war, oppression, and exploitation. There are at least as many songs (not to mention novels and movies) about love gone bad as there are about the excitement and promise of new love. Moreover, our capacity to love gasps for air in the kind of social order we live in. "In a society where competition for the basic cultural goods is a pivot of action people cannot be taught to love one another, for those who do cannot compete with one another except in play."[1] In our world, the "basic cultural good" and "pivot of action" is money.

Nevertheless, as W.H. Auden wrote in1939 as the catastrophe of war loomed in Europe, "We must love one another or die." This ultimatum applies not only to nations, but to all of us, unable to fully live because unable fully to love.

But is it really possible to turn our lives around in the direction of love? A brand of herbal tea furnishes each bag with a tag inscribed with an uplifting maxim, one of which is "Love is a source of bliss and infinity." What are we supposed to do with such advice? How available is love? We are too often invited to assume that we can

---

1 Henry, *Culture Against Man*, p. 295.

turn it on at will—just "love everyone starting now!" Anyone who has suffered through the end of a marriage, for example, knows it's not that easy.

So what kind of love could save us, and what stands in its way?

Most of us are not strangers to love. For at least the first year or two of our lives, most (but *not* all) of us were loved and held by our parents. Our experience of them and the world around us was still unmarked by the Symbolic. Our world was globally, amodally, and dynamically whole, not divided up by the imperatives of language into utilitarian categories. The child was in love with *living*, with simply *being*. Living and loving were one.

The infant carries on a "love affair with the world",[2] and it is not difficult to see this love alive in children, from the infant falling blissfully asleep at the breast described by Freud,[3] to the giddy play of children that goes on in a different universe from our own, one unmarked by time intervals.

> The days of the child seem to unfold in some sense outside of our time. These days of childhood—let each recall them— seem to the child as if they were eternal.... Of course the important persons who bring up the child strictly impose the scheme of their time on him... but he feels the imposition of adult time by adults as an alien intrusion into his own time, which is essentially in some sense infinite.[4]

---

2 According to Margaret Mahler, cited in Benjamin, Jessica, "Recognition and Destruction: An Outline of Intersubjectivity."

3 "No one who has seen a baby sinking back satiated from the breast and falling asleep with flushed cheeks and a blissful smile can escape the reflection that this picture persists as a prototype of the expression of sexual satisfaction in later life" Freud, *Three Essays on the Theory of Sexuality,* p. 48. Freud says "sexual satisfaction"; I say satisfaction, period.

4 Marie Bonaparte, *Chronos, Eros, Thanatos,* quoted in Brown, *Life Against Death,* p. 94.

The days of the child get structured as we are inducted into the regulated, measured ways of acting, seeing, thinking, and feeling that make us intelligible and manageable. We are sworn to a common fealty to the big Other, enforced by the over-I that addresses us as delinquent children.

Moreover, even in the midst of our love affair with the world, there are the minor and major injuries that afflict every child in different ways—from the infant's terrors of being left alone too long in the dark to being physically and/or emotionally abused or neglected. All this sets up at least some degree of unconscious resentment of the way things are (the big Other), and often a seething undertow of rage that gets its release in cruelty directed at those weaker than ourselves—including that inner child (Bukowski's "bluebird"[5]) we also feel ourselves to be.

Love is blocked by both these factors—being dragged out of our sensuous immersion in the world to take up our posts as responsible, recognizable persons; and the mistrust that comes from the failure—in our infantile eyes—of the grownups to keep us safe from the terrors of childhood. We are also made mistrustful by the adult responsibility of enforcing the rules of the symbolic on others. Just as police and prison guards adopt distrust as a basic approach to their jobs, so to the extent that we identify with the big Other, we all become wary and suspicious of each other.

"All Who Live Need Help From All the Rest"[6]

There is also a larger dimension that makes love difficult for us. We live in a world order that systematically blocks and constrains our ability to love. It is said that the more you freely give your love away,

---

5 See Chapter 16, Appendix 2
6 Bertholt Brecht, "Of the infanticide Marie Farrar" [*Von der Kindesmörderin Marie Farrar*] (1920) from *Devotions* (1922-1927); trans. Sidney H. Bremer in *Poems, 1913-1956*, p. 92

the more of it you have: the more you actively love, the more loving you become and the more love you will receive. But with money and what it buys, the opposite is true: We give up our money only in exchange for something of equal or greater value. Money is the key to every thing, a necessary (though far from sufficient) condition for meeting all our needs and desires. Unless one is born wealthy, money is acquired either by manipulating others into turning over to us as much of it as possible in exchange for as little as possible; or by selling our life energy by the hour or the week or the year to an employer in exchange for the money we need to sustain ourselves and our families. In this zero-sum game, my interests are always contrary to yours, and each of us must put our own ahead of others'. Having no other way to live and be recognized than to play this game, we now live in "a voracious, atomized, polarized, turbulent, often violent culture, one that insists each of us be in competition with every other" (Doug Henwood).[7] It is a culture that "has too often taught us to see ourselves as little more than singular, gratification-seeking units, out to maximize our narrow advantage... "(Naomi Klein).[8]

If we dream, as I believe we do, of a world we could love again as we did (at least some of the time) as children, then we are dreaming of a world that runs on love and is not regulated by money.

Getting what we desire always depends, directly or indirectly, on the cooperation of many other people. What brings about that cooperation? Outside the circle of family and good friends, it is the exchange of money. The many long trains of cooperation that bring food to our tables, clothing to our bodies, roofs over our heads, and music to our ears are *metered* by the circulation of money, money we receive on the dicey condition that the managers of capital can profit from our labor. Those with little or no money go hungry, cold and homeless—or as is the case for half of the population of the

---

7 Henwood, *Wall Street.*
8 Klein, *This Changes Everything.*

US,[9] they are one paycheck away from losing their housing, which means living under the constant threat of destitution while always aware that there are some whose desires can run to the ends of the earth because they have unlimited access to money. Can we conceive of a world that fulfilled the dream of childhood, a world in which no one had to live with the ontological insecurity that comes from the knowledge that one's existence depends on maintaining the always tenuous hold on money?

I said this would be a world that ran on love. What does that mean? Consider the possibility that the desire to help people do what they are doing, whether it's opening a door for someone laden with packages or finding homes for refugees of war, something in us wants to be of use, to facilitate the activities of others. A personal example: sitting at a counter facing a window near the door of a coffee shop, I saw a man pushing a hand truck loaded with boxes approaching the door. As he struggled to get the door open, I felt myself moved towards getting up to help, but as I hesitated, he managed to get through the door on his own. He went back for another load, and this time, I allowed my impulse to move into action and got up to hold the door for him. I did not deliberate about my obligations; I seemed to be acting out an impulse of my vitality rooted in my body. Most of us regularly act in similar ways and observe others doing so as well.

It turns out that we are in good company—the company of toddlers. "When infants 18 months old see an unrelated adult whose hands are full and who needs assistance opening a door or picking up a dropped clothespin, they will immediately help," according to psychologist Michael Tomasello.[10]

It really *is* possible that the world at large could be organized cooperatively, resulting in a sustainable way of life run by love,

---

9 Fottrell, "Most Americans Are One Paycheck Away from the Street."
10 Wade, "Some Biologists Find an Urge in Human Nature to Help." referring to Tomasello, *Why We Cooperate*.

not by the single minded drive to accumulate capital, to "grow the economy." A cooperative world would be one constructed and organized around the meeting of everyone's basic needs so that no one would be materially insecure, just as is done in good families. For that to happen, the resources and the institutions that feed, clothe, shelter, educate, and care for us when we are sick would need to be dedicated to making all our lives better rather than to accumulating wealth for the few who are now perversely permitted to manage those resources in their own narrow interests. In conditions of personal security, most parenting could be quite "good enough;" we would have less to fear, and our inner demons would not take so much of our energy.

We know such a world is possible, and that is what makes it so frightening to those whose way of life depends on there being plenty of people who have no way to live except by renting themselves out to do the bidding of their employers. The people who live from the labor of others pay those who educate us to make sure that the idea of cooperative labor and the sharing of labor's fruits is regarded as absurd and dangerous. The Cold War was not just a war against a competitor for global domination, but a war against a simple and attractive idea. This is the "specter of communism": the possibility that the world's people could work to satisfy their needs without some form of threat and coercion from above and that the fruits of the earth and human labor should be shared out according to need. How well nearly everyone has learned to smack down this idea can be observed in the comment sections of most public affairs websites.

We have no guarantee that a world order based on love and cooperation can or will come about. But rather than decide in advance that it cannot, why not do all we can to make it happen? The course we are on leads to human, social, and planetary catastrophe.

Love Under Siege

In spite of all the obstacles, love finds ways. Psychoanalyst Harry Guntrip says, "man's need of a love-relationship is the fundamental thing in his life." And, he adds, "the *love-hunger* and *anger* set up by frustration of this basic need ... constitute the two primary problems of personality on the emotional level."[11] So love persists, but even as we seek it, we are wary of it, afraid of being hurt again as we were as infants—and knowing that the world at large is not a welcoming place.

We can think of our life-long search for love as the desire to reclaim some fragments of the intense and all-consuming love we experienced as babies and children (unless, of course, we had little or none, in which case we may spend our lives avoiding the love we know we desire). So most of us manage to love at least some other people and to act sometimes on that love without considering material self-interest. Parents often love their children in this way even when their children disappoint them.

Although we still desire the love we once felt and knew as babies, we are forced to settle for the fragmented and partial kinds of love the world makes available: romantic love, the pursuit of wealth, luxury and power; love of God as represented by a religious institution or leader; love of country, or patriotism; love for a political cause and its leader.

These loves are exclusive and preferential, and so they lead to conflict. We fall in love with one person and then demand that he or she care only for us. Or we identify with a sect or a nation that must exist in violent opposition to others, requiring us to take that violence into ourselves. To love God often means hostility towards nonbelievers and towards those who love God differently. When the nation is associated, as it often is, with a dominant religious,

---

11 Guntrip, *Schizoid Phenomena, Object-Relations and the Self.*

racial, or ethnic group, then patriots will find one or more groups to hate—Jews, Blacks, immigrants, or Muslims, for example.

Many people's lives are intensely energized by nationalism, patriotism, and militant religious commitment forcing the mighty river of their love into a system of concrete canals and pipes with valves, constricting it so that it shoots out into the world with such intensity that it destroys more than it nourishes. We invest all the love that really wants to flow into all the nooks and crannies of life into an unambiguous, symbolically demanding big Other that promises to lead us down a straight and narrow path of right action and belief, free of doubt and insecurity, blinding us to everything that doesn't fit. Things that don't fit become the objects of hatred, giving us a licensed target for all the unconscious anger stemming from the frustrations of love.

So the partial and exclusionary love that is most readily available to us is not the love that might save our lives. Is there a way to revive our love affair with the world—that love of life and living that we experienced as children—and to possibly free ourselves from our inner demons?

To do so, we would have to dethrone the big Other, the phantom that cripples our love and unleashes the demons. So let's return one last time to the big Other and the grip it has on us. What would it take to make it let go—or for *us* to let it go?

Dethroning the big Other

The big Other is the vast complex of norms, practices, and vitality habits by which we make sense of ourselves for ourselves and for others and that enable us to communicate and cooperate. We could not be the social beings we are without it. Yet it is also, for most of us, our supreme object of fear. It looms over us as having an absolute, unchallengeable authority over and above us. Even the thought of violating its imperatives can set off tremors of guilt, which, as we have seen, is the fear of the inner bully ripping our souls to shreds. We cannot abolish or abandon the big Other, but we might be able bring it down from its throne to live on more amicable terms among us. The power of the big Other is virtual, not absolute; like the power of money, the Other's power is produced and maintained by our own habits and practices. So why can we not treat its commands as we do the rules of the games we play, knowing that they are games and that the rules are up to us and open to negotiation? (If the players in a poker game agree that the game is better if one-eyed jacks and deuces are not wild, then those cards are no longer wild.) What keeps us in bondage to the big Other?

It is very rare that any of us comes out of the Garden of Infantile Catastrophe feeling whole and secure. We all suffered what felt to us at the time like some degree of neglect or abuse, leaving our vitality riddled with anxiety, rage, and doubts about whether we are welcome in the world. As we are inducted into language and the scenarios of adult social life, the scripts of those scenarios make the claim, implicitly and explicitly, that there is *a* way we are supposed to be, down to our very core. The big Other is that way. At some level of awareness, I know that my soul rebels against complete obedience to any ideal and that there are forces within me that I can neither understand nor control. This is a fundamental source of guilt—the feeling that I am not what I am supposed to be. I don't love as I am supposed to, and I am angry at the world and at those whose love I need. This is the source of guilt and existential anxiety. And on top of all that, I must find my way in a universe of differing and competing beliefs and ways of living.

We tamp down this terrifying insecurity about what we should be and do by seizing upon some absolute doctrine that will relieve our anxiety about how to live—some authorized version of the big Other. Looking for salvation—the release from guilt—we may dedicate ourselves to serving this big Other, demonstrating loyalty to it by our hostility towards its enemies. Our vitality becomes saturated with some mixture of disgust and hatred in relation to others. These attitudes boil up in the comment sections of many websites, where it becomes clear that the big Other takes many forms, including sectarian religion, patriotism, nativism, the "free" market, possessive individualism, and other forms of moral absolutism, both left and right. There are also those who rebel in rage against the way things are, and their lives can take many paths, from violence and murder to misanthropic reclusion.

To dethrone—to *demystify*—the big Other would be to accept that we can never be certain about such questions as Who am I? and How am I supposed to live? We would have to admit that there are no answers to these questions that can be delivered to us from some source other than our own tentative and fallible struggles to make sense of our souls and our lives with each other. The Symbolic is not engraved in stone or woven into the fabric of reality. What can give us the courage to accept this universe without a ruler, without a God, a world in which we have only each other to turn to?

Doesn't the question contain the answer? We have each other to turn to.[12]

But do we? In this world organized around the competitive struggle for power and wealth, we do not really have each other to turn to beyond, if we are lucky, a small circle of friends and family. Only if we can count on the wide-spread love of life—of all life—is there enough love and trust to free ourselves from the big Other and to rely on ourselves, that is, on each other.

The big Other is too big for any of us to escape from it all by ourselves. If we are lucky in our circumstances and our fortitude, we may be able to find ways to think, feel, perceive and act more independently of the big Other. Some people do. But it should be clear by now that, just as we cannot play tennis outside the structure of

---

12 This seems to be the suggestion of Žižek's film, directed by Sophie Fiennes, "The Pervert's Guide to Ideology." Fiennes, *The Pervert's Guide to Ideology.*

the game of tennis, we cannot think, feel, perceive, and act outside the social order we inhabit. The big Other gets its power not from the free and unfettered choices made by single individuals, but from established practices and institutions within which we are socialized and educated every waking minute of every day.[13] The big Other is deeply entrenched in our souls, and the only way we can ever be really free of it is with its demystification. It needs to be brought down to earth where we can deal with it as our own work, our own organization of our lives and our souls. The project of building a better social world has to be, at the same time, a new way of cultivating our own souls, of altering our habits of vitality.

But that will not happen quickly.

Consider Nietzsche and the "death of God". In his book *The Gay Science*, a madman asks "Where is God?" and answers, "We have killed him—you and I. All of us are his murderers."[14] In the modern scientific and skeptical world, very few people are able to believe in a God-centered universe and practice a God-centered life in the way that our ancestors might have. There are still churches, synagogues, temples and mosques, but they and what goes on them are peripheral to the everyday concerns of the lives we now live.

In another passage, Nietzsche writes,

---

13 Social institutions and practices produce in each of us what sociologist Pierre Bourdieu calls "habitus". Paraphrasing Bourdieu, Steve Valsey characterizes habitus as "a hard-to-change, widely applicable set of habits of acting, seeing, and talking that are learned from these patterns in our social environment and, through their repeated use, tend to recreate similar environmental patterns over time. These habits lead people to behave in regular and predictable ways even though they aren't following conscious rules. People thus seem to be successfully pursuing goals even though they aren't consciously pursuing them and even though they can't articulate the steps necessary to achieve them. The end result is that social patterns get recreated over time as if someone were coordinating things even though no one is actually coordinating them at all." Hirschman, "Translating Habitus from Bourdieu to English."

14 Nietzsche, *The Gay Science,* §125.

God is dead; but given the way of men, there may still be caves for thousands of years in which his shadow will be shown. — And we — we still have to vanquish his shadow, too.[15]

The shadows that darken the sky over all of us today are big institutions and institutionalized ideas like the market, money, property, human nature, America, and destiny. They claim to be the authoritative guides to what is possible and impossible in the world. They are shadows cast by the institutions, practices, and habits of real people, all of us, who cooperate in a world order that makes us all servants of capital. These will not disappear or lose their grip on our lives as the result of what we do or refrain from doing individually. We may come to appreciate that we live in chains that are only virtually real. But they do not melt away with this understanding. Freedom from any form of the big Other depends on unforeseeable historical circumstances making possible a movement of people who are willing and able to build a world organized and directed by love.

In the meantime, we can try to clear the way towards those circumstances by showing up and cooperating in each others' lives with as much compassion and mercy as we can find for all the souls in our lives including our own.

---

15 Ibid, §108.

BIBLIOGRAPHY

Aiken, Conrad. *Blue Voyage*. New York: Charles Scribner's Sons, 1927.

Als, Hilton. "The Good-Bye Girl." *The New York Review of Books*, December 18, 2014. http://www.nybooks.com/articles/archives/2014/dec/18/diane-keaton-good-bye-girl/.

Althusser, Louis. *Lenin and Philosophy*. Monthly Review Press, 1971.

Aristotle. *Nicomachean Ethics*. Translated by Martin Ostwald. 1st edition. New Jersey: Pearson, 1999.

Arthur Kleinman. *Rethinking Psychiatry: From Cultural Category to Personal Experience*. New York: The Free Press, 1988.

Atwood, Margaret. *The Year of the Flood*. Reprint edition. New York: Anchor, 2010.

Auster, Paul. *Sunset Park: A Novel*. New York: Picador, 2011.

Beauvoir, Simone de. *The Ethics Of Ambiguity*. Princeton, N.J.: Citadel, 2000.

Becker, Ernest. *The Denial of Death*. New York: Free Press, 1997.

Benjamin, Jessica. "Recognition and Destruction: An Outline of Intersubjectivity." In *Like Subjects, Love Objects: Essays on Recognition and Sexual Difference*. New Haven: Yale University Press, 1995.

———. *The Bonds of Love: Psychoanalysis, Feminism, & the Problem of Domination*. First Edition edition. New York: Pantheon, 1988.

Bettelheim, Bruno. *Freud and Man's Soul: An Important Re-Interpretation of Freudian Theory*. Vintage Books ed edition. New York: Vintage, 1983.

Bierman, A.K., Logic: A Dialogue. San Francisco: Holden-Day, 1964.

Boime, Jerome. *Violence and Utopia: The Work of Jerome Boime*. Edited by Boime, Albert. Lanham, Md: UPA, 1996.

Borges, Jorge Luis. *Other Inquisitions, 1937-1952*. Translated by Ruth L. C. Simms. Austin: University of Texas Press, 1975.

Briggs, Robert. *Ruined Time: The 1950's and the Beat*. Scappoose, Oregon: RBA Publishing, 2006.

Brown, George Mackay. *Greenvoe*. Edinburgh: Birlinn Ltd, 2004.

Brown, Norman O. *Life Against Death*. Vintage, 1959.

———. *Love's Body*. Reprint edition. Berkeley: University of California Press, 1990.

Bukowski, Charles. *Run With the Hunted: A Charles Bukowski Reader*. New York, NY: HarperPerennial, 1994.

Burns, John Horne. *The Gallery*. New York: NYRB Classics, 2004.

Carse, James P. *Death and Existence: Conceptual History of Human Mortality*. Edited by Irving I. Zaretsky. New York: John Wiley & Sons Inc, 1980.

Conrad, Joseph. *Lord Jim*. Scholastic Library Edition, 1965.

Cross, Amanda. *Sweet Death, Kind Death*. New York: Ballantine Books, 1995.

Damasio, Antonio. *The Feeling of What Happens: Body and Emotion in the Making of Consciousness.* New York: Mariner Books, 2000.

Descartes, René. *Descartes: Discourse On Method.* New York: Macmillan/Library of Liberal Arts, 1956.

Descartes, René. *Descartes: Meditations on First Philosophy: With Selections from the Objections and Replies.* Edited by John Cottingham. Revised edition. Cambridge, England: Cambridge University Press, 1996.

Dewey, John. *Art as Experience.* New York: Perigee Books, 2005.

Dick, Philip K. *The Man in the High Castle.* Reissue edition. Boston: Mariner Books, 2012.

Dickenson, Emily. "Poems of Emily Dickinson: Series Two; Nature, Poem 24: The Snake." *Lit2Go,* n.d. http://etc.usf.edu/lit2go/115/the-poems-of-emily-dickinson-series-two/4460/nature-poem-24-the-snake/.

Dostoevsky, Fyodor. *Notes from Underground.* Translated by Richard Pevear and Larissa Volokhonsky. Reprint edition. New York: Vintage, 1994.

Eagleton, Terry. "Bakhtin, Schopenhaur, Kundera," n.d.

Egan, Jennifer. "Finding a Voice, a Review of Norah Webster by Colin Toibin." *New York Times Book Review,* October 5, 2014.

Ellison, Ralph. *Invisible Man.* 2d ed. Vintage, 1995.

Feher, Michel, Sanford Kwinter, and Jonathan Crary, eds. *Zone 1/2: The [Contemporary] City.* New York: Zone Books, 1987.

Fiennes, Sophie. *The Pervert's Guide to Ideology.* Documentary, 2013.

Fingarette, Herbert. *Self-Deception.* First Edition, With a New Chapter edition. Berkeley, Calif: University of California Press, 2000.

Fitzgerald, F. Scott. *The Great Gatsby.* New York: Scribner, 2004.

Flannery, Tim. "What Is a Tree?" *The New York Review of Books,* February 15, 2007. http://www.nybooks.com/articles/archives/2007/feb/15/what-is-a-tree/.

Fottrell, Quentin. "Most Americans Are One Paycheck Away from the Street." *MarketWatch.* Accessed September 9, 2015. http://www.marketwatch.com/story/most-americans-are-one-paycheck-away-from-the-street-2015-01-07.

Freud, Sigmund. *Civilization and Its Discontents.* Translated by James Strachey. New York: W.W. Norton, 1962.

———. *Three Essays on the Theory of Sexuality.* Translated by James Strachey. Mansfield Centre, Conn.: Martino Fine Books, 2011.

Furbank, P.N. "The Love of a Pessimist: Review of Leonard Woolf: A Biography by Victoria Glendinning." *New York Review of Books,* December 21, 2006.

Gardam, Jane. *Old Filth.* New York: Europa Editions, 2006.

Gilmore, Mikal. *Shot in the Heart.* Reissue edition. New York: Anchor, 1995.

Ginsberg, Allen. *Howl and Other Poems.* Reissue edition. San Francisco: City Lights Publishers, 2001.

Goffman, Erving. *Encounters: Two Studies In The Sociology Of Interaction.* Edited by Robert McGinnis. Indianapolis: Literary Licensing, LLC, 2011.

————. *The Presentation of Self in Everyday Life.* New York, NY: Anchor, 1959.

Goldstein, Rebecca. *The Mind-Body Problem.* New York: Penguin Books, 1993.

Guntrip, Harry. *Schizoid Phenomena, Object-Relations and the Self.* New York: International Universities Press, 1969.

Habermas, Jürgen. *The Theory of Communicative Action, Volume 1: Reason and the Rationalization of Society.* Translated by Thomas McCarthy. Boston: Beacon Press, 1985.

Hegel, G. W. F. *Phenomenology of Spirit.* Translated by A. V. Miller. 1st edition. Oxford: Oxford University Press, 1977.

Hendel, Hilary Jacobs. "It's Not Always Depression." *Opinionator,* March 10, 2015. http://opinionator.blogs.nytimes.com/2015/03/10/its-not-always-depression/.

Henry, Jules. *Culture Against Man.* New York: Vintage, 1965.

Henry, Jules. "Golden Rule Days: American Schoolrooms." In *Culture Against Man.* New York: Vintage, 1965.

Henwood, Doug. *Wall Street: How It Works and for Whom.* London: Verso, 1998.

Hirschman, Dan. "Translating Habitus from Bourdieu to English." *Scatterplot*. Accessed September 9, 2015. https://scatter.wordpress.com/2015/09/08/translating-habitus-from-bourdieu-to-english/.

"Invictus by William Ernest Henley : The Poetry Foundation." Accessed May 12, 2015. http://www.poetryfoundation.org/poem/182194.

Jaynes, Julian. *The Origin of Consciousness in the Breakdown of the Bicameral Mind*. Houghton Mifflin, 1990.

Jenks, Chris. *Transgression*. London: Routledge, 2003.

Kavenna, Joanna. "Things Fall Apart: A Spanish Master's Quizzical Unravelings. Review of Dublinesque by Enrique Vila-Matas." *The New Yorker*, September 3, 2012.

Keaton, Diane. *Let's Just Say It Wasn't Pretty*. New York: Random House, 2014.

Kerr, Sarah. "The Unclosed Circle." *The New York Review of Books*, April 26, 2007. http://www.nybooks.com/articles/archives/2007/apr/26/the-unclosed-circle/.

Klein, Naomi. *This Changes Everything: Capitalism vs. The Climate*. Simon & Schuster, 2015.

Koppelman, Alex. "Memo to Bill O'Reilly: More Immigrants Equals Less Crime." Accessed May 12, 2015. http://www.salon.com/2007/04/10/geraldo_2/.

Laing, R. D. *The Politics of Experience*. 7th THUS edition. Ballantine Books, 1971.

Laing, R.D. *The Divided Self*. Pelican, 1965.

Langer, Susanne K. *Mind: An Essay on Human Feeling.* Baltimore: Johns Hopkins University Press, 1984.

Larkin, Philip. *Collected Poems.* Edited by Anthony Thwaite. New York: Farrar, Straus and Giroux, 2004.

Lawrence, D. H. *Sons and Lovers.* Ware: Wordsworth Editions Ltd, 1997.

Longenbach, James. "A Music of Austerity: The Poetry of Wallace Stevens." *The Nation,* August 26, 2009. http://www.thenation.com/article/music-austerity-poetry-wallace-stevens.

Louis Althusser. "Marxism and Humanism." In *For Marx,* translated by Ben Brewster. London, n.d.

Loy, David. *Lack and Transcendence: The Problem of Death and Life in Psychotherapy, Existentialism, and Buddhism.* Amherst, N.Y.: Prometheus Books/Humanity Books, 2000.

Lyng, Stephen. "Edgework: A Social Psychological Analysis of Voluntary Risk Taking." *American Journal of Sociology* 95, no. 4 (1990): 851–86.

———. , ed. *Edgework: The Sociology of Risk-Taking.* New York: Routledge, 2004.

Mailer, Norman. *Some Honorable Men: Political Conventions, 1960-1972.* 1st edition. Boston: Little Brown, 1976.

Mann, Thomas. *Buddenbrooks: The Decline of a Family.* New York: Vintage, 1994.

McGowan, Todd. *The Impossible David Lynch.* New York: Columbia University Press, 2007.

McIlvanney, William. *Laidlaw*. London: Hodder and Stoughton, 1979.

———. *Weekend*. Main edition. Canongate UK, 2014.

Mead, George H. *Mind, Self & Society: From the Standpoint of a Social Behaviorist*. Fifth Impression edition. The University of Chicago Press, 1946.

Miller, William Ian. *Faking It*. Cambridge; New York: Cambridge University Press, 2005.

"Mind Games." *This American Life*. Accessed September 12, 2015. http://www. thisamericanlife.org/radio-archives/episode/286/mind-games?act=1.

Minor, Kyle. "Behind the David Foster Wallace Myth." *Salon*, September 12, 2012. Behind the David Foster Wallace myth.

"Mirror Neuron." *Wikipedia*. Accessed August 14, 2016. https://en.wikipedia. org/wiki/Mirror_neuron.

Mitchell, Stephen A. *Hope And Dread In Pychoanalysis*. New York, N.Y.: Basic Books, 1995.

Mosley, Walter. *Little Scarlet*. ORION, 2004.

Murdoch, Iris. *Bruno's Dream*. First Dell Printing, Worn edition. Dell, 1970.

———. *Nuns and Soldiers*. New York: Penguin Classics, 2002.

———. *The Nice and the Good*. St. Louis: Penguin Books, 1978.

———. *The Sea, The Sea*. London: Penguin Classics, 2001.

Murphy, Sara, Huguette Glowinski, and Zita M. Marks. *A Compendium of Lacanian Terms*. London ; New York: Free Association Books, 2001.

Narvaez, Darcia, Tracy Gleason, Lijuan Wang, Jeff Brooks, Jennifer Burke Lefever, and Ying Cheng. "The Evolved Development Niche: Longitudinal Effects of Caregiving Practices on Early Childhood Psychosocial Development." *Early Childhood Research Quarterly* 28, no. 4 (October 2013): 759–73. doi:10.1016/j.ecresq.2013.07.003.

Nietzsche, Friedrich. *Beyond Good and Evil: Prelude to a Philosophy of the Future*. Translated by R. J. Hollingdale. Revised edition. London, England ; New York, New York, USA: Penguin Classics, 1990.

———. *On the Genealogy of Morals and Ecce Homo*. Edited by Walter Kaufmann. Reissue edition. New York: Vintage, 1989.

———. *The Gay Science: With a Prelude in Rhymes and an Appendix of Songs*. Translated by Walter Kaufmann. New York: Vintage, 1974.

———. *Thus Spoke Zarathustra: A Book For None and All*. New York: Penguin Books, 1983.

"Nina Simone - Don't Let Me Be Misunderstood - YouTube." Accessed September 12, 2015. https://www.youtube.com/watch?v=9ckv6-yhnIY.

Oliver, Kelly. *Witnessing: Beyond Recognition*. Minneapolis, MN: Univ Of Minnesota Press, 2001.

Perec, Georges. *W, or the Memory of Childhood*. Boston, Mass: David R Godine, 2010.

Phillips, Adam. *On Flirtation*. Cambridge, Mass.: Harvard University Press, 1996.

Powell, Alvin. "Children Need Touching and Attention, Harvard Researchers Say," April 9, 1998. http://news.harvard.edu/gazette/1998/04.09/ChildrenNeedTou.html.

Proust, Marcel. *Swann's Way*. Translated by Lydia Davis. New York: Viking Adult, 2003.

Ratcliffe, Matthew. *Feelings of Being: Phenomenology, Psychiatry and the Sense of Reality*. 1st edition. Oxford ; New York: Oxford University Press, 2008.

Robinson, Kim Stanley. *Red Mars*. Spectra, 1993.

Rutsala, Vern. *A Handbook for Writers: New & Selected Prose Poems*. First Edition edition. Buffalo, N.Y: White Pine Press, 2004.

———. *The Mystery of Lost Shoes*. Amherst, Mass. : Berkeley, Calif: Lynx House Pr, 1985.

Ryle, Gilbert. *The Concept of Mind*. Barnes & Noble, 1964.

Sabato, Ernesto. *El Tunel / The Tunnel*. Poc edition. Barcelona: Planeta Publishing, 2003.

Singer, Michael A. *The Untethered Soul: The Journey Beyond Yourself*. 1st edition. Oakland, CA: New Harbinger Publications/ Noetic Books, 2007.

Stein, Sadie. "Childish Things." *Paris Review Daily*, August 28, 2013. http://www.theparisreview.org/blog/2013/08/28/childish-things/.

Stern, Daniel N. *Forms of Vitality: Exploring Dynamic Experience in Psychology and the Arts*. Oxford ; New York: Oxford University Press, 2010.

————. *The Interpersonal World Of The Infant A View From Psychoanalysis And Developmental Psychology*. New York: Basic Books, 2000.

Sullivan, Harry Stack. "The Illusion of Personal Individuality." In *The Fusion Of Psychiatry and Social Science*. New York: W. W. Norton & Company, 1971.

Szabo, Magda. *The Door*. Translated by Len Rix. New York: NYRB Classics, 2015.

Thomas, Elizabeth Marshall. *The Hidden Life of Dogs*. New York: Mariner Books, 2010.

Tomasello, Michael. *Why We Cooperate*. Cambridge, Mass: The MIT Press, 2009.

Tykwer, Tom, Andy Wachowski, and Lana Wachowski. *Cloud Atlas*. Drama, Sci-Fi, 2012.

Vonnegut, Kurt. *Mother Night: A Novel*. New York, N.Y: Dial Press Trade Paperback, 1999.

Wade, Nicholas. "Some Biologists Find an Urge in Human Nature to Help." *The New York Times*, November 30, 2009. http://www.nytimes.com/2009/12/01/science/01human.html.

Warren, Robert Penn. *All the King's Men*. Bantam Modern Classic Edition 23rd Printing edition. Bantam Books, 1968.

Wegner, Daniel. *The Illusion of Conscious Will*. 1st edition. Cambridge, Mass.: A Bradford Book, 2003.

Wharton, Edith. *The Age of Innocence.* CreateSpace Independent Publishing Platform, 2015.

White, Edmund. *The Married Man: A Novel.* New York: Vintage, 2001.

Winnicott, D. W. *Winnicott On The Child.* Cambridge, MA: Da Capo Press, 2002.

Winters, Ben. *World of Trouble: The Last Policeman Book III.* Philadelphia: Quirk Books, 2014.

Wittgenstein, Ludwig. *Philosophical Investigations.* Translated by G. E. M. Anscombe. 2d edition. Oxford: Basil Blackwell, 1958.

———. *Tractatus Logico-Philosophicus.* Translated by C. K. Ogden. Mineola, NY: Dover Publications, 1998.

Wolfe, Thomas. *Thomas Wolfe's Look Homeward, Angel.* Bantam, 1970.

Zacharek, Stephanie. "'Alfie.'" Accessed May 12, 2015. http://www.salon.com/2004/11/05/alfie/.

Zafón, Carlos Ruiz. *The Shadow of the Wind.* Translated by Lucia Graves. Princeton, N.J.: Penguin Books, 2005.

Žižek, Slavoj. *Event: A Philosophical Journey Through A Concept.* Brooklyn, NY: Melville House, 2014.

———. *How to Read Lacan.* New York: W. W. Norton & Company, 2007.

———. *The Sublime Object of Ideology.* Second Edition. London: Verso, 2009.

———. *Violence: Six Sideways Reflections.* New York: Picador, 2008.

ACKNOWLEDGMENTS

"As Bad as a Mile" and the excerpt from "Aubade" from COLLECTED POEMS by Philip Larkin. Copyright © 1988, 2003 by the Estate of Philip Larkin. Reprinted by permission of Farrar, Straus and Giroux, and Faber and Faber.

"the bluebird" from THE LAST NIGHT ON EARTH POEMS by Charles Bukowski. Copyright © 1992 by Charles Bukowski. Reprinted by permission of HarperCollins Publishers.

Born At The Right Time
Copyright © 1990 Paul Simon
Used by permission of the Publisher: Paul Simon Music

DON'T LET ME BE MISUNDERSTOOD
Words and Music by BENNIE BENJAMIN, SOL MARCUS and GLORIA CALDWELL
Copyright © © 1964 (Renewed) CLAUDE A. MUSIC CO.,
ROSE MARCUS PUBLISHING DESIGNEE and CHRIS-N-JEN MUSIC
All Rights for CLAUDE A. MUSIC CO. Administered by CHAPPELL & CO., INC.
All Rights for ROSE MARCUS PUBLISHING DESIGNEE Administered by WB MUSIC CORP.
All Rights Reserved
Used By Permission of ALFRED MUSIC

"Gee, I didn't know..." Cartoon
© Bizarro: (c) 2012 Dan Piraro. Distributed by King Features Syndicate, Inc.

"Guilt", Vern Rutsala, *A Handbook For Writers: New & Selected Prose Poems*, White Pine Press (2004). Used by permission.

My Mind's Got A Mind Of Its Own
Words and Music by George Hancock
Copyright © 1991 Two Roads Music
All rights Administered by BMG rights Management (US) LLC
All Rights Reserved Used by Permission
Reprinted by Permission of Hal Leonard LLC

There's A World
Words and Music by Neil Young
Copyright © 1971 by Silver Fiddle Music
Copyright Renewed
All Rights Reserved Used by Permission
Reprinted by Permission of Hal Leonard LLC

"There She Goes" by John Prine
© 1978 Bruised Oranges ASCAP admin. by Wixen Music Publishing, Inc.
All Rights Reserved. Used by Permission.

"What Are You Planning to be for Halloween?" Photo by Alan Wieder. Used by permission.

INDEX

A

adverse childhood experiences
(ACEs), 195-96, 204
affect attunement (vitality matching), 162, 167-74
aggression. See rage
anger. See rage
anxiety, 98-101, 214-22
attunement, 162, See affect
attunement

B

big Other, the, 81-91, 177-88
abolishing the, 236-40
God as, 87
inner bully as, 88-89, 185-88
brain, 10-11

C

communion, 142-43, 152, 162
compassion, 226-27
confession, 56-58, 218-19
Conrad, Joseph. See *Lord Jim*
conscious choice, 8, 98n
illusion of, 110-11
consciousness, 28, 108-09, 137-41,
See also unconscious, the; and
self-consciousness
cruelty, 185-88

D

death, 188-89
fear of, 219-22
depression, 96n
desire, 22-23

E

emotions, 93-96, 104-06, 112-13;
unconscious, 108-09, 119
See also inner demons
expression. See expressive discourse
expressive discourse, 125-30

F

Fingarette, Herbert, 114n, 117n
free will. See conscious choice, illusion of
free-floating anxiety. See anxiety

G

garden of infantile catastrophe, 43,
113, 144-45, 195, 225, 237
God, 59n, 87, 88n, 198, 235-40. See
also big Other
guilt, 97-98
analysis of, 190-203

H

hailing (interpellation), 47-52

Photo by Jackie Lemieux

Clayton Morgareidge is Professor Emeritus of Philosophy at Lewis & Clark College. Since retiring from teaching in 2002, he has been thinking and writing about our inner demons as well as contributing to the Old Mole Variety Hour heard on KBOO community radio in Portland. He sings with the duo Clayton & Ernie and with Satori Men's Chorus. He lives in Portland with his wife Jackie Lemieux and a cat named Nicky.

www.ingramcontent.com/pod-product-compliance
Lightning Source LLC
Chambersburg PA
CBHW062131280526
45788CB00001B/128